RUSSIAN ROULETTE

Other Books by the Author

The Dynamics of Détente
The Myths of National Security
Prospects for Peacekeeping

RUSSIAN ROULETTE
The Superpower Game

Arthur Macy Cox

with a Soviet Commentary by Georgy Arbatov

Times
BOOKS

Published by TIMES BOOKS, a division of
Quadrangle/The New York Times Book Co., Inc.
Three Park Avenue, New York, N.Y. 10016

Published simultaneously in Canada by
Fitzhenry & Whiteside, Ltd., Toronto

Library of Congress Cataloging in Publication Data

Cox, Arthur M.
  Russian roulette.

  Includes bibliographical references and index.
  1. Atomic warfare. 2. United States—Military
policy. 3. Soviet Union—Military policy. 4. World
politics—1975-1985. 5. Disarmament. I. Title.
UF767.C68   1982   355'.0217   81-84899
ISBN 0-8129-1011-7   AACR2

Manufactured in the United States of America
10 9 8 7 6 5 4 3 2 1

For My Children
Stephen, Timothy, Anthony, Heather

Contents

RUSSIAN ROULETTE

Chapter I

Accidental Nuclear War

At 11:00 A.M. on June 3, 1980, the Air Force officers monitoring the early warning system deep underground inside Cheyenne Mountain, Colorado, were struck with terror. The fluorescent display screens connected to the Nova Data General computer were flashing a warning: The Soviet Union had launched a large attack from its land-based missiles and strategic submarines. The submarines had launched their missiles from positions close to the coast of the United States; the missiles would reach their targets in less than ten minutes.

The alert was immediately fed into computers of the Strategic Air Command in Omaha, the National Military Command Center in the Pentagon, and the Alternate Military Command Center underground in Mount Weather, fifty miles northwest of Washington. Pilots and crews of 116 B-52 nuclear bombers at airfields across the United States raced to their planes, gunned the engines, and began to taxi for takeoff. Nuclear submarine commanders at sea were alerted for action. At the underground launch centers near silos housing the American intercontinental ballistic missiles, officers strapped themselves into jolt-resistant swivel chairs, unlocked strongboxes, removed verification codes, and inserted launch keys into their slots. (When two keys ten feet apart are twisted within two seconds of each other, the missiles blast off toward their targets in the Soviet Union.)[1] Unlike a bomber, which

3

can be called back, an ICBM, once launched, continues irretrievably on its terrible mission.

Fortunately for our planet this computer error was discovered in time. But it was only one of three serious computer failures in eight months which placed the United States on nuclear alert. Incredibly, the June 3 incident was followed by another alarm on June 6, reported by the same faulty computer. According to a Pentagon briefing, these false alarms were caused by the failure of an electronic chip, about the size of a dime, which costs forty-six cents. Eight months earlier a war game tape was fed into the computers and unaccountably interpreted as the real thing. It took six minutes before the command and control officers determined that the attack was simulated.

During this time the pilot and crew of the E-4 command center plane which is always on runway alert at Andrews Air Force Base to allow the President to escape early nuclear attack and still be able to direct retaliation from the skies took off without President Carter. In fact, the plane was in the air before the President had even been informed of the alert.

As attested by a report prepared by the Senate Armed Services Committee, there were 3,703 alarms in the eighteen-month period from January 1979 to June 1980. Most of these were routinely assessed and dismissed, but 147 false alarms were serious enough to require evaluation of whether or not they represented a potential attack.

The Pentagon code word for an accident involving nuclear weapons is "broken arrow." The Defense Department has publicly acknowledged thirty-two "broken arrows," the most recent of which was the Titan II missile explosion in Damascus, Arkansas, on September 19, 1980. So far we have never had a nuclear explosion, but we have been lucky. In 1950 a B-29 carrying a nuclear bomb crashed on takeoff. In 1961 a B-52 with two nuclear weapons crashed near Yuba City, California. Also in 1961, another B-52 with two nuclear bombs went out of control near Goldsboro, North Carolina. When Air Force bomb experts reached the scene of the accident, they found that five of the six safety interlocks on one of the weapons had been set off by the force of the crash; only one remaining switch prevented the twenty-four-megaton bomb from detonating and spreading destruction and fallout over a wide area. In 1966 a B-52 crash near Palomares, Spain, resulted in dispersal of plutonium over an extensive agricultural area. The United States cleaned up the damage at a cost of $50 million. In 1968 a B-52 crashed and burned near Thule Air Force Base in Greenland. The bomber carried four nuclear weapons, all of which were destroyed by fire. During a four-month operation 237,000 cubic feet of radioactively contaminated ice, snow, and water were removed to an approved storage site in the United States.

The Pentagon says that new safety features now make an accidental nuclear explosion almost impossible. However, there is still the possibility of radioactive contamination if a nuclear weapon is consumed by fire or shattered by accidental detonation of nonnuclear explosives which are part of each nuclear device. And there are 30,000 nuclear weapons in the United States, stored in more than 200 locations in forty states.[2] The safety record has been remarkable, but the risks are growing.

One of the greatest risks we face is accidental launch of nuclear weapons resulting from breakdowns in the communications systems and insufficient time for reliable human decision making. After the two false alarms in June 1980 Secretary of Defense Harold Brown told a Senate inquiry: "I can assure that our strategic command and control system is configured to insure that a false alert could not result in a nuclear launch." Pentagon specialists said the key is a human judgment that must be made at each phase of an alert: Human decision is intended to prevent machinery alone from ordering a nuclear strike. Assistant Secretary of Defense Gerald P. Dinneen, the top expert on the U.S. early warning system at that time, declared: "There is no chance that any irretrievable actions would be taken on the basis of ambiguous computer information."

According to Dinneen, duty officers in various command posts make initial judgments that are passed back to Washington and up to the President, "who alone has the authority to order nuclear retaliation." A Pentagon report to the Senate was more specific: "The last stage of a nuclear alert is the convening of a missile attack conference that brings in all senior personnel, including the President. No such conference has ever been convened." All this information might be reassuring if we could continue to have the time necessary to implement the system, or if the Russians continue to fail to react to our false alerts, or if we can continue to maintain the record of extraordinary good luck that has marked the past thirty years.

But the next decade will be very different from the past thirty years. Unless the nuclear arms race is reversed, the probability of accidental nuclear war will increase sharply. The next round of nuclear weapons systems will make both superpowers fearful, with reason, of surprise attack. Some nuclear weapons based in Europe will be able to reach their Soviet targets with great accuracy in as little as six minutes. No system of command and control can possibly insure presidential decisions under those circumstances. Both sides will be on a continuous hair-trigger alert. In times of major political crisis the danger of accident will be probable rather than possible, as it is today.

Under such circumstances, imagine the Soviet reaction to one of our false alerts when their intelligence tells them that our B-52's are in the air and our ICBMs are being prepared for launch. If they have only six minutes to launch their missiles before their command and control system is destroyed, the odds are very strong that they will fire before an attack has been completed. This is known as launch under attack or launch on warning.

An indication of Soviet jumpiness came after the U.S. false alarm of November 1979. Tass commentator Alexander Dmitryuk said: "The Pentagon may have set off a false alarm about a Soviet nuclear attack deliberately to see the reaction of the Russians." And, he added, "there were other false alarms at the end of the 1950's and 1960's, and each could have ended in a catastrophe. . . . This incident shows once again on what a thin thread security now hangs and how this thread is tested for strength by irresponsible people in the United States."

Accidental Nuclear War

As the danger grows, the flawless function of our command and control system becomes ever more vital. But the system today is error-prone to the point of gigantic risk. A team of U.S. government auditors concluded in 1980 that the computers installed nearly a decade ago cannot be used effectively for military command purposes. They said the Pentagon spent $1 billion trying to make its World Wide Military Command and Control System work. In the opinion of the auditors, the system, called Wimex, remains "unacceptably slow and unreliable."

An Associated Press story by Michael Putzel reports that John H. Bradley, an electronics engineer who helped test the computer network during development, says that he was fired after he went over his bosses' heads to warn the White House that the President should not depend on Wimex to warn him of Soviet attack.

The Pentagon says the President does not depend solely on Wimex because there are two other faster systems designed to detect a nuclear strike. However, a task force of computer industry experts which reported to President Carter's Office of Management and Budget in 1979 found that at least one of the other systems "suffers frequent power interruptions due to electrical storm activity in Colorado." In 1979 the General Accounting Office (GAO), watchdog for Congress, evaluated the World Wide Military Command and Control System. Developed during the 1960's Wimex consisted of 158 different computer systems in operation at eighty-one separate locations. The GAO review had been requested to determine the extent to which the Department of Defense had been able to improve the computer and data communications support of command and control activities. The conclusion was that "little, if any, improvement was noted. Planned future expenditures of the Department of Defense will not resolve the problems unless major changes are initiated:

In view of major software deficiencies, we believe that for the near term consideration should be given to stopping or curtailing the development of new Wimex software. Our experience has shown that major software design deficiencies and associated problems cannot be corrected after the fact—even with expenditure of considerable time, effort, and money.[3]

In other words, the General Accounting Office was saying that a bad system cannot be made effective and reliable by patching and improvisation. A new system is needed. Since the computer systems of our command and control organization represent the heart of our nation's security, the findings of the GAO are chilling indeed.

Unlike our Strategic Air Command and our ground-launched strategic missiles, which are served by the central communications systems, the strategic submarines require a separate mechanism. A report by the GAO states that "the Navy maintains two squadrons of TACAMO aircraft for communications with strategic submarines during an emergency. This system is considered the Navy's only survivable link to the strategic submarine force." Since the TACAMO planes are aging and will be pulled out of service during the eighties they must be replaced by new aircraft. The Navy plans to have the new planes equipped with an extremely low-frequency communications system. But the GAO finds that "the proposed modified extremely low frequency system is no more survivable than existing day-to-day communication systems and there is doubt that the system will work as planned even if it is needed."[4] Since strategic submarines are the most secure leg of our strategic weapons triad, their communications system should never be in doubt.

The Reagan administration took a long look at the U.S. command, control, and communications (C^3) system and agreed with the verdict that it is dangerously vulnerable. The President and Secretary of Defense Caspar Weinberger have decided to spend more than $18 billion during the next ten years to modernize the system. This is part of a $180 billion program to expand and improve the entire U.S. strategic nuclear capability. The new program, the Pentagon has announced, "is intended to enable the United States to regain nuclear superiority over the Soviet Union within this decade. The Administration intends to build a capacity to fight nuclear wars that range from a limited strike through a protracted conflict to an all-out exchange."[5]

According to high-ranking Pentagon officials, the new program, when completed, will permit "the President to order a retaliatory nuclear strike against the Soviet Union without risking an accidental nuclear war, after ascertaining that Soviet missiles are definitely heading towards the United States. This response, known as 'launch under attack,' is currently possible but has not been adopted because the strategic warning system's accuracy cannot be trusted. The new plan's goal is to make the system so reliable that evidence of an attack would be unmistakable."[6] It would be reassuring to know that such a system is contemplated, if it were possible to achieve. But it is terrifying to know that we are prepared to run the risk of building first-strike weapons during a ten-year period when we know that our command and control and communications system is not survivable. First-strike weapons such as the MX, Trident II, and Pershing II force the Soviets into a hair-trigger response, greatly increasing the risk of accidental launch.

All experts now agree that C^3 is one of the most vital elements of our national security. It is a conglomerate of communications systems, satellites, AWACS, airborne command centers (E-4's), shipboard tracking stations, radars, and sensors. One of the reasons the present C^3 system would not survive a nuclear attack is that it would be crippled by electromagnetic pulse (EMP). Defense strategists say "that a single Soviet warhead detonated 200 miles above Nebraska would perform an electromagnetic lobotomy on computer memories, knocking out unprotected communications systems from coast to coast."[7]

At a meeting sponsored by the Defense Department to discuss the plans of the Reagan administration to improve C^3, it was agreed that the command and control of U.S. strategic forces would be a primary Soviet target. Charles A. Zraket, executive vice-president of MITRE, a coporation engaged in systems engineering for the Air Force, said it is essential that "the Soviets know they cannot decapitate the strategic defense system and have a cheap ride to victory."[8] What is usually left out of these discussions is the fact that the Soviet C^3 is even more vulnerable and more prone to error than the U.S. system because of the relative inferiority of their computers and because of the concentration of their locations.

Despite the advances of technology, serious doubts have been raised about the ten-year $18-billion plan to make the U.S. C^3 secure. A 1981 study by the International Institute of Strategic Studies in London entitled "Can Nuclear War Be Controlled?" raises serious doubts. The study demonstrates that there will inevitably be too many uncertainties. Some of its findings follow:

1. The U.S. nuclear command and control system (like the Soviet system) is an uncoordinated hodgepodge that is unsuited to conduct, moderate or end nuclear war.

2. The command and control system is inherently vulnerable to jamming, spoofing (sending spurious signals) or destruction, and no amount of hardening of facilities can alter this fact.

3. It would, in any case, take two to keep a nuclear war limited, and Soviet military doctrine has shown no interest in such a concept. [Soviet Defense Minister Dimitri Ustinov was quoted in *Pravda* on July 25, 1981, as saying, "Could anyone in his right mind speak seriously of any limited nuclear war? It should be quite clear that the aggressor's actions will instantly and inevitably trigger a devastating counterstroke by the other side. None but completely irresponsible people could maintain that a nuclear war may be made to follow rules adopted beforehand, with nuclear missiles exploding in 'gentlemanly manner' over strictly designated targets and sparing the population."]

4. The likelihood that the U.S. could keep a superpower nuclear war limited is therefore remote.

5. C^3, because it depends on establishing communications between two or more points around the globe, generally requires large, fixed and soft facilities that are easy to destroy. Radars are easy to knock out. Even superhardened command centers are as vulnerable to a direct hit—given today's accuracies—as are any fixed targets. [This means that the underground U.S. Strategic Command

Center in Colorado would be obliterated by a direct hit.]
And airborne command centers—which are now deemed
the only survivable solution—are limited to some three
days use by crew fatigue, engine oil depletion, and probable destruction of landing fields.[9]

AUTHORITY TO LAUNCH
NUCLEAR WEAPONS

As the danger of accidental nuclear war increases, the command and control of these weapons become paramount in
considering our security. Supposedly only the President of
the United States, as Commander in Chief, can authorize the
use of nuclear weapons. Long ago it became clear that in
matters of nuclear war the constitutional powers of Congress
would be bypassed. The Constitution gives Congress the
power to declare war, but time will not permit any such
declaration in a nuclear war. The Vietnam War was never a
declared war, so in order to avoid any future Vietnams, Congress approved the War Powers Act in 1973. Because of that
act in the absence of a declaration of war the President is
required, within forty-eight hours of committing U.S. forces
into hostilities, to submit a report to Congress explaining his
action.

But the War Powers Act also allows the President to conduct a war (nuclear or conventional) for sixty days without
congressional approval, with the stipulation that Congress
can take action to terminate it within that time. Now it is
conceivable that a nuclear war between the superpowers
might last long enough for Congress to decide to terminate it,
but the possibility is remote. Some U.S. strategic planners
discuss the prospect of waging limited nuclear wars, but Soviet doctrine unambiguously rejects any possibility of limitation. The Soviets make it clear that if they are ever attacked
with nuclear weapons, their response will be total.

Thus any decision to launch nuclear weapons will probably
be only in the executive branch. The responsibility for such
a decision is the most awesome in the history of man, and the
procedures for controlling the command of communications

11

involving the possible use of nuclear weapons are vital to our survival. Wherever he goes, the President is always followed by a man with a black bag containing the codes by which the chief executive can authorize the launch of nuclear weapons. One of the most frightening aspects of the television coverage of the shooting of President Ronald Reagan at the Hilton Hotel in Washington was the sight of the man with the black bag running in one direction as the presidential limousine drove off in another.

Imagine what might have happened if the Soviets had accidentally launched a nuclear weapon while the President was in surgery and Vice President Bush was airborne, returning from Texas. It was not reassuring at the time to see a trembling Secretary of State Alexander Haig appear on television screens reporting from the White House: "I am in control here." Actually the command of the black bag runs from the President to the Vice President to the secretary of defense, not to the secretary of state.

This delegation of authority is contrary to the provisions for succession to the presidency, which provide that the speaker of the House of Representatives and the president pro tem of the Senate are next in line after the Vice President. In fact, the whole question of the delegation of authority for employing nuclear weapons is shrouded in secrecy. In testimony before a subcommittee of the House International Relations Committee in 1976, retired Vice Admiral Gerald E. Miller, former director of the Joint Strategic Planning Staff of the Department of Defense, testified that:

it would be virtually impossible for a military commander to use the weapons in his command without Presidential release authority.

One exception of the delegation of authority has to do with the North American Air Defense (NORAD) Commander who has been delegated such authority only under severe restrictions and specific conditions of attack. . . . Weapons he might launch would be in response to a threat of "first use" by the opposition and under actual war conditions. . . . I understand that action is

underway in the Department of Defense to revoke this
authorization in the near future.[10]

It is important to know whether the NORAD commander
still has the delegation of authority because it would clearly
permit him to order the use of nuclear weapons in the event
of an accidental Soviet launch or even of a false alarm that was
not ascertained in time to be false.

The difficulty in communicating with our strategic submarines has always posed the risk of accident. The submarines
can communicate with headquarters only at set times when
they rise near the surface to send and receive messages. They
are out of contact with Washington and the President during
the hours when they are cruising deep under water.[11] In a
CBS television series entitled *The Defense of the United States*
the following remarkable exchange occurred between CBS
correspondent Bob Schieffer and Admiral Powell Carter:

> SCHIEFFER: Only the submarines thousands of miles from
> the U.S. mainland would be unaffected by a surprise
> attack. But communicating with the subs—difficult
> under ideal conditions—might become impossible. It is
> for this reason that we suspected a submarine comman-
> der might be able to fire his nuclear missiles without
> codes released by the President. We know that land-based
> missiles and bombers cannot be launched independently.
> They have built-in technical safeguards. But what about
> the submarine? It has never been admitted publicly be-
> fore, but Admiral Powell Carter confirmed to us for the
> first time that, yes, a submarine commander and his crew
> have the capability to launch their nuclear missiles in a
> crisis—if they have lost communications with the com-
> mand structure.
>
> Let's say there was a total blackout in communications.
> Would you have to have information from the command
> authorities or from some outside source in order to
> launch, or couldn't you, in fact, go ahead and launch?
> ADMIRAL CARTER: There is nothing on a submarine sys-
> tem that prevents that mechanically, through some sort
> of a—an interlock system that has to receive electromag-
> netic pulses from outside the submarine, to enable the

missile to be launched. No, that's not the case. The whole thing is vested in the—in the—

SCHIEFFER: Integrity of the crew?

ADMIRAL CARTER: Crew. Crew.

SCHIEFFER: Even though it would take the cooperation of practically the entire crew to fire the missiles, the fact remains that these men have the capability to wage a nuclear war all by themselves. Any Soviet planner contemplating a surprise attack must take into account that the subs would be out there. The subs might be out of contact for a while, but they would be able on their own to continue and expand the war.[12]

As the danger of accidental nuclear war increases, the question of who has the finger on the nuclear trigger becomes critical. Our nation should be paying much more attention to the possible consequences of the assassination or incapacitation of our President. Our history demonstrates that the risks are great. Scenarios involving launch of nuclear weapons by delegated authority, by ambiguous authority, or by mistake are far more plausible than the worst-case war games played in the Pentagon which presently serve as the basis for spending hundreds of billions of dollars on new strategic weapons systems.

Inevitably command and control of nuclear weapons are not a risk-free business because the whole system, though mechanized, involves human beings, thousands of them, all along the line from the President down to the men in the missile silo who wear sidearms to be able to shoot their partners if they should go insane while on the job. The following story is revealing:

On July 9, 1973, Major Harold L. Hering, U.S. Air Force, asked a question. He was a student at Vandenberg Air Force Base in California where officers learn how to launch nuclear missiles from their underground silos. According to Major Hering, it seemed like a logical question, so he raised his hand and asked. What he wanted to know was this: If he got an order to fire the missiles how could he be sure it was a lawful order? How, for example, could he be sure it wasn't fake, sent by someone other than the President? Or could he be sure the President himself hadn't gone crazy? Major Hering never got an answer.

Instead, the Air Force dropped him from the course, stopped his promotion to Lieutenant Colonel and began proceedings to kick him out of the service. Major Hering, a 21-year veteran who received the Distinguished Flying Cross in Vietnam, was given an administrative discharge from the Air Force for "failure to demonstrate acceptable qualities of leadership." He had, the Air Force said, a "defective mental attitude toward his duties."[13]

Obviously, if the system is going to work, the officers who are responsible for putting the keys in the slots and turning them must act without question when they receive the correct coded signal. However, history demonstrates that Major Hering was asking valid questions. The three major computer errors in 1979 and 1980 set in motion alarms that could conceivably have resulted in commands to launch. There have been episodes in our history when Presidents of the United States were not fully in control of their faculties, either physical or mental. There have been other times when Presidents have been under severe emotional stress. In 1974, when Congress was considering impeachment proceedings, President Richard Nixon called several members of the House to the White House to seek their support. The President was very emotional as he asserted that his work for peace had been much more important to the nation than any "little burglary at Watergate." Then he said something very frightening, perhaps to demonstrate what a responsible leader he had been: "Why, I can go into my office and pick up the telephone, and in 25 minutes 70 million people will be dead."[14]

The CBS television documentary *The Defense of the United States* included the following exchange:

BOB SCHIEFFER: More disturbing, perhaps, is the ease with which strategists talk about first strike. Limited nuclear war has made the horror of a nuclear exchange seem somehow manageable, even commonplace. That

15

suggests we have finally learned to live with the bomb.

Out in the missile fields of North Dakota, where men control warheads hundreds of times more powerful than the bomb dropped on Hiroshima, it is just another day at the office.

CREWMAN: I have Echo, November, Alpha, Bravo, Lima, Echo.

CREWMAN: Okay. Let's coordinate the command with everybody else.

CREWMAN: Everybody is coordinated.

CREWMAN: Coordinated!

CREWMAN: Okay. I'm launching at this time. (Buzzer) I have missile away.

SCHIEFFER: It must be an enormous responsibility. You must . . . to be in charge, as you two gentlemen are, of the most powerful weapon that man has ever devised?

CREWMAN: Yes, sir, it is a definite challenge. It's more responsibility than I could obtain in a civilian world. And to me that is job satisfaction.

SCHIEFFER: Do you guys actually know which missiles out there in the silos are yours?

CREWMAN: Yes, sir, we certainly do.

SCHIEFFER: And do you know the targets that they are targeted for?

CREWMAN: No, sir, we do not.

SCHIEFFER: You don't know?

CREWMAN: No, sir.

SCHIEFFER: Do you ever wonder?

CREWMAN: Yes, sir, sometimes I do. I wonder what the target is. You know, are the people over there thinking the same way I am? . . . But to actually know where the target is for each missile, I really wouldn't want to know. Personally I wouldn't want to know.

SCHIEFFER: Why not?

CREWMAN: Well, I—I really don't—I don't have to know to start with. Secondly, I would—I would feel kind of—kind of emotional about what kind of people I'd be destroying.[15]

* * *

COUNTERFORCE AND LAUNCH ON WARNING

There are many reasons why accidental nuclear war is becoming progressively more likely, but the most important is the emergence of the doctrine of counterforce and the directly related policy of launch on warning. "Counterforce" is a term for the capability to attack the military forces of an enemy. In strategic lingo it means the ability to attack the strategic nuclear weapons systems of the enemy. "Launch on warning" is the term used, especially with respect to intercontinental land-based nuclear weapons, to describe action taken to prevent destruction of the weapons before they can be used. Today the U.S. and Soviet ICBMs are housed in hardened missile silos. Rather than permit the missiles to be destroyed in their silos, they would be launched at first warning of attack.

We and the Soviets are on the brink of developing strategic counterforce capabilities, which means that we both are moving toward launch on warning. When we have arrived at that point, our nuclear weapons systems will be on hair-trigger alert. Both sides will know that the other side has the capacity to launch a first strike which could destroy not only missiles but the command and control and communications system of the other side as well.

We have gotten ourselves into this dilemma partly because of the inventiveness of man and the momentum of technology, but mostly we have reached this extraordinarily dangerous point in history by bad thinking, limited leadership, and failed diplomacy. Both the Russians and the Americans have sought security through military buildup and a continuing arms race. As a result, each year both superpowers become less secure. We have reached the point of diminishing returns. There is no such thing as nuclear superiority anymore.

In order to change course, it is important to know how we arrived at this point. Nuclear weapons have been used only twice: at Hiroshima and Nagasaki, Japan, at the end of World War II. After the Soviets succeeded in building nuclear weapons, our doctrine became avoidance of nuclear war through

17

deterrence. At first our nuclear superiority permitted us to guarantee our NATO allies that if they were ever attacked by Soviet forces, we would strike the USSR with nuclear weapons. But as the Soviet nuclear arsenal grew, we adopted a deterrence policy of mutual assured destruction. This meant that both the United States and the USSR would be mutually deterred from attacking the other side because no military advantage could be achieved. After an attack both sides would continue to have a sufficient number of remaining nuclear weapons to destroy the other assuredly. The assurance was particularly secure for the United States, which maintained a well-balanced triad of strategic weapons, including ICBMs, strategic submarines, and strategic bombers.

In 1969 the United States made one of its most dangerous and most expensive strategic errors. The arms control process was under way with negotiations to limit and control strategic nuclear weapons. The United States had developed the technology for deploying multiple independently targeted reentry vehicle (MIRV) warheads on its nuclear missiles. There was a debate within the Nixon administration whether to deploy or to negotiate with the Soviets a total ban on MIRV. Since the United States had a five-year lead over the Soviets in MIRV technology, the President and Kissinger decided to authorize the deployment of multiple warheads. If instead we had negotiated a ban on multiple warheads, we would not be faced today with the threat to our ICBMs and the terrible dangers of counterforce weapons on both sides.

The SALT (strategic arms limitation talks) I agreement signed in Moscow in 1972 placed some limits on numbers of ICBMs and strategic submarines. The Soviets were allowed more of both these categories because the United States had multiple warheads and thus four times as many warheads as the Soviets and also because the agreement did not include strategic bombers, in which the United States maintains a three to one lead. SALT I was an interim agreement for a five-year period.

The most significant arms control achievement reached at the 1972 summit was the antiballistic missile (ABM) treaty which insured the continuation of mutually assured destruction. It meant that neither side could build a defense to protect its cities from ballistic missile attack. The ABM treaty enhances deterrence and has also saved tens of billions of dollars for both sides. Even so, as we have seen, some members of the Reagan administration are opposed to renewing the treaty because they advocate building an antiballistic missiles system in their search for the chimera of superiority.

In 1974, when James Schlesinger was secretary of defense, a new U.S. strategic doctrine began to emerge. It was clear by then that the Soviets would soon have multiple warheads on their huge rockets. At first the United States had built very large missiles, such as the Titan II's, with nine-megaton warheads, which are still deployed. But as U.S. technology advanced, especially in miniaturization and computers, the United States moved to smaller, much more accurate missiles. The Minuteman III has three warheads which are relatively small but are still several times larger than the bomb that obliterated Hiroshima.

The Soviets did not have the technology to build these small, accurate missiles, so they relied on their much bigger city busters. With MIRV it became hypothetically possible for them to place enough warheads on their large SS-18 and SS-19 missiles with enough accuracy and explosive power to blow up most of our ICBMs, most of our strategic bombers which were not in the air, and most of our strategic submarines not at sea. Such a hypothetical first-strike capability, Schlesinger claimed, would put a U.S. President in the position of facing "surrender or suicide." If the United States should counterattack with its nuclear submarines at sea and with its airborne bombers, the Soviets would still have enough weapons left to destroy our cities. Schlesinger admitted that it was unlikely that the Soviet leaders would attack, knowing that our strategic submarines at sea could destroy all their cities; nevertheless, he claimed that the perception of a strategic advantage might give them the capability for political blackmail.

Schlesinger set in motion the notion that we needed to develop counterforce weapons which would permit us to destroy Soviet strategic weapons. He spoke of a "selective first strike" policy and the capability for "nuclear war fighting." Testifying before the Senate Foreign Relations Committee, Schlesinger said: "What we are seeking is the ability to conduct constrained nuclear warfare, so that if deterrence were to fail . . . the use of nuclear weapons would not result in the kind of orgy of destruction to which members of the committee have referred."[16] This concept of limited nuclear war was the second major error in U.S. strategic policy, second only to the MIRV decision.

When the Carter administration moved into the White House in 1977, Secretary of Defense Harold Brown categorically rejected the validity of limited nuclear war as a rational basis for policy. But then, unaccountably, Brown backed a series of expedient decisions which, in effect, reversed his common sense and gave support to a drift toward irrationality. As a sop to the Joint Chiefs of Staff to obtain their backing for the SALT II treaty, Brown supported a decision to build and deploy the MX missile. The MX is so large and so accurate that when deployed, it will be capable of destroying most of the Soviet strategic weapons, if they have not been launched on warning. Along with the Trident II submarine-launched missile, the MX is a counterforce weapon.

But even more disastrous, from the standpoint of U.S. national security, was Secretary Brown's role in developing a new strategic concept which was declared in Presidential Directive 59. PD 59, as it is known, was released to the public in August 1980, just before the Democratic National Convention.

On August 20, describing the presidential directive at the Naval War College, Brown said: "The overriding objective of our strategic forces is to deter nuclear war . . . fashioning strategic nuclear policy that will lead us away from nuclear war and not toward it." But Brown and the Carter administration had fashioned a doctrine, and the authority to build weapons to implement that doctrine, which ran counter to their professed "overriding objective." The new doctrine, because it accepted the concept of fighting limited nuclear wars, reduced the credibility of strategic deterrence, increased the possibility of accidental nuclear war, and undercut the prospects for strategic arms control.

Brown had been struggling with this central issue ever since he became secretary in 1977, as evidenced by his annual reports to Congress. In his report of January 1979, he said: "In the interests of stability, we avoid the capability of eliminating the other side's deterrent . . . In short, we must be quite willing—as we have been for some time—to accept the principle of mutual deterrence, and design our defense posture in light of that principle." Brown acknowledged that it was difficult to maintain a balance: "It is all well and good to say that we want both deterrence and stability. But how do we know when we are strong enough to deter, but not so strong as to drive the other side to actions detrimental to both?"

Of course, the best answer to that question is through strategic arms control, but now we are moving on a course which will make realistic, verifiable arms control virtually impossible. Secretary Brown said that we need new weapons systems to be in a position "to attack, in a selective measured way, a range of military, industrial and political control targets, while retaining an assured destruction capacity in reserve." Brown wanted to "ensure that the Soviet leadership knows that if they chose some intermediate level of aggression, we could, by selective, large (but still less than maximum) nuclear attacks, exact an unacceptable high price."

Why, if the Soviets know we have assured destruction, would they be so insane as to launch "some intermediate level" of nuclear attack? Brown himself demonstrated how implausible this thinking is. He said:

In adopting and implementing this policy we have no more illusions than our predecessors that a nuclear war could be closely and surgically controlled. There are, of course, great uncertainties about what would happen if nuclear weapons were ever used again. . . . My own view remains that a full-scale thermonuclear exchange would constitute an unprecedented disaster for the Soviet Union and for the United States. And I am not at all

21

persuaded that what started as a demonstration, or even a tightly controlled use of strategic forces for larger purposes, could be kept from escalating to a full-scale thermonuclear exchange.

Brown frequently asserted that a strategic nuclear attack is "the least likely military contingency we face." And he admitted that preparing for limited nuclear war may appear to be "contrary to the precepts of common sense, but in an arena where the stakes are so high and the uncertainties so great, common sense is not always an infallible guide. It may be reasonable in daily personal life to equate the implausible with the impossible; nuclear calculations involving the survival of the nation require us to distinguish between the two." But by preparing to fight a most implausible limited nuclear war, we make nuclear war more possible and deterrence much less stable. All the logic of Brown's principles of deterrence was contradicted.

U.S. doctrine had been changing since 1974, when then Secretary of Defense James Schlesinger launched his ideas about counterforce and limited nuclear war fighting. As Brown said: "Presidental Directive 59 codifies our restated doctrine, and gives guidance for further evolution in our planning and systems acquisition." Indeed it does. It provides authority and momentum for all the new counterforce weapons.

It has delighted those strategists who wistfully long for the days of U.S. nuclear superiority, who believe that the threat of nuclear confrontation could persuade or coerce the Soviets to back down—as was claimed by some to be the case in the Cuban missile crisis, though it was not. Even though some of them acknowledge that nuclear superiority may not again be attainable in any meaningful sense, they believe the exploitation of our technological advantages can exert useful political pressure on the Soviet system.[17]

President Reagan and his advisers have rejected the SALT II treaty. Reagan says that he would like to negotiate deep cuts in the nuclear forces of the two superpowers but asserts that before such a negotiation can be successful, the United

States needs to build up its strategic forces considerably. The Reagan administration has accepted the failed logic of Carter's Presidential Directive 59 and has moved ahead with all the counterforce weapons, including the MX, Pershing II, and Trident II.

In July 1980 a meeting was held at the National Defense University to consider "Rethinking U.S. Security Policy for the 1980's." Among those attending were several participants who were soon to be Reagan advisers, including Paul Nitze, now chief negotiator for the United States in the medium-range nuclear weapons talks, and General Edward L. Rowny, the SALT negotiator for the administration. The group reached some ominous conclusions from the standpoint of those who believe in controlling and reducing strategic nuclear weapons. They agreed that no weapons programs should be deferred merely because they would interfere with future control of strategic weapons. Moreover, they concluded that we should not "fiddle with systems in order to make them more inspectable, verifiable, or countable" in future agreements. They urged that we "do what makes sense operationally and worry later whether some future SALT process can accommodate these systems."

In other words, these are men who have rejected serious strategic arms control and reduction as an essential part of our national security. They believe that our security is better protected by building counterforce weapons. Some of the counterforce weapons and some of the cruise missiles are almost impossible to monitor because they are so small and/or so mobile. But adequate verification is an essential part of any arms control agreement. So when we cease being concerned whether nuclear weapons are countable or verifiable, we are no longer seriously interested in the limitation and reduction of nuclear weapons by negotiation.

This rejection of meaningful arms control was rationalized at the conference in a paper entitled "Strategic Stability Reconsidered," written by Colin S. Gray, now an adviser to the Reagan Defense Department. Mr. Gray rejects the concept of mutual assured destruction and asserts that the strategic balance would be stable "were it to permit Western governments to enjoy not-implausible prospects of defeating the enemy (on his own terms) and of ensuring Western political-social survival and recovery. . . . Forces which do not lend themselves to *politically intelligent* employment in war, are unlikely to suffice to deter [emphasis added]."[18] The tragedy about Mr. Gray and other Reagan strategists who share the same view is that they are taken seriously.

They will not understand until the holocaust comes that there is no such thing as "politically intelligent" employment of strategic nuclear weapons. At this stage in history it is recklessly irresponsible to take the risk of trying to build the weapons necessary to destroy the Soviet nuclear arsenal and at the same time attempt to ensure our own political-social survival and recovery. That is suicidal fantasy. That is Russian Roulette.

During the Senate hearings on SALT II former Secretary of State Henry Kissinger and present Secretary of State Alexander Haig both asserted that it is immoral to rely any longer on a doctrine of mutual assured destruction. They want to replace the policy, which has successfully deterred war for more than twenty-five years, with a new policy which would permit us to destroy Soviet strategic weapons without hitting Soviet cities. If the Soviets ever launched a first strike against our strategic weapons without attacking our cities, it would be immoral, they claimed, for the United States to counterattack against Soviet cities.

This concept of fighting clean nuclear wars limited to military targets is incredible. Nobody has ever made a persuasive explanation of how to keep a nuclear war limited because it is most probable that whichever side is losing will always escalate to the next level of nuclear attack. Furthermore, there is no such thing as a surgical first strike. If either side attacks the strategic weapons of the other, millions of people would be killed by blast, fire, and radiation in fallout. As we have seen, the Soviets have made it clear that any limited attack on their territory would elicit an all-out counterattack on their part. Edward Luttwak, a young protégé of James Schlesinger and an adviser to the Reagan Pentagon, has expressed doubt about taking the Soviets' doctrine seriously. If the United States launches a limited attack in a real conflict, Luttwak believes Moscow will "know what the U.S. is up to and will show restraint."[19] The off-the-cuff opinions of such strategists as Luttwak provide a fragile basis upon which to rest the security of the United States.

Clearly the existence of nuclear weapons in the arsenals of both sides has helped prevent a war between the superpowers. But if the idea that some forms of nuclear war are more moral than others is ever accepted, the deterrent to nuclear war could be eroded seriously. The best deterrent to nuclear war is the unmistakable knowledge, by both sides, that any nuclear attack will bring a counterattack against all major cities. That knowledge is the most exacting assurance there is that nuclear weapons will never be used. Any attempt to modify, refine, or limit that assurance diminishes the deterrence.

A strategic nuclear attack by the Soviets is the least likely military contingency we face, yet we continue to press ahead for counterforce weapons which make an accidental launch by the Russians a real possibility. The first U.S. strategic counterforce weapons are scheduled for deployment in Germany in early 1984. Pershing II missiles, which will be deployed there, are very accurate and will be capable of blowing up Soviet command and control, and some Soviet missiles, within six minutes of being fired. Since the Soviets will not want to risk the consequences of such a strike, they will almost certainly adopt a policy of launch on warning. In other words, the deployment of Pershing II missiles will virtually guarantee a much greater risk of accidental Soviet launch. So a decision taken ostensibly to enhance the security of NATO will, instead, undermine it.

In his annual reports to Congress in 1979 and 1980 former Secretary of Defense Brown dealt with the growing vulnerability of U.S. ICBMs by observing that the Soviets could never be sure that we hadn't adopted a policy of launch on warning. In June 1980 Fred Ikle, former director of the Arms Control and Disarmament Agency under President Ford and now undersecretary of defense for policy, wrote an article attacking Brown for *The Washington Post* entitled "The Growing Risk of War by Accident." He said:

> The more we rely on "launch-on-warning" (or, for that matter, the more the Soviets do), the greater the risk of accidental nuclear war. Anyone who tries to explain that this tactic could be implemented in a totally reliable and safe way is a fool. He does not even know how little he knows. No one can understand in sufficient detail all the possible malfunctions, unanticipated events and human errors that might interact someday to confound the "redundant" warning systems or to bypass the "safeguards" against an unintended release of the command to launch a missile salvo.
>
> The crux of the matter is that the more important it becomes to "launch on warning," the more dangerous it will be. The tightening noose around our neck is the requirement for speed. The more certain one wants to be that our missile forces could be launched within minutes and under all circumstances, the more one has to practice the system and to loosen the safeguards. And remember: As in June, 1980, there will be false alerts.[20]

Mr. Ikle's warning is apt, and it applies even more to the Soviets, who have a less advanced system of command and control, than to us.

Under those circumstances it is almost unbelievable that we are still pressing for deployment of the Pershing II missiles. As Mr. Ikle notes, "the tightening noose around our neck [but especially the Soviet neck] is the requirement for speed." A six-minute launch on warning system will have to be controlled by computers. Unfortunately we refuse to sell our more advanced computers to the Soviets on grounds of national security. Our computer technology is well ahead of the Soviets', but as we've already noted, even our computers make errors.

Shortly after the Ikle article Secretary Brown was interviewed by *The Wall Street Journal* about the possible consequence of the false alarms in the U.S. strategic warning system. He was asked at what point after a warning we would launch a counterattack. He replied:

> I think the idea of dependency on launch under attack is a bad idea . . . we ought not to let computers make the decision as to when to go to war.
> There are two problems with a doctrine of "launch under attack." One is the false alarm problem. The other is: Can you really do it? Can you make all the decisions that you would have to make in a short time, be it 10 minutes, 15 minutes, 25 minutes? I think we can't be certain we would be able to do that. That is why we shouldn't depend on it.[21]

Brown recognizes that a system of launch on warning would risk "going to war by computer." Yet we are willing to risk forcing the Soviets into that position.

Richard De Lauer, undersecretary of defense for research and engineering in the Reagan administration, told the Senate Armed Services Committee: "We are not changing our consistently held view that launch under attack is a good capability . . . but a dangerously destabilizing strategy to depend on. We do not, and we will not, depend on it." To those who suggest that the Soviets might adopt such a strategy De Lauer said: "That suggests that the Soviets are not as rational as we, and I reject that view. I believe my Soviet counterpart can see the flaws and related potential for accidential catastrophe as clearly as I, and he will have no part of it."[22] There is one course of action which could make Mr. De Lauer's hopes become reality, and that would be for both sides to make deep cuts in their nuclear forces and to avoid the deployment of counterforce weapons which force the other side into a corner from which there is no escape.

Apparently Mr. De Lauer has not done his homework on developments in U.S. policy from the standpoint of launch under attack. Here is what some top U.S. leaders said on the CBS documentary *The Defense of the United States:*

> SCHIEFFER: About a third of the [B-52] fleet is always on alert—that is, loaded with bombs, crews standing by for

27

immediate takeoff. And they seem ready for any contingency, even taking off with drapes drawn.

FREDERICK JAICKS: Well, as these airplanes sit on alert, we would probably launch under attack on a survivability launch, and we would be under the effect of a nuclear attack, probably or possibly, and we'd want to keep the pilot from becoming flash blind. . . .

SCHIEFFER: Launch under attack has never been official U.S. policy, but the truth is we practice it every year in war games like this one: Operation Global Shield . . .

LIEUTENANT GENERAL KELLY BURKE: The United States never has and, in my opinion, never should, renounce the possibility—of launching its missiles and forces on a confirmed warning of a Soviet attack. But it's an altogether different state of affairs than to structure your forces in such a manner that they can survive only based on that—that launch on warning. . . .

DAN RATHER: But your basic recommendation is that we must be prepared—we must at least be prepared—to do a launch under attack.

SECRETARY [of Defense Caspar] WEINBERGER: . . . it gives undue emphasis to single out any one particular kind of option and say that that is the one we're considering. We're considering them all. We aren't eliminating anything. . . .[23]

George Kistiakowsky, science adviser to President Dwight Eisenhower and one of the world's most authoritative experts on nuclear weapons, had this to say:

Given the present geopolitical trends and the quality of political leaders that burden mankind it would be a miracle if no nuclear warheads were exploded in anger before the end of this century and only a bit smaller miracle if that did not lead to a nuclear holocaust.[24]

Chapter II

The Soviet Blunder

The leaders of the Soviet Union, by indulging in a series of military adventures in the Third World, have committed a devastating blunder which can be repaired only by a fundamental shift in policy. Soviet involvement, either indirect or direct, in intervention with external combat forces in Angola, Ethiopia, South Yemen, and Afghanistan, combined with continuing support for the Vietnamese invasion of Cambodia, has resulted in a disastrous setback for the highest priorities of Soviet national security policy. The Soviets failed to grasp the enormous political consequences of the U.S. defeat in Vietnam, and they seriously misestimated the probable response of the United States to their aggressive adventures in the Third World.

President Leonid Brezhnev's national security priorities call for the avoidance of war with the West through peaceful coexistence and arms control agreements. Soviet policy emphasizes, especially, measures to prevent direct military confrontation between the superpowers. In other words, the Soviets give highest priority to national survival. However, their actions in the Third World during the past seven years have inspired a response in the United States which has rekindled the arms race, revived the cold war, and blocked the strategic arms (SALT) process. U.S.-Soviet relations are at their lowest ebb since the Stalin era, and the danger of unintentional or accidental nuclear war increases every day.

This terrible historical retrogression should never have occurred. In many ways both powers have reverted to the cold war reflexes of the 1950's. But the technology of weapons, especially nuclear weapons, has advanced to the point where the nonsense of the fifties is a luxury in which neither power can afford to indulge. Of course, there have been destructive forces at work on both sides, but the primary responsibility must be attributed to those in the Kremlin who were willing to take the risks implicit in the dispatch of combat forces to Third World disputes. The Soviets have presented elaborate explanations for their actions, but no matter what the reasons, the consequences, in terms of blocking more important Soviet interests, should demonstrate them to be wrong to Soviet leaders—doubly wrong because they ensured the political victory of cold warriors and confrontationists in the United States.

The worst mistake of Soviet policy makers was their failure to make a correct evaluation of the American experience in Vietnam. A fundamental change took place in the United States, not only in public opinion but in government policy in both the executive branch and the Congress. The vast majority of Americans wanted peace, wanted to end the cold war, and, above all, wanted to avoid sending American boys abroad to intervene in foreign wars. During the cold war the United States frequently supported military intervention, either with its own troops, as in Korea, Lebanon, the Dominican Republic, and Vietnam, or with covert paramilitary operations, proxy or so-called volunteer forces. At one time there were 550,000 U.S. military personnel in Vietnam.

But after Vietnam the American people wanted foreign military intervention to end. This was a deep, widely held feeling throughout the country. National polls from 1970 to 1975 reflected a noninterventionist opinion of more than 80 percent. Those Americans who were alarmed that the Soviets might take advantage of U.S. abhorrence of military intervention referred to this powerful sentiment as a kind of national sickness—the "Vietnam syndrome." It was clear, however, that it would take a very serious threat to American security to change the noninterventionist sentiment. Soviet actions during the last half of the 1970's, helped along by the distorted interpretations of American hawks, have reversed the "Vietnam syndrome." Détente has been a dirty word in the United States for several years because most Americans think the Soviets cheated. This happened primarily because of bad Soviet judgment.

When Richard Nixon moved into the White House in January 1969, he announced that he was gradually going to bring the boys home from Vietnam and that he would change the U.S. stance toward the Soviet Union from confrontation to negotiation. This was received enthusiastically throughout the United States and Russia as well. The process of negotiation proceeded smoothly, and by May 1972 Presidents Nixon and Brezhnev were able to hold a summit meeting in Moscow, where they signed the antiballistic missile treaty and the SALT I interim agreement, setting limits on intercontinental ballistic missiles (ICBMs) and on submarine-launched ballistic missiles (SLBMs). They agreed to start SALT II negotiations based on the "principle of equality and equal security."

They also signed an agreement called the "Basic Principles of Relations between the USSR and the USA" which acknowledged that in an age of nuclear weapons there is no alternative to "peaceful coexistence." This is the term that the Soviets prefer, though it is interchangeable with the word "détente." The "Basic Principles" committed the two powers to "refrain from efforts to obtain unilateral advantage at the expense of the other." The principles were seen as broad ground rules for the inevitable competition that would continue between the two superpowers in an era of détente and negotiation. The results of the Moscow summit inspired a mood of harmony and euphoria in most of the world. In subsequent speeches Brezhnev frequently asserted that "détente is irreversible."

Détente had its roots, even before the Moscow summit, in the *Ostpolitik* of West German Chancellor Willy Brandt from 1969 to 1972, which transformed the major cold war issues of Europe. This included a nonaggression treaty between West Germany and the USSR, a four-power agreement in Berlin significantly reducing the political pressure there, and diplomatic recognition and expanded trade and cultural relations between West Germany and Poland and Czechoslovakia. But the most momentous act of *Ostpolitik* was the recognition of East Germany by West Germany as a sovereign, independent state. This recognition, which was followed by that of the United States and the other nations of Western Europe, virtually eliminated the dangerous political pressures for reuniting Germany.

The spirit of détente prevailed for almost eighteen months until Egypt and Syria broke the tranquillity. They launched a surprise attack on Israeli positions on the Jewish holy day of Yom Kippur in October 1973. The short war resulted in serious losses of soldiers and weapons for both sides. The Soviets had armed the Egyptians and Syrians and were widely suspected of being aware of the plans for attack. Since Israel is so closely allied to the United States, the war was interpreted by many as evidence of Soviet willingness to risk a damaging blow to détente. Democratic Senator Henry Jackson of Washington said the Yom Kippur attack demonstrated the "speciousness of détente."

Henry Trofimenko, a top Soviet specialist on U.S. foreign policy, writing in the Summer 1981 issue of *Foreign Affairs*, had this to say about Soviet involvement:

> The massive transfers of Soviet military hardware at the most generous financial terms and the assistance rendered by Soviet military specialists helped to build up the impressive military potential of Egypt and Syria that made it possible for them to counter Israeli military force with their own. After the 1973 war in the Middle East, Soviet military aid helped to compensate for wartime losses of the Arabs. . . .[1]

The war was a standoff, but the prestige of Anwar Sadat was considerably enhanced. The American Jewish community was angered and hostile toward not only the Arabs but also the Russians.

Détente continued to flourish despite the war. Nevertheless, serious damage had been done, with repercussions soon to come. The crisis of Watergate overshadowed everything else in American politics at the time. But during 1974 U.S.-Soviet contacts grew, with more scientific, cultural, and tourist exchanges than ever before. Trade, especially U.S. grain sales, increased considerably, and more export licenses were granted by the United States for Soviet purchases of advanced technology. Moscow ordered an end to the jamming of U.S. radio broadcasts, so that Russians were able to listen freely to American interpretation of the news.

Most important of all, real progress was being made in the SALT II talks. Gerald Ford, who had replaced Nixon as President, and Secretary of State Henry Kissinger went to Vladivostok in November 1974 for another summit meeting with President Brezhnev. They reached an agreement on a limit of strategic weapon launchers, for each side, of 2,400, 1,320 of which could have multiple warheads (MIRV). This ceiling on strategic weapons was preposterously high, but it did, for the first time, establish a formula of rough numerical equality. The Soviets made significant concessions, accepting less than actual parity. They agreed to drop their demands that British and French strategic forces, and U.S. forward-based systems in Europe capable of striking the Soviet Union, should be included in the strategic balance.

According to Soviet sources, one of the reasons they agreed to compromise was a promise from Henry Kissinger that the United States would agree to a major trade agreement, including most favored nation (MFN) status for the USSR and substantial credits from the Export-Import Bank. But it was not to be. Capitalizing on lingering feelings inspired by the Yom Kippur War, Senator Jackson sponsored an amendment to the U.S.-Soviet trade bill which would grant the USSR MFN status only if it allowed a substantial increase in the emigration of Jews. Secretary Kissinger tried to circumvent any formal stipulation by assurances contained in a letter he sent to Jackson.

Kissinger, having worked out a complex deal through diplomatic channels, said that it was the U.S. assumption that the Soviets would increase the level above the 35,000 Soviet Jews permitted to emigrate in 1973. Jackson didn't accept this formula, saying in his reply to Kissinger that "60,000 emigrants a year would be considered a benchmark—a minimum standard of initial compliance." Both houses of Congress decisively passed the trade bill, with the Jackson-Vanik amendment attached. Congress also enacted an amendment to curb Export-Import Bank loans to the USSR. The Soviets angrily rejected the trade bill, saying that they would not submit to the humiliation of interference in their internal affairs, even in return for badly needed American technology and favorable tariff treatment. That was in December 1974; by 1976 Jewish emigration had dropped from an annual rate of 35,000 to 10,000.[2]

According to Boris Rabbot, a high-level Soviet defector now at Columbia University, the Jackson amendment represented a severe setback to President Brezhnev's policy of détente with the United States. Former KGB chief Alexander Shelepin, who was Brezhnev's major opponent in the Politburo in 1974 and 1975, said the Jackson proposal would "amount to selling human beings, an unacceptable affront." Shelepin recommended aggressive counteraction. The Caetano dictatorship had collapsed in Portugal with a prospect for revolution, so Shelepin urged the Politburo to send "volunteers" on the model of Soviet support for the Republican forces in the Spanish Civil War nearly forty years before.

Brezhnev's political position had been deteriorating, along with his health. He retreated to his dacha, where he rested and licked his wounds, trying to counter the moves of Shelepin. He emerged with a different idea—sending Cuban troops to assist the Communist side in the civil war in Angola. The Politburo accepted the new policy, and Brezhnev emerged victorious. On April 16, 1975, *Pravda* announced that Shelepin had retired. So, as Rabbot interpreted it, the real Soviet response to the Jackson amendment was the adventure in Angola. The collapse of the dream that significant trade and aid would be coming from the United States "intensified the struggle between 'hawks' and 'doves' in the Soviet leadership."[3]

THE ANGOLAN INTERVENTION

A struggle for power among various factions had existed in Angola starting in the early 1960's. By 1973 three major political organizations had emerged. The National Front for the Liberation of Angola (FNLA) was led by Holden Roberto. The FNLA, by 1975, had the strongest military position partly because it was supported by military assistance from China and a 120-man military training mission led by a Chinese major general. The second group, led by Jonas Savimbi, was the National Union for the Total Independence of Angola (UNITA). It too received early support from the Chinese as well as other anti-Soviet elements. The third faction, the Popular Movement for the Liberation of Angola (MPLA), was directed by Agostinho Neto, a Marxist, who had been supported for several years by Soviet and Eastern European training and arms as well as by the Portuguese left.

The United States government did not become actively involved in Angola until 1975. In January the 40 Committee, responsible for reviewing covert operations for the National Security Council, authorized the CIA to funnel $300,000 to the FNLA. In the spring of 1975 the FNLA launched an offensive, which moved to Luanda, the capital of Angola. Holden Roberto purchased the largest newspaper in Luanda and a television station through which he tried to establish his political leadership.

As the Soviets stepped up their shipments of military supplies to Neto, the United States responded by expanding its clandestine shipments to both the FNLA and UNITA. By mid-1975 the CIA had been authorized to arrange transfers of more than $30 million of military hardware. In late October, as the Portuguese Army left Angola, Soviet military technicians and Cuban combat forces began to arrive. At the same time a South African expeditionary force launched a surprise attack from South West Africa. There were 1,200 South African Army regulars, equipped with armored cars and helicopter gunships, joining forces with UNITA and Portuguese mercenaries. They were able to drive the MPLA out of the southern half of Angola.

However, on Independence Day, November 11, the MPLA announced in Luanda the creation of the People's Republic of Angola, which was immediately recognized by the Soviet Union. The Soviets began to carry out Brezhnev's plans, developed earlier that year, in detail. From that day forward Cuban combat troops were airlifted into Angola in huge Soviet transport planes. By sea and air the Soviets also dispatched T-54 and T-34 tanks, 122-millimeter rockets, and tons of other sophisticated weapons.[4]

By December Congress had gotten wind of the details of the CIA operations. Black African nations were highly critical of the involvement of the white South African troops. The military and political situation looked bad for U.S. interests. By a vote of 54 to 22 the Senate banned all further covert aid to Angola. The House also voted, in January, not to authorize any overt support which Kissinger had requested to strengthen the FNLA-UNITA forces in hopes of achieving a military stalemate. The vote against the Kissinger plan was 323 to 99. U.S. critics of the congressional action said that it reflected American impotence inspired by the "Vietnam syndrome."

The Angolan struggle was, by then, certain to end as a Communist victory. The South African involvement ensured that most of black Africa would support Neto. The congressional action brought an end to further U.S. support, but most decisive of all was the growing presence of well-trained, well-equipped Cuban combat troops. Furthermore, there could be no question that the Cubans were serving as proxies of the Soviet Union. They were airlifted and sealifted in Soviet planes and ships, and they were trained, equipped, and financed by the Soviet Union. They were also assisted by Soviet military advisers who had been dispatched to Angola.

The Angolan War represented the first time the Soviet Union had been responsible for sending third-party combat troops anywhere in the world outside Eastern Europe. The Soviets had given military equipment to the North Koreans in the Korean War, the North Vietnamese in the Vietnam War, the Egyptians and Syrians in the Yom Kippur War, but those were indigenous forces. The Cubans were external forces. Henry Kissinger, especially, was alarmed and angry—angry because of his feelings of impotence.

Kissinger was a strong proponent of what has become known as linkage. He believed that U.S. policy toward the Soviet Union should be based on an interrelationship of rewards for behavior acceptable to the United States and punishments for unacceptable behavior. He adopted the view that Soviet behavior in the external world should inevitably be linked to progress in arms control from the standpoint of balance of power and practical considerations in U.S. domestic politics. The SALT negotiations had reached a critical point when Kissinger went to Moscow in January 1976. But Kissinger believed that the SALT deal he had in mind should be linked to a Cuban withdrawal from Angola.

When Kissinger discussed the issues with President Brezhnev, the latter replied mockingly that he hardly knew where Angola was and that in any event he was not prepared to negotiate with the United States matters which were the internal affairs of the government of Angola. When Kissinger later pressed the point, Foreign Minister Andrei Gromyko told Kissinger that the Cuban intervention was a decision which the Cubans had made themselves. He pointed out that Cuba has natural historical ties with Africa. Finally, Gromyko rejected the concept of linkage with the arms control negotiations since equal, verifiable limitation of strategic weapons is just as advantageous to the United States as to the Soviet Union. At the end of the conversation Kissinger informed Gromyko that he was making a serious mistake. He said the Cuban adventure in Angola in time would have deleterious repercussions for the Soviet Union.[5]

When Kissinger returned to the United States, he made one more try to persuade the Congress. He asserted that Angola represented a post-Vietnam test of U.S. will. He told a Senate subcommittee that "the Soviet Union must not be given any opportunity to use military forces for aggressive purposes without running the risk of conflict with us."[6] Taking his case to the public in a major address in San Francisco, he said:

If the Soviet Union is permitted to exploit opportunities arising out of local conflicts by military means, the hopes we have for progress towards a more peaceful international order will ultimately be undermined. This is why the Soviet Union's massive and unprecedented intervention in the internal affairs of Africa with nearly 200 million dollars of military equipment, its advisors, and its transport of the large expeditionary force of 11,000 Cuban combat troops must be a matter of urgent concern.

Angola represents the first time that the Soviets have moved militarily at long distance to impose a regime of their choice. It is the first time that the U.S. has failed to respond to Soviet military moves outside the immediate Soviet orbit. And it is the first time that Congress has halted national action in the middle of a crisis. . . . After the Senate vote to block further aid to Angola, Cuba more than doubled its forces and Soviet military aid was resumed on a large scale. . . . [It] can never be in our interest to let the Soviet Union act as the world's policeman. . . . If the United States is seen to waver in the face of massive Soviet and Cuban intervention, what will be the perception of leaders around the world as they make decisions concerning their future security?

And what conclusions will an unopposed superpower draw when the next opportunity for intervention beckons? Where are we now? The Government has a duty to make clear in the Soviet Union and Cuba that Angola sets no precedent, that this type of action will not be tolerated again.[7]

Unfortunately Kissinger's warnings were insufficiently heeded in both the Soviet Union and the United States. The Cuban troop buildup in Angola continued at an unrestrained pace, reaching a figure of 19,000 to 20,000 troops, augmented by 4,000 Cuban civilian technicians. Détente, at least as the Soviets defined it, continued in a somewhat less robust condition. A major achievement for President Brezhnev had been the Helsinki summit meeting in July 1975, when the chiefs of state of all the governments of Europe (except Albania) and the United States and Canada signed a "Declaration on Security and Cooperation in Europe." The declaration had been a major goal of Soviet foreign policy since World War II. It was one of several important steps that Brezhnev wanted to accomplish before the 1976 Soviet Communist Party Congress.

The Helsinki agreement is not legally binding, but it had tremendous symbolic and political importance to the Soviets. It recognized the European boundaries established by World War II and pledged nonintervention in the affairs of other states. For totalitarian regimes which remain in power because of their secret police and military forces, the Helsinki declaration provided added security. It certainly was discouraging to potential resistance movements. The future of communism seemed to be further solidified in Eastern Europe by the fact that the Western leaders had signed the declaration.

In his speech to the Twenty-fifth Congress of the Soviet Communist Party on February 24, 1976, Brezhnev emphasized the priority he gave to détente, but he made it clear that he rejected any linkage of the events in Angola with his concept of peaceful coexistence:

> Our party supports and will continue to support peoples fighting for their freedom. In so doing the Soviet Union does not look for advantages, does not hunt for concessions, does not seek political domination or exact military bases. We act as we are bid by our revolutionary conscience, our Communist convictions. . . . Some bourgeois leaders affect surprise and raise a howl over the solidarity of Soviet Communists, the Soviet people with the struggle of other peoples for freedom and progress. This is either outright naivety, or more likely a deliberate befuddling of minds. We make no secret of the fact that we see détente as the way to create more favorable conditions for peaceful socialist and communist construction.[8]

But the intervention of Cuban combat forces into the fighting in Angola was not "peaceful" Communist construction. And that is the central issue. Soviet statements for years, including the exchanges with the Americans at the Moscow summit of 1972, have made it clear that the Soviet Union would give support to so-called liberation movements. However, at no time have the Soviets claimed a right to intervene with combat forces. It is this distinction which has remained so fuzzy in the rhetoric that has proved disastrous for Soviet policy. For Americans the Soviet interventionist actions have spoken louder than their less belligerent words.

Brezhnev has consistently maintained that a struggle between the superpowers is inevitable because the two systems have such different values and goals. In a speech before the party congress he said: "Competition and rivalry between the two systems in the world arena continues. The crux of the matter is only to see to it that this process does not develop into armed clashes between the countries, into the use of force in relations between them, that it does not interfere with the development of mutually advantageous cooperation between states with different social systems."[9]

Of course, Brezhnev was correct that competition between the powers is inevitable, but under his doctrine the competition should not reach a point where it interferes with mutually advantageous cooperation, nor should it lead to armed confrontation. Brezhnev and his advisers got away with the adventure in Angola, but they were playing with fire. Not only were they risking their paramount goal of mutually advantageous strategic arms limitation, but they were also increasing the prospect of armed collision with the United States sometime in the future.

SOVIET ADVENTURES IN THE HORN OF AFRICA

During the early 1970's the Soviet Union manifested growing interest in the Horn of Africa and the Indian Ocean. Moscow established close relations with the government of Somalia, which was led by Siad Barre, a Marxist-oriented politician. The Somali Army became almost wholly dependent on Soviet military equipment and was trained by approximately 5,000 Soviet military advisers. In 1974 the two governments signed a treaty of friendship and cooperation which strengthened the relationship and granted the Soviets access to the Somali ports of Berbera and Kismayu. But the pledge of Soviet-Somali friendship was not a lasting commitment.

In 1974 Emperor Haile Selassie of Ethiopia was ousted and replaced by a Marxist named Mengistu Haile Mariam. Ethiopia had been a close ally of the United States, so close in fact that the United States was permitted to maintain some very sensitive military and intelligence equipment at secret installations there. But under Mengistu, Ethiopia gradually turned to the Soviet Union for assistance. In late 1976 the Soviets agreed to send $100 million in military assistance to Ethiopia. In April 1977 Ethiopia terminated its military relationship with the United States. In September of that year it signed with Moscow a new military agreement in which the Soviets agreed to send Ethiopia military hardware valued at $385 million, including 48 MiG-21 fighter planes, 400 tanks, SAM 3 and SAM 4 missiles.[10]

By late 1977 the Ethiopian government was confronted by a growing civil war in the province of Ogaden, where rebel forces were supported by invading troops from Somalia. Mengistu asked the Soviet Union for help, and almost immediately 11,000 Cuban combat troops and several hundred Soviet military advisers, including a high-ranking Soviet general, were dispatched by air to Ethiopia. Clearly the Soviets were not paying attention to the warning of Henry Kissinger that the Angolan adventure must not be repeated.

Quite the contrary. On October 7, 1977, the Soviet Union adopted a new Constitution which contained an entire chapter setting forth the foreign policy goals of the Soviet state. Among the expressed foreign policy aims were "consolidating the positions of world socialism and supporting the struggle of peoples for national liberation and social progress." The previous Constitution, issued in 1936, had contained no special section on foreign policy and no reference to liberation movements. According to Brezhnev and other Soviet spokesmen, the Soviet policy of support for liberation movements made it completely consistent for Moscow to respond decisively to Ethiopia's request for help. Here again, though, there was a great difference between sending military supplies and sending external troops to engage in combat.

While all this was going on, a transition had taken place in the U.S. government. Kissinger was gone. Gerald Ford had been replaced by Jimmy Carter in January 1977. Carter's first year of dealing with the Soviet Union had been a learning process marked by some dubious experiments and some serious divisions among his policy makers. At the outset Carter had given priority to rhetoric about the lack of human rights within the Soviet system. He also offered a new SALT package which was so inequitable that it was rejected on the spot by the Soviets when Secretary of State Cyrus Vance took it to Moscow in March. The repercussions were so great that it took about six months to get the SALT negotiations back to where they had been when Ford called off the talks in 1976.

It was not until March 1978 that U.S. reaction to the Soviet intervention in Ethiopia began to dominate the news. Throughout most of 1977 there had been disagreement between Secretary of State Vance, arms control negotiator Paul Warnke, and Soviet affairs adviser Marshall Shulman, on the one hand, and national security adviser Zbigniew Brzezinski, on the other, on whether to link the conduct of SALT negotiations with Soviet behavior in Africa. Vance and his team were strongly opposed to linkage and had persuaded the President to reject the Kissinger approach on the logical ground that since SALT was just as much in our security interest as the Soviets', the treaty should not be viewed as some sort of reward for Soviet good behavior.

However, on March 1 Brzezinski told reporters at the White House that "if tensions were to rise because of the unwarranted intrusion of Soviet power, that will inevitably complicate the process of concluding a new SALT accord, not only the negotiating process itself, but any ratification that would follow the successful conclusion of the negotiations. . . . We are not imposing linkages, but linkages may be imposed by unwarranted exploitation of local conflict for larger international purposes."[11] The White House press secretary confirmed that Brzezinski reflected President Carter's position. This was the first time that the Carter administration had tied the fate of SALT to its concern with the Soviet and Cuban military presence in the Horn of Africa.

The Soviets immediately rejected the Brzezinski warning, calling it dangerous and unacceptable because it amounted to "crude blackmail" which would jeopardize progress in negotiations dealing with the main problems of international security and détente. The Soviets consistently refused to accept any relationship between their aggressive behavior in Africa and the increasingly fragile progress in the SALT talks. Already there were abundant signals for Soviet observers of the American scene that even if a SALT treaty were successfully negotiated, its ratification in the United States Senate might be in doubt.

Senator Henry Jackson, the leading critic of the SALT negotiations in the Senate, said the administration had delayed too long in coming to grips with the Soviet intervention in Africa. He said the strains in U.S.-Soviet relations as seen by the public and the Congress were now so fundamental that in his view, the Senate would not recommend ratification of a new SALT treaty even if it were signed by the President during 1978. Senator Howard Baker of Tennessee, the Republican minority leader, went even further, demanding that President Carter break off the SALT talks until the Soviets and Cubans were withdrawn from Africa.[12]

The Republican National Committee issued a broadside attack on the Carter administration, calling for an end to all diplomatic contacts with Cuba and for provision of military and economic assistance to all African states opposing the presence of Cuban forces in Africa. Fred Ikle, chairman of the Republican Advisory Council on National Security and International Affairs (and presently undersecretary of defense for policy) issued a statement charging the Carter administration with flinching on direct linkage of the SALT negotiations with Soviet actions in Africa.[13]

It was apparent that U.S.-Soviet relations were in a state of profound disarray. Differing interpretations of events were polarizing opinion in both Washington and Moscow. Soviet Ambassador Anatoly Dobrynin was called home. Georgy Arbatov, the top Soviet expert on the United States and an adviser to Brezhnev, wrote a 3,400-word article in *Pravda* setting forth a grim portrayal of Soviet-American relations in which he said there was a rapid slide backward. He said the SALT negotiations had reached the crucial stage of "whether the agreement is to be or not to be. This is not merely the question of just another agreement—the question is actually about selecting the road for years to come."

Arbatov described the Carter administration as torn between two political forces with one striving to build up tensions, while the other (the Vance team) displayed "strong tendencies toward détente." Arbatov rejected the concept of linkage, adopting the standard Soviet position:

> The two countries could not have failed to realize from the outset that they were divided by deep-seated ideological and social differences and by their approaches to many international questions. Were the two countries to wait for all the political storms to calm down and contradictions to be resolved of their own accord so that nothing would mar the atmosphere? Had the Soviet Union and the United States opted for this approach, they would have, no doubt, remained in the cold-war period, and the situation, if anything, would have become even more dangerous.[14]

Arbatov and other senior Soviet officials failed to comprehend that most Americans considered the Soviet adventures in Angola and Ethiopia the very essence of cold war behavior—the opposite of détente and relaxation of tensions. Tragically the Soviets badly misestimated abundant evidence that their Third World interventions were providing American opponents of SALT with the necessary ammunition for almost certain defeat of the treaty. Instead, the Soviets continued their military expansion, unchecked, with a steady flow of Cuban combat forces and Soviet military advisers. By mid-1978 there were 19,400 military troops and economic technicians from the Soviet Union, Eastern Europe, and Cuba in Ethiopia.

Of course, Soviet and Cuban military involvement in all Africa was a tiny fraction of the 550,000 troops the United

States had deployed in Vietnam at one time. One senior Soviet official referred to American protests as "making the world safe for hypocrisy." But there was a very important difference: Since the withdrawal from Vietnam no American combat troops or American-sponsored combat troops had been sent into any dispute anywhere in the world. Most Americans thought that détente meant the avoidance of intervention with combat troops.

Early in 1978 there had been talk in Washington, especially in the State Department, that President Carter might attempt to make the forthcoming United Nations Special Session on Disarmament an opportunity for U.S. initiatives for genuine arms reduction. But deteriorating U.S.-Soviet relations made such aspirations unrealistic. In fact, the United States merely went through the motions at the UN. Instead, at the NATO ministers' meeting in Washington in May 1978 the United States sponsored a declaration calling for all NATO members to increase their defense spending 3 percent a year, beyond inflation, for the next five years. It was adopted unanimously. The Soviets had been increasing their defense spending 3 percent in real terms for several years, while U.S. defense spending had actually dropped after Vietnam.

Just before the NATO meeting Zbigniew Brzezinski had returned from China. In an exclusive interview with *The New York Times* he endorsed a "masterful analysis" given by Hua Kuo-feng, leader of the People's Republic of China. Brzezinski said that he discussed a secret White House memorandum describing American worldwide security objectives. This was the most profound and candid consultation since the United States and China reestablished diplomatic contact in 1971. It was the sort of meeting calculated to disturb the men in the Kremlin.

The day after the interview Brzezinski joined President Carter and Secretary Vance for a four-hour meeting at the White House with Soviet Foreign Minister Gromyko. Originally the meeting had been scheduled to attempt to resolve the last few remaining issues of the SALT II treaty. But now it was much more wide-ranging and included some vigorous charges and countercharges about Soviet aggressive moves in

Africa. Following the Gromyko encounter, Brzezinski appeared on nationwide television on *Meet the Press*, on Sunday, May 28. He described Moscow's behavior in Africa as "a shortsighted attempt to exploit global difficulties, not compatible with what was once called the code of détente." Brzezinski said: "I do not believe that this kind of Soviet-Cuban involvement ought to be cost-free. There are a variety of ways in which concerned countries can convince the Soviets and Cubans that their involvement, their intrusion, is not only conducive to greater international instability, but in fact carries with it consequences which may be inimical to them as well." Here Brzezinski was joining Kissinger in the same warning—i.e., that the African adventures might destroy the much higher Soviet priorities of détente and SALT.

Speaking of SALT, Brzezinski said: "An agreement is within grasp, if reason prevails. The United States has made very proper, balanced proposals to conclude a new treaty limiting intercontinental missiles and bombers. If they are accepted, we could have agreement within days. If they are not accepted, we will wait until they are accepted." A high-ranking Soviet official commented, "That is not negotiating, that is an ultimatum."[15] Brzezinski was riding high, apparently more influential with President Carter than was Secretary Vance, who still pursued the priority goal of achieving a balanced SALT agreement and whose rhetoric was always restrained.

On June 8, 1978, President Carter gave a major address on Soviet-American relations which reflected the views of both Vance and Brzezinski. Carter said:

> We must realize that for a very long time our relationship with the Soviet Union will be competitive. . . . Détente between our two countries is central to world peace. . . . Both nations must exercise restraint in troubled times. Both must honor meticulously those agreements which have already been reached. . . . Our long term objectives must be to convince the Soviet Union of the advantages of cooperation and of the cost of disruptive behavior. . . . A SALT agreement which enhances the

46

security of both nations is of fundamental importance.
. . . I am glad to report to you today that the prospects
for a SALT II agreement are good.

And then came the Brzezinski section:

> The abuse of basic human rights in their own country,
> in violation of the agreement at Helsinki, has earned
> them the condemnation of people everywhere who love
> freedom. . . . Their cultural bonds with others are few
> and frayed. Their form of government is becoming in-
> creasingly unattractive to other nations so that even
> Marxist-Leninist groups no longer look on the Soviet
> Union as a model to be imitated. . . . In Africa we and our
> African friends want to see a continent that is free of
> dominance of outside powers. . . . The persistent and
> increasing military involvement of the Soviet Union and
> Cuba in Africa could deny this hopeful vision. We are
> deeply concerned about the threat to regional peace and
> to the countries within which these foreign troops seem
> permanently to be stationed. . . . We have no desire to link
> the negotiation for a SALT agreement with other com-
> petitive relationships. In a democratic society, however,
> where public opinion is an integral factor in the shaping
> and implementation of foreign policy, we do recognize
> that tensions, sharp disputes or threats to peace will com-
> plicate the quest for a successful agreement. The Soviet
> Union can choose either confrontation or cooperation.
> . . . We would prefer cooperation through a détente that
> increasingly involves similar restraints for both sides,
> similar readiness to resolve disputes by negotiation and
> not by violence, similar willingness to compete peace-
> fully and not militarily. Anything less than that is likely
> to undermine détente and this is why I hope that no one
> will underestimate the concerns that I have expressed
> today.[16]

The President's speech was very clear and very balanced.
He affirmed his desire to compete with the Soviet Union in
the framework of détente, preferring cooperation to confrontation. He made it clear that a SALT agreement still repre-

sented a high priority and that he had no desire to link the SALT negotiations with other competitive relationships, but he did note that in the U.S. political process it was very difficult to gain public support for vital strategic agreements with the Soviet Union while it was indulging in military action in the Third World. The President set forth most of the key points essential to improving U.S.-Soviet relations.

However, if the men in the Kremlin were listening, they either failed to understand or dismissed his arguments out of hand. Undoubtedly there were some who understood, and some who agreed; but they were an obvious minority. The Soviet Union continued to pursue, unchecked, its reckless course in the Third World. There was no attempt to reduce the combat forces in Angola and Ethiopia. Furthermore, the Soviet Union became more directly involved in South Yemen.

The People's Democratic Republic of Yemen was embroiled in conflict over the future path of its foreign policy. President Salem Robaye Ali was working for closer relations with North Yemen, Saudi Arabia, and the West in general. His goal was a unification of the two Yemens under Saudi sponsorship. Abdel Fattah Ismail, leader of the opposition, was negative, wanting rather to establish a new Marxist party modeled after the Communist Party of the Soviet Union. When Robaye Ali tried to establish relations with North Yemen leader Ahmad al-Ghashmi, Ali was arrested and executed by Ismail's forces. Shortly thereafter al-Ghashmi was assassinated also. This was in July 1978.

Whether the Soviet Union had anything to do with these events is pure speculation, but since the 1978 coup the Soviets have moved swiftly to ensure their control. In the period 1954–1977 Soviet economic aid to Aden totaled only $39 million. In 1978 alone, it was raised to $204 million. Soviet, East European, and Cuban economic advisers were increased to 1,075. Soviet, East European, and Cuban military advisers, including some troops, were increased from 700 in 1977 to 1,550 in late 1978. Subsequently a treaty of friendship and cooperation, similar to the one with Ethiopia, was signed between the USSR and the People's Democratic Republic of

Yemen. Reportedly the Soviets received access to military facilities in Aden and the island of Socotra, which compensated for their loss of bases in Somalia and allowed them to maintain access to the Indian Ocean and the Red Sea.[17]

Clearly the Soviet move into South Yemen was not anywhere as consequential as the interventions in Angola and Ethiopia, but when combined with Soviet support for the Vietnamese invasion of Cambodia in 1979, it seemed to be part of a worldwide strategy whereby the Soviet Union, through direct or indirect military intervention, was increasing its power and influence. Whether there was a broad strategic concept associated with Soviet ambitions for world conquest or merely a response to events and limited opportunities made little difference. The fact was that the Soviet Union was engaging in a series of aggressive actions involving the use of military force. The American opponents of SALT were presented with invaluable ammunition with which to sustain their arguments. Even proponents of SALT, including the original negotiator, Henry Kissinger, became progressively more concerned about Soviet behavior.

In January 1979 *Time* magazine published two important interviews in the same issue, one with Kissinger, the other with Brezhnev. Kissinger said:

> The Soviet Union must understand, or must be brought to understand that a relaxation of tensions is not compatible with a systematic attempt to overturn the geopolitical equilibrium. . . . So the first necessity is to bring home to the Soviet Union that to us détente means a restrained international conduct, and if we cannot achieve that, then we will have to confront expansionism where it takes place, however indirect it is.

In response to a question asking how the United States could halt the Soviets, Kissinger said: "By imposing penalties and risks that they are not willing to accept. . . . I simply cannot believe that it can be beyond the capacity of the United States to stop Cuban expeditionary forces thousands of miles from home."[18]

RUSSIAN ROULETTE

President Brezhnev had a definition of détente and the conduct which it implies very similar to that which President Carter expressed in his Annapolis speech. Brezhnev said:

> When we say "relaxation of tension," or simply "détente" for short, we mean a state of international relations opposite to a state which is commonly termed "cold war. . . ." Détente means a willingness to resolve differences and disputes not by force, by threats or saber rattling, but by peaceful means, at the negotiating table. Détente means a certain degree of trust and ability to reckon with each other's legitimate interests. . . .
>
> We . . . actively work toward strengthening the process of détente . . . in all regions of the world, including . . . Africa and the Middle East. But it would be unfair and unrealistic to expect the peoples of those or any other regions to give up the struggle for their legitimate rights in the name of a concept of détente that some people falsely interpret.[19]

This last sentence is the heart of the matter.

Of course, it would be unrealistic to imagine that struggles for political control or for liberation will not continue all over the world. Nor can one object to the Soviet Union's giving support and encouragement to factions it may favor. However, there is serious objection to support through the intervention of third-party combat forces. Soviet doctrine and Soviet policy are very ambiguous and murky on this point. Kissinger is correct: The Soviets must be made to understand. Either Brezhnev is being disingenuous or he mistakenly believes that he can have his cake and eat it, too.

Despite the growing tension and mistrust in superpower relations, the negotiations for a SALT II treaty became even more intensive during the early months of 1979. Finally, a breakthrough was achieved, and the few remaining issues were resolved in compromise. Presidents Carter and Brezhnev met in Vienna, where they signed the treaty and agreed to provisions for the next round of negotiations, which called for substantial reductions and qualitative controls to ensure that neither side would ever again be so threatened by strategic weapons. Even at the summit, celebrating the achievement of SALT II, there were sharp differences between Carter and Brezhnev over Soviet military intervention in the Third World.

Brezhnev told Carter again that "solidarity with liberation struggles is a principle of Soviet policy." Carter replied that "we must restrict military intervention either directly or through third parties in regional disputes and we must protect each nation's vital interest in access to crucial natural resources."[20] Here Carter was groping for new rules of competition that went beyond the ambiguities of the "Basic Principles" of 1972. One of the great errors of the Carter administration was that it never entered into diplomatic negotiations with the Soviets on these matters. The SALT treaty completely dominated U.S.-Soviet diplomacy, except for a few protests and rhetorical thrusts contained in speeches or press conferences.

Opposition to the SALT treaty had been growing in the U.S. Senate for months. Only thirty-four negative votes were required to block ratification. But the Carter administration mounted a skillful and effective campaign to win the battle, even though some of the compromises considered essential ran counter to the goal of limiting and reducing strategic weapons. President Carter had announced a decision to go ahead with the large MX missile and its complicated multiple-basing racetrack system of deployment. He also indicated a willingness to increase the next defense budget by 5 percent above the rate of inflation. A story was leaked from the White House that the President had signed a new presidential directive which stated that the United States would not allow arms control agreements to block the deployment of any strategic weapons considered essential to U.S. national security. All this was balm to the hawks, especially those influential Democratic senators, such as Sam Nunn of Georgia, who had been wavering in support for SALT.

The hearings went well during July. The administration brought in all its big guns with testimony demonstrating that the treaty was at least as advantageous to the United States as the Soviet Union, perhaps more so. The Joint Chiefs of Staff testified as individuals and unanimously endorsed the treaty as a modest step in the right direction which would contribute to the security of the United States. The treaty was approved by a large majority in the Senate Foreign Relations Committee. The national polls showed more than 70 percent of the public favoring Senate ratification. By the time Congress adjourned for its August recess there was optimism among treaty proponents that the final vote, though close, would be affirmative.

Then, a month later, a disaster occurred—at least from the standpoint of those who believe in the importance of controlling and reducing the possibility of nuclear war. U.S. intelligence photos from a satellite showed a Soviet military brigade on maneuvers in Cuba. The President and Secretary of State Vance were out of Washington on vacation. Those left in responsibility decided that Frank Church of Utah, the Democratic chairman of the Senate Foreign Relations Committee, should be informed immediately. Church, who was in serious trouble in his efforts to win reelection, immediately went on national television with an impassioned and ill-advised statement that as long as the Soviet combat brigade remained in Cuba he saw no likelihood that the Senate would ratify SALT. Shortly thereafter President Carter asserted that the combat brigade would have to be withdrawn. The President, too, was permitted to act before he had all the facts.

Recalling the Cuban missile crisis of 1962, opponents of SALT claimed that the Soviets were indulging in one more act of blatant aggression in violation of the agreement that had been reached between Nikita Khrushchev and John Kennedy. The Soviets were astounded by the entire furor and referred to it as a hoax perpetrated by the opponents of SALT. Actually the Soviet brigade had been in Cuba for years. In fact, in 1962 the Soviets had had almost 40,000 troops in Cuba; in 1979 they had fewer than 3,000. The entire matter had been mishandled by the Carter team. After a month of frenzied negotiation, during which the Soviets refused to budge, the White House decided to back away as gracefully as possible.

On October 1 the President gave an address to the nation:

The Soviet Blunder

Recently we have obtained evidence that a Soviet combat brigade has been in Cuba for several years. The presence of Soviet combat troops in Cuba is of serious concern to us. . . . This is not a large force, nor an assault force. (It has about 2,600 men.) It presents no direct threat to us. It has no airborne or seaborne capability. In contrast to the 1962 crisis, no nuclear threat to the U.S. is involved. . . . My fellow Americans, the greatest danger to American security tonight is certainly not the two or three thousand Soviet troops in Cuba. The greatest danger to all the nations of the world—including the United States and the Soviet Union—is the breakdown of a common effort to preserve the peace, and the ultimate threat of a nuclear war. I renew my call to the Senate of the United States to ratify the SALT II treaty.[21]

The President was trying to get back on the track, but it was too late. The damage could not be repaired. Carter was immediately attacked by critics for vacillating, for backing down on his demand that the Soviets withdraw their combat brigade. The Church statement had so eroded Senate leadership that there was no chance of obtaining the necessary sixty-seven votes to ratify the treaty. The Soviets were exasperated and alarmed. The turn of events seemed to indicate that more than six years of patient, exacting negotiation were about to be dissipated. To make matters worse, from the Soviet standpoint, Vice President Walter Mondale visited China in September for talks with Chinese leaders. Mondale indicated a willingness to sell military-related equipment to China. All this was calculated to exacerbate Soviet anxieties.

Moreover, there were growing press reports that the United States intended to move ahead with its plans to install 570 nuclear missiles in Europe capable of striking targets in the Soviet Union. The Soviets interpreted these weapons to be an extension of the U.S. strategic arsenal, but increasing the danger to Soviet security because some of the rockets could reach their targets in a much shorter time than those based in the United States. Furthermore, the Soviets considered the plan to be in direct conflict with the intent of the SALT II treaty. In October, President Brezhnev made an address in Berlin in which he announced the unilateral withdrawal of one Soviet division and 1,000 tanks from Soviet forces in East Germany. He also indicated a willingness to dismantle unilaterally an unspecified number of Soviet medium-range missiles in return for a U.S. agreement to start immediate negotiations on European-based nuclear weapons.

Brezhnev's speech was dismissed as a propaganda maneuver by Washington. U.S. officials made clear their view that any serious discussion with the Soviets at that point would delay, if not destroy, the possibility for an affirmative NATO decision on the new missiles. Even so, when the NATO ministers met in Brussels on December 7, 1979, there was a seven-hour debate before a decision could be reached. It was agreed that the U.S. missiles would be deployed, but that negotiations would be started as soon as possible between the United States and the USSR to agree on limits and reductions of medium-range nuclear weapons in Eastern and Western Europe within the context of the SALT treaties.

AFGHANISTAN

On December 24, 1979, the Soviet Union launched a massive invasion of Afghanistan, by airlift and by land across the Soviet-Afghanistan border, which ultimately numbered 85,000 Soviet troops. U.S.-Soviet relations, already very bad, plummeted to the lowest level since the Stalin era. This was the first time that the Soviets had directly employed their combat troops in territory beyond the boundaries established by World War II. It was an ominous precedent which confirmed the arguments of those who maintained that the Soviet Union intended to expand its global reach through military power. The Soviets claimed that they were merely responding to a call from the Afghan government for help. But such claims were farcical.

Afghanistan had a long history of friendly neutrality with its big neighbor. Since 1955 it had been militarily dependent on the Soviet Union, but it had remained nonaligned until 1978. In April 1978 President Sardas Mohammad Daoud was overthrown in a Soviet-encouraged military coup. Nur

Mohammad Taraki was named prime minister of the Democratic Republic of Afghanistan. In December 1978 a treaty of friendship and cooperation was signed with the Soviet Union. In the spring and summer of 1979 tribal rebellion spread in Afghanistan. Foreign Minister Hafizullah Amin took over from Taraki as prime minister, while the latter became president. In September Taraki attended the nonaligned nations' conference in Havana. He returned via Moscow and a meeting with Brezhnev. Upon reaching Kabul, he attempted to replace Amin but was killed when the coup failed.

Amin was a Marxist but was very strong-willed and independent, not given to following Soviet instructions. He moved relentlessly to crush the tribal rebellions and to impose his authority. During this period General Ivan Pavlovsky, a deputy minister of defense and chief of Soviet ground forces, had been in Kabul, along with twenty-three other Soviet generals, assessing the results of the Amin government.[22] Apparently the generals did not like what they saw. Shortly after they had reported to the Politburo in Moscow, action was taken. There was a large buildup of Soviet divisions on Afghanistan's northern borders. Then on December 8 and 9 some Soviet troops were airlifted to the airport in Kabul, preceding the all-out invasion on the twenty-fourth. On December 27 Amin was "tried" and executed by a new Soviet-installed regime, headed by a former deputy to Taraki, Babrak Karmal, who had been in exile in Czechoslovakia.

World reaction was swift, and much more vigorous than the Soviets had anticipated, especially in the United States. President Carter said that the invasion was "the greatest threat to world peace since 1945." At a special emergency session of the United Nations General Assembly the Soviet action was condemned by an overwhelming margin, which included almost all the members of the nonaligned movement. The speeches by representatives of the Third World governments removed any remaining illusions that the Soviet Union had a popular role to play among the nonaligned. Only a month before, at the nonaligned movement meeting in

Havana, where Castro had replaced Tito as chairman of the movement, the Soviets were anticipating a new era of Third World influence. Afghanistan changed all that.

Any lingering aspirations about détente within U.S. opinion disappeared. The anti-Soviet mood deepened further when Andrei Sakharov, the greatest dissident leader, was exiled from Moscow and placed under house arrest. President Carter ordered that the SALT II treaty be placed on hold with no further attempt to gain Senate ratification. The United States decided not to attend the Olympic Games scheduled for Moscow in the summer and mounted a campaign to persuade other nations to join in the boycott. The United States cut off most of its grain and all its technology from Soviet trade. Cultural and scientific exchanges were ended. In fact, it soon became clear that U.S. relations with the Soviet Union were being placed in a deep freeze.

In his State of the Union message on January 23, 1980, President Carter said: "Let our position be absolutely clear: An attempt by any outside force to gain control of the Persian Gulf region will be regarded as an assault on the vital interests of the United States of America. And such an assault will be repelled by any means necessary, including military force." This so-called Carter Doctrine gave immediate impetus to building a rapid deployment force, to a search for bases in the Persian Gulf area, and to a considerable strengthening of the U.S. fleet in that part of the world. It was clear that the Afghanistan invasion, unlike the Czech invasion of 1968, had inspired a course of action which would not soon change.

Why would the Soviets take such a risk to gain control of a country that has no important natural resources but that has a barren mountainous terrain, a primitive economy, and warring tribes that have never been successfully dominated by an outside power? The hawks in the United States have asserted that the only rational basis for the invasion was to establish a military base to facilitate a strike into the oil fields of the Persian Gulf and possibly an invasion of Iran if the Ayatollah Khomeini regime is overthrown. The Soviet explanation from Brezhnev, Gromyko, and others in formal speeches and informal discussions has been different.

The Soviet Blunder

The Soviets acknowledge that General Pavlovsky did bring back a negative assessment from his investigation in Kabul. It was clear that Amin was hated by the Afghan populace and would soon be overthrown, with a strong possibility that his replacement would be anti-Soviet and perhaps pro-Chinese. The Soviets were especially alarmed at the thought of growing Chinese influence in Afghanistan and claimed that both the Chinese and the CIA were giving support to the rebellious tribes. Thus, after a long debate the Politburo decided to enforce the Brezhnev doctrine. After the Czech invasion in 1968 Brezhnev asserted that once a country becomes socialist (Communist), it is essential that it remain Communist and not be allowed to stray into the capitalist camp. It was essential that Afghanistan remain Communist and pro-Soviet, he claimed.

In the view of the Soviets, relations with the United States had deteriorated to such a point that there was no benefit to be gained from restraint. They listed a series of actions that had eroded détente, starting with the NATO decision in 1978 to increase the defense budgets each year by 3 percent above inflation, the failure to ratify the SALT II treaty, the hoax over the Soviet brigade in Cuba, the growing rapprochement between the United States and China, and especially the NATO decision in December 1979 (shortly before the decision to invade Afghanistan) to base additional U.S. nuclear weapons in Europe capable of striking the Soviet Union.

There probably was another fundamental reason for the Soviet action. It was consistent with their ideology. The Politburo is still composed, for the most part, of old Bolsheviks who hold on to long-discredited tenets of Marxism-Leninism such as the concept of world communism. Furthermore, the Soviet leaders made a serious misestimate of the consequences of the U.S. defeat in Vietnam from the standpoint of their adventures in the Third World. Because they were able to get away with the interventions in Angola, Ethiopia, and South Yemen without any disastrous repercussions, they may have anticipated a similar response to their invasion of Afghanistan. They were certainly handicapped, in any case, by attempting to rationalize their actions through ideological mumbo jumbo.

The Soviet ideologists assert that the so-called correlation of forces differs fundamentally from concepts of balance of power. Maintaining that class struggle is inevitable, they say that international politics is a struggle and interaction of class, political, national, and other factors, with class factors always playing the decisive role. Through the liberation struggle the working class, governed by the principles of Marxism-Leninism, will emerge dominant. Soviet doctrine calls for support of the liberation movement. They maintain that it is impossible to put a freeze on world sociopolitical development to preserve a Western concept of détente. Nor, they claim, can any international agreements alter the laws of class struggle.[23]

Shortly after the invasion of Afghanistan, Boris Ponomarev, secretary of the Central Committee of the Soviet Communist Party, wrote in *Kommunist:*

Soviet people, of course, are not indifferent to the sociopolitical orientation by the various trends in the developing world. The devotees of scientific socialism have no intention of denying their spiritual closeness to the progressive forces in Asia, Africa and Latin America. Sympathy for fighters for true freedom is natural for Marxist-Leninists and internationalists. Where such forces exist and are struggling they have the right to depend on our solidarity and support.

If the ideology expressed by Ponomarev were applicable to the invasion of Afghanistan, then, by logical extension, the Soviet Union could rationalize an invasion, with the Red Army, anywhere in the Third World where a struggle for power was in process.

Henry Trofimenko wrote:

The continuing stormy events in the Third World, generated by the objective process of development, specifically by the newly free countries' struggle for an equal place under the sun, are inevitable. This process has developed and will develop against the background of the continuing competition between the two world systems, the capitalist and the socialist, for influence on its course and outcome. It is only an unbiased and businesslike approach of all non-local forces to the political crisis situations arising in this zone that can ensure their not leading to the military involvement of great powers, to another world war.[24]

Trofimenko is certainly correct about the continuing competition. But when that competition involves the direct or indirect use of combat forces, it can hardly be described as "an unbiased and businesslike approach." No interpretation of Soviet ideology can rationalize intervention with external military forces. The Soviets have gone too far, so far in fact that their highest goals of national security have been placed in serious jeopardy. Henry Kissinger said the SALT II treaty began to die in Angola. Zbigniew Brzezinski said the SALT treaty died in the Ogaden desert of Ethiopia.

Now the Reagan administration has moved into the White House with a unanimous view that the SALT II treaty is unacceptable. President Reagan and his advisers say that they will link Soviet behavior in the world with any further negotiations for arms control. The Reagan administration has decided that the only way to respond to Soviet military adventures is by a gigantic buildup of U.S. military power.

Secretary of State Alexander Haig says that the United States wants Moscow to observe an agreed code of international conduct as a condition of future negotiations. "All new Soviet-American agreements," Haig said, "including arms control, trade and financial credits, will be held up until there is a new understanding on the limits of Moscow's activities throughout the world."[25] These developments were certainly not anticipated by the Soviet Politburo when it launched its Third World adventures.

It is evident that Soviet leaders learn from history no better than U.S. leaders. It is to be hoped that Soviet actions in recent years are manifestations of a dying ideology soon to be replaced by more realistic policy with greater attention to the priorities of national survival and the interests of people living in the Soviet Union. Surely it is apparent, even to old Bolsheviks, that there is no such thing as the correlation of forces if that means the advance of world communism supported or controlled by the Soviet Union. Over the years China, Yugoslavia, and Albania have left the Soviet bloc.

The largest Communist party in Western Europe, located in Italy, is no longer responsive to Soviet leadership. Rumania and to a considerable degree Hungary are becoming increasingly independent. In the Third World the Soviet Union has had a series of important setbacks where Marxist-oriented governments have been replaced by regimes that have rejected Soviet domination or influence. These include Indonesia, Ghana, Guinea, Algeria, Mali, Sudan, Egypt, and Somalia. The 1981 meeting of the ninety-two member nonaligned nations' movement in New Delhi adopted by decisive margins resolutions calling for the "withdrawal of foreign troops from Afghanistan" and "foreign forces from Cambodia." So much for the correlation of forces.

In Angola today there are still nearly 20,000 Cuban military and 7,000 civilians. Jonas Savimbi and his UNITA forces are still waging guerrilla warfare against the Soviet-backed government. But ironically, the main financial support for the Neto regime comes from taxes and royalties paid by the American Gulf Oil Company, which pumps 100,000 barrels a day from its enclave in Abinda, Angola. In 1979 Gulf paid $320 million for its 49 percent share. During the next four years Gulf will have invested $500 million more in the Angolan base. So the Marxist regime survives with the know-how and resources of American capitalism.

In Ethiopia about 12,000 Cuban troops remain, and the fighting continues sporadically in the Ogaden and Eritrea. The government is more stable than in 1978, but at considerable cost. There are still 90,000 Soviet troops in Afghanistan, facing resistance from tribal forces that will probably never submit to Soviet control. The Vietnamese aggression in Cambodia continues.

The drain on the Soviet budget, each year, from these four interventions is substantial. It is clear that the Kremlin has gained very little in the process, while suffering severe political and financial loss. Military intervention in the Third World is a dangerous, unprofitable game for the superpowers. The Third World states have made it clear that they want the superpowers to stay out. Neither the United States nor the Soviet Union can be world policeman. New rules for world security need to be negotiated.

Chapter III

Victory for the American Hawks

Soviet military adventures in the Third World, culminating with the invasion of Afghanistan, ensured political victory for the American hawks. Détente is dead in the United States, and the process of genuine arms control lies dormant. Even if the Soviets had not indulged in their interventionist excursions, however, the battle against détente and SALT in the United States would have been almost equally ferocious. The outcome might have been different, but it would have been a very close call because the hawks have always been a powerful force in American politics, at least since World War II.

The emergence of détente in the United States became possible because of two important related factors: the U.S. defeat in Vietnam and the negotiations with the Soviets conducted by Richard Nixon and Henry Kissinger, both Republican conservatives with well-established records of anticommunism. It is difficult to recall today that Kissinger was known as Mr. Détente. After the triumphs of Peking and Moscow and the successful withdrawal of U.S. forces from Vietnam, Kissinger's reputation skyrocketed. A Gallup poll showed him to be the most popular man in the United States; a British international poll named him the most popular man in the world; he shared the Nobel Prize for peace, and a *Newsweek* magazine cover story portrayed him in the costume of Superman.[1]

Thereafter the media frequently referred to him as Super Henry. When Gerald Ford succeeded Nixon in the White House, his first appointment was Kissinger, as both secretary of state and national security adviser. Now all that has changed. Kissinger is out of power and no longer advocates détente, largely because of Soviet military interventions in the Third World. Richard Nixon has returned to the aviary of the hawks, demonstrating his anti-Soviet stance in a book called *The Real War*.

There were some Americans, though, who opposed détente and the strategic arms agreements from the outset. These were the unreconstructed cold warriors who believed that the cold war had never ended—at least, they didn't want it to end. During the cold war there was a vast American consensus which supported the policy of containment. Most Americans believed that the United States could serve as the world's policeman and should maintain sufficient military power to contain any Soviet aggressive moves beyond the boundaries that had been established by World War II and the agreements reached at Yalta and Potsdam. But the Vietnam debacle destroyed this U.S. foreign policy consensus.

Nixon and Kissinger decided to get out of Vietnam and to replace confrontation with negotiation and competitive coexistence. The cold warriors were opposed. They saw a policy of nonintervention and negotiated compromise with the Soviets as the "Vietnam syndrome," a sickness which could be cured only by a massive buildup of American military power, a return to confrontation and containment, a return to the cold war. In these days of Reagan Republicanism it is noteworthy that the two most influential leaders of the return to the cold war are Democrats.

They are Senator Henry Jackson, from the state of Washington, and Paul Nitze, a dominant figure in national security affairs since World War II. These two men, through the years, have probably had more influence on the direction of U.S. national security policy than any other Americans, including Nixon and Kissinger. Scoop Jackson, as he is known in Washington, has emerged as the most powerful man in the U.S. Senate in military affairs and matters of national security. On military matters Jackson seldom loses a debate, even to other powerful senators such as Edward Kennedy of Massachusetts or Alan Cranston of California.

Jackson has been a consistent advocate of U.S. military superiority. His goals have fitted in well with those of the huge Boeing industries which have headquarters in the state of Washington. This relationship has earned Jackson the title of the senator from Boeing. U.S. strategic forces are dominated by Boeing products. The B-52 bomber is produced by Boeing. The major ICBM, the Minuteman, is built by Boeing. And now the huge Trident submarine, the third leg of the strategic triad, will have its home port in Washington. Jackson led the fight in the Senate to build the Trident, which barely passed, 49 to 47, after a struggle lasting several weeks. But it would be inaccurate to characterize Jackson's enthusiasm for military superiority as mere political opportunism. He has been a passionate opponent of the Soviet Union throughout his years in Congress. He believes that our military power is the only force that can contain its ambitions for world domination.

Like Jackson, Paul Nitze has been a cold warrior ever since he entered the government after World War II. In fact, Nitze, a brilliant intellectual, could be considered the American cold war guru. As head of the State Department policy planning staff under Secretary Dean Acheson, Nitze was principal drafter in 1950 of the U.S. cold war manifesto. Known as NSC-68, the policy contrasted the Soviet desire for world domination with the U.S. desire for an environment in which free societies could exist and flourish. The analysis of the Soviet threat combined Marxist-Leninist doctrine with the power of the Soviet state into "an aggressive expansionist drive which found its chief opponent and, therefore, target in the antithetic ideas and power of our own country. It was true and understandable to describe the Russian motivating concept as being that 'no state is friendly which is not subservient,' and ours that 'no state is unfriendly which, in return for respect for its rights, respects the rights of other states.' "[2]

NSC-68 said that:

the policy of containment is one that seeks by all means short of war to (1) block further expansion of Soviet power, (2) expose the falsities of Soviet pretensions, (3) induce a retraction of the Kremlin's control and influence, and, (4) in general, so foster the seeds of destruction within the Soviet system that the Kremlin is brought at least to the point of modifying its behavior to generally accepted international standards. . . . Without superior aggregate military strength, in being and readily mobilizable, a policy of "containment"—which is in effect a policy of calculated and gradual coercion—is no more than a policy of bluff.

Thirty-two years later both Nitze and Jackson believe that this policy and this analysis are still essentially sound.

Nitze, through the years, has been a consistent advocate of more military power to contain the Soviet threat. He has been a modern Paul Revere calling at the top of his voice, "The Russians are coming, the Russians are coming." There has often been a tendency to exaggerate the dimensions of the threat on grounds that unless the public has a sufficient sense of danger, Congress and the executive branch will not spend the necessary money. Thus, there was discovered in the mid-1950's a bomber gap in which the Soviets would soon have the advantage. But intelligence later demonstrated that no gap existed.

In 1957 President Eisenhower authorized an independent study which was called "Deterrence and Survival in the Nuclear Age." Later called the Gaither Report, because the chairman of the study group was H. Rowan Gaither, Jr., it became the most influential policy paper since NSC-68. Not surprisingly, Paul Nitze was one of the most persuasive members of the Gaither Committee and a major draftsman of the study. The report concluded that the Soviets would achieve a sufficient ICBM force by 1959 to wipe out the U.S. strategic bombers. The claim that the Soviets would win the race to develop ICBM's was known as the missile gap. Much to the dismay of President Eisenhower, the conclusions of the Gaither Report were leaked to the press. Eisenhower had rejected much of the analysis.

65

RUSSIAN ROULETTE

John Kennedy used the missile gap as an important prong of his campaign to defeat Richard Nixon in 1960. Paul Nitze was a policy adviser to Kennedy and emerged after the election as assistant secretary of defense in charge of international security affairs. Not long after the Kennedy inauguration, U.S. intelligence had sufficient photographic evidence to report that the missile gap was nonexistent. But another finding in the Gaither Report, calling for a major U.S. civil defense program to defend against possible Soviet nuclear attack, continued to have important influence on policy. After President Kennedy's meeting with Khrushchev in Vienna in June 1961, there were rumblings of another Berlin confrontation. For several months thereafter there was a frenzied national preoccupation with civil defense, including backyard shelters.

An indication of Nitze's thinking on the Berlin problem appeared in a speech he gave in 1959 in which he said that in the event of another Berlin blockade we should "put SAC [the Strategic Air Command] on full alert and *evacuate our cities* [emphasis added], both to indicate the full measure of our determination and to be in the best possible position to survive the likely consequences if the Russians choose to challenge that determination." Nitze also stressed that we should not be the first to shoot and that the use of nuclear weapons, whether strategic or tactical, should "be avoided at all cost." In fact, Nitze at the time was an opponent of placing tactical nuclear weapons in Europe.

The resolution of the Cuban missile crisis of 1962 followed by Kennedy's conciliatory and balanced speech at American University and the partial test ban agreement in 1963 brought to an end, temporarily, the preoccupation with nuclear war. Nitze moved on to become secretary of the navy and then deputy secretary of defense. As an advocate of containment he was a strong supporter of Lyndon Johnson's intervention in Vietnam. But as American involvement grew to 550,000 troops, and a substantial portion of the U.S. Air Force and fleet, Nitze began to worry about becoming overextended, especially to the detriment of our commitment in Europe. Indeed, if the Soviets had ever contemplated an invasion of Europe, it would have been at the height of the Vietnam War.

With the demise of Johnson and the arrival of Nixon and Kissinger, Nitze continued to have an important role in matters of national security. He became the representative of the Department of Defense on the U.S. SALT delegation. As a leading representative of the view that the Soviets respect only military power and that therefore, the United States should maintain military superiority, Nitze was not a likely supporter of negotiating agreements which, of necessity, had to be based on the principle of parity or equality. His role was more that of a watchdog than an advocate.

NIXON, FORD, AND KISSINGER

After the Moscow summit of 1972 the Senate voted 89 to 2 to ratify the antiballistic missile (ABM) treaty and to endorse the interim SALT I agreement. But even then the resistance of Senator Jackson was much in evidence. He raised strong objections to the SALT I agreement, claiming that the Soviets were granted a strategic advantage because they were permitted 1,618 ICBM's to 1,054 for the United States and were allowed 62 missile-firing submarines with 950 launch tubes, while the United States would have 44 strategic subs with 710 launch tubes. Jackson proposed a qualification to the SALT I approval which asked the administration not to accept any future SALT agreement that limited the United States to an inferior number of weapons in any category.

The Senate approved Jackson's "qualification" by a vote of 56 to 35. This was a considerable political victory for Jackson because it established in the media and public opinion the view that Nixon and Kissinger, in their eagerness to advance détente, had accepted an interim agreement which was less than equal. As will be demonstrated in the next chapter, the truth was exactly the opposite: SALT I gave the United States a clear advantage, but Jackson got away with his ploy.

It is widely acknowledged in Washington that an important reason for Jackson's long-standing dominance in the Senate on matters of national security is his excellent staff work. And the man given credit for much of that success is Richard Perle, who for years was Jackson's specialist on defense. Perle, now forty, has become Jackson's key man in the Pentagon as assistant secretary of defense in charge of arms control, Soviet affairs, and NATO policy. Perle joined Jackson when he was only twenty-eight and became like a son to the senator. He is credited with the staff work which put the Trident submarine program through the Senate and with the qualification to the SALT I idea. As we shall see, Richard Perle had a substantial role in the defeat of détente.

In view of the no-holds-barred struggle that emerged between Jackson and Kissinger, it is ironic to recall that when Nixon was elected in November 1968, his first offer of the position of secretary of defense went to Scoop Jackson. Nixon had long admired Jackson's record as a cold warrior and a leading supporter of increased defense budgets. Jackson didn't accept the offer because he wanted to run for President as a Democrat. He nevertheless remained close to Nixon on defense matters, and when Melvin Laird left the Defense Department, Jackson recommended his old friend James Schlesinger.

Leslie Gelb, writing in *The New York Times Magazine*, said of Schlesinger's appointment: "He had the right two patrons, Senators Henry M. Jackson, who packs a great deal of influence in the White House and Congress and General Alexander Haig, Jr., formerly Henry Kissinger's deputy at the White House and now the President's [Nixon's] Chief of Staff."[3] So Jackson had his own man running the Pentagon.

Schlesinger and Jackson made quite a team, waging an effective struggle against Kissinger's priorities of arms control and détente. The Yom Kippur War in October 1973, followed by the Arab oil embargo and long lines at the gas stations, contributed to the souring mood in the United States. Jackson and Perle moved swiftly to exploit the situation. Both Jackson and Perle are as passionate supporters of Israel as they are enemies of the Soviet Union.

Perle is the grandson of émigrés from Russia. He was the man behind the scenes in developing the Jackson-Vanik amendment to the U.S.-Soviet trade bill which withheld most favored nation tariff status from the Russians unless they granted the right of emigration to their citizens. He admits that he has had a role in "innumerable little operations to affect the way things turned out." Perle and two other congressional staffers were credited with designing the amendment and persuading a majority of both houses of Congress to support it before the Nixon administration could organize means to counter it. The amendment resulted in a Soviet rejection of the trade agreement and remains to this day an important source of friction in U.S.-Soviet relations.[4]

During 1974 the Democratic neoconservative movement emerged in full bloom. It was given impetus by the Yom Kippur War but reflected essentially the cold war views held by those who opposed the notion of détente and the SALT process. The movement included most of the members of the Coalition for a Democratic Majority, which had been formed to back Scoop Jackson for President in 1972 and included such leaders as Daniel Patrick Moynihan, Ben Wattenberg, and former Undersecretary of State Eugene Rostow. The movement also included such intellectuals as Norman Podhoretz, editor of *Commentary,* the voice of the American Jewish Committee, and Irving Kristol, editor of the neoconservative *The Public Interest.*

In June 1974 Paul Nitze resigned from the U.S. SALT delegation and was urged by Jackson to explain his action before the Senate Armed Services Committee. Nitze said he couldn't, in good conscience, participate any longer in a process which was based on "the myth of détente." When his old friend Eugene Rostow released a report entitled "The Quest for Détente," which was published by the Coalition for a Democratic Majority, Nitze gave his full support. The paper was a broadside attack on Kissinger's negotiations with the Soviets, maintaining that the Russians cannot be trusted in matters of weapons control which are so important to our national security. In a personal letter to Kissinger after the report had been released, Rostow said: "And we think it is not only wrong but dangerous to lull Western public opinion by proclaiming an end of the Cold War, a substitution of negotiation for confrontation and a generation of peace."

On August 8, 1974, the Watergate scandal reached its logical conclusion with the resignation of Richard Nixon. His successor, Gerald Ford, still fully supported the arms control goals of Henry Kissinger. In November, Ford and Kissinger went to Vladivostok for a summit meeting with Brezhnev, and they agreed to equal ceilings for strategic weapon launchers and for an equal limit on launchers that could have multiple warheads. Senator Jackson vigorously attacked the new levels as too high, demanding that they be reduced in categories which would increase the relative lead of the United States.

Both Jackson and Schlesinger had been highly critical of the throw-weight advantage that the SALT I agreement allegedly had given to the Soviets. (Throw-weight is the amount of megatonnage of nuclear weapons that can be delivered on opposing targets.) In his 1974 report to Congress, Schlesinger asserted that:

> the lack of equality can become a source of serious diplomatic or military miscalculation. Opponents may feel that they can exploit a favorable imbalance by means of political pressure, as Hitler did so skillfully in the 1930's, particularly with Neville Chamberlain at Berchtesgaden. Friends may believe that a willingness on our part to accept less than equality indicates a lack of resolve to uphold our end of the competition and a certain deficiency in staying power. Our citizens may doubt our capacity to guard the nation's interests.

Schlesinger's comparison of the United States, which had assembled the mightiest military arsenal in history, with the almost impotent Britain of the 1930's was a gargantuan absurdity.[5] Nevertheless, a major theme of the American hawks has been to equate SALT agreements with Munich.

Schlesinger observed that because the Soviets had such large missiles, the time would soon come when they would have enough large multiple warheads (MIRVs) with enough accuracy to blow up, in a first strike, most of our land-based missiles (ICBMs), submarines in ports, and bombers which had not left airfields. Therefore, it was essential, Schlesinger asserted, for the United States to build the necessary counterforce weapons so that it would also have the capability of destroying Soviet strategic systems. Schlesinger announced a targeting doctrine which would permit the United States to have a selective and flexible response to any attack. This doctrine advanced the concept of limited nuclear warfare and set in motion plans for the deployment of Mark 12A warheads to increase the payload and accuracy of the Minuteman III missile and longer-range plans for the MX missile and the Trident II submarine missile—all of which are counterforce weapons.

At this time the director of the Arms Control and Disarmament Agency was Fred C. Ikle, and the deputy director was John Lehman. Both men have been vigorous hawks all of their professional careers. It was ironic that they should be responsible for arms control since both were proponents of a U.S. capability for nuclear war fighting and of building the weapons essential to create that capability. Ikle was close to Schlesinger and supported his hard-line stance, as did Lehman, who is a close friend of Richard Perle. Ikle and Lehman both let it be known around Washington that they opposed the policy of détente.

So Kissinger found himself surrounded by tough, dedicated, skillful opposition in the Pentagon, in the Arms Control and Disarmament Agency, in the Senate Armed Services Committee, especially from Jackson and Perle, and elsewhere from men like Nitze, Rostow, and the neoconservatives. After Vladivostok, progress in the SALT II talks had slowed perceptibly. A major problem had emerged because the United States was rapidly developing the technology for long-range cruise missiles. The Soviets insisted that such weapons be banned or counted in the strategic aggregates of SALT. The Pentagon countered with a demand that the new Soviet Backfire bomber be counted as strategic, too. The Soviets insisted that the Backfire was a medium-range bomber, but U.S. experts maintained that it could reach the United States, flying at subsonic speed on a one-way trip and landing at bases in Cuba. If it were equipped with additional gas tanks, it could be refueled in air and fly round trip to the United States. As a result of the Backfire controversy, an impasse was reached. That was fine with the hawks, who were opposed to SALT and wanted to build long-range cruise missiles.

Kissinger was trying desperately to resolve the dilemma by working on proposals for complex negotiating compromises. But it was becoming clear that Jackson and Schlesinger were going to succeed in blocking him. Then, suddenly, came the so-called Halloween Massacre, on the weekend of November 1 and 2, 1975. President Ford took dramatic action. He fired Schlesinger. He replaced CIA Director William Colby with George Bush. Kissinger was to remain, but with only his State Department hat. The national security adviser post was filled by Brent Scowcroft, who had been NSC deputy. Ford's White House chief of staff, Donald Rumsfeld, became secretary of defense. Explaining his decisions on national TV, Ford said: "I need to have my own team."

Certainly Rumsfeld was Ford's man, while Schlesinger clearly was Jackson's man. But the issue was more fundamental: Kissinger could not make progress on SALT while being undercut by the Jackson-Schlesinger coalition. On the night that Schlesinger was fired, he told a journalist friend that "Henry is always tough with everybody, but the Russians."[6] Schlesinger didn't believe in negotiating with the Russians on the basis of equality. He wanted the United States to maintain superiority. Kissinger thought our security was better served by restraining the arms race. But Henry Kissinger was never soft on the Russians, and President Ford knew it.

Kissinger tried one more time to proceed with SALT when he had talks with Brezhnev and Gromyko in January 1976. He worked out a formula based on slight adjustments in the Vladivostok numbers, an agreement to limit and count long-range cruise missiles, and an agreement to limit and control the Backfire bomber, which would be outside the SALT treaty. The Soviets were ready to make a deal. But it was too late. The Soviet-Cuban intervention in Angola had had profound repercussions in American opinion. "Détente" had become a dirty word which President Ford no longer used. The election campaign had begun, and the Reagan forces were on the attack. U.S. policy toward the Soviet Union was a major issue. Ford decided to put the SALT negotiations on the back burner.

Victory for the American Hawks

At the 1976 Republican National Convention Kissinger was given humiliating treatment by the Reagan team. Schlesinger, on the other hand, had become a hero to the American right and was acting as an adviser to Reagan. Rostow had been writing to Schlesinger with suggestions of possible speeches which Reagan might give to attack the Ford-Kissinger position. The foreign policy planks adopted at the convention were a virtual repudiation of Kissinger. It was almost inconceivable that only four years before, Kissinger had been Super Henry and the darling of the convention. Ford won the nomination in a close fight, but so much damage had been done that the Kissinger policies were in shambles. Even if Ford were to win the election, the prospects for recovery were dim.

Even so, the hawks had one last act to play during the remaining months of the Ford-Kissinger term. The Foreign Intelligence Advisory Board had recommended that President Ford and CIA Director George Bush commission an independent, outside examination of the CIA annual estimate of Soviet military strength and intentions. This is far and away the most important CIA intelligence estimate. Ford and Bush agreed, but instead of appointing a balanced group of experts, Bush appointed a team of ten non-CIA men, almost all of whom were superhawks. They were: chairman Richard Pipes, professor of Russian history at Harvard, now Soviet specialist on the Reagan National Security Council staff; Paul Nitze, now chief of the U.S. delegation to the talks on intermediate-range nuclear weapons in Geneva; William R. Van Cleave, professor of international relations at the University of Southern California, who was head of the Reagan transition team for the Department of Defense; Paul D. Wolfowitz, who was in the Arms Control and Disarmament Agency, under Ikle, and is now chief of policy planning in the State Department; Seymour Weiss, who was ousted by Kissinger as head of the State Department Bureau of Politico-Military Affairs; Daniel O. Graham, retired Army lieutenant general and former director of the Defense Intelligence Agency, who is now on the National Strategy Committee of the American Security Council, a private lobby which advocates increased defense spending and cold war policies; Foy D. Kohler, former U.S. ambassador to Moscow, 1962–66, and now a think tank associate of General Graham; Thomas Wolfe, longtime specialist on Soviet military affairs at the Rand Corporation, a think tank substantially funded by the U.S. Air Force; John W. Vogt, Jr., retired Air Force general who commanded the Seventh Air Force in Vietnam; Jasper A. Welch, Jr., Air Force brigadier general, assistant chief of staff, who has helped prepare SALT positions for the Joint Chiefs.

The selection of these ten men to review the CIA intelligence estimates represented the first time in the history of national intelligence estimates that such a step had been taken. The group rapidly became known as Team B, contrasted with the CIA intelligence professionals, who were known as Team A. Team B was, not surprisingly, in sharp disagreement with the findings of the regular CIA estimate. Accordingly there ensued a battle which was described by Team B members as "bloody, but healthy, and long overdue." Critics called the exercise a "bludgeoning" which further damaged the already demoralized and battered agency.

Ray Cline, a former deputy director of CIA and a director of State Department Intelligence until he was ousted by Kissinger, said he deplored the Team B experiment. Cline, himself a hard-liner, said that the process of making national security estimates "has been subverted by employing a kangaroo court of outside critics all picked from one point of view."[7]

The Team A, Team B process was expected to last until February 1977, when it would be reviewed by the Foreign Intelligence Advisory Board, according to Leo Cherne, the board's chairman. At that time the intelligence board would weigh the relative merits of the official national estimate and the Pipes report and make a recommendation to the CIA director and the President. But Jimmy Carter won the election in November, and a new team, including a new CIA director, would soon be in power. So in late December the whole Team B story, including the major findings, was leaked to the press. The first news report in the *Boston Globe* described the confrontation as a "crushing victory for the Pipes group over the CIA intelligence estimators."

At this point George Bush, the head of the entire U.S. intelligence community, granted an interview with *The New York Times*. In the past CIA directors always refused to comment on national intelligence estimates, which are top secret, even when reporters may have picked up pieces of information that might have a bearing on the contents of the estimates. But Bush told *The New York Times* that "new evidence and a reinterpretation of old information contributed to the reassessment of Soviet intentions." Bush made it clear that the Team B report had been adopted as the official CIA estimate. The *Washington Star* said that the Bush interview gave the Team B estimate "an official stamp. It guaranteed that the revision in evaluating the Soviet challenge would become known with an authoritative ring which will profoundly affect the future of the defense dialogue in Washington."[8]

Herbert Scoville, Jr., a former CIA deputy director for science and technology, said: "I think this whole thing was clearly an attempt to leave a legacy for the new administration which would be very hard to reverse. . . . Now the integrity of the estimating process has been questioned it is extremely difficult for the CIA regulars to stand up to the pressure of a biased point of view when the people at the top want to prove something."[9] Clearly George Bush wanted to leave the Carter administration with a well-publicized message that might influence defense spending for years to come.

THE CARTER YEARS

Jimmy Carter had campaigned with speeches frequently asserting the theme that nuclear weapons must be controlled and reduced eventually to a point where they are abolished. He had also pledged to cut back defense spending, on an annual basis, by $5 to $7 billion. But as he approached his inauguration, he was hit broadside by the Team B conclusions, which were: that the Soviet Union intended to achieve military superiority over the United States and was rapidly approaching that goal; that the Soviet Union was pursuing a very different strategic doctrine from that of the United States because it believed that nuclear war could be fought and won; and that the Soviets were seeking a war-fighting capability because they still endorse the view of the Prussian general Karl von Clausewitz that war "is a continuation of political relations by other means."

The evidence for the Team B findings was said to be a new CIA estimate that the Soviets had doubled their defense spending from a rate of 6 to 8 percent of their gross national product (GNP) to a new rate of 11 to 13 percent of GNP. It was claimed that the Soviet Union was outspending the United States by 50 percent. The evidence that the Soviets were preparing to fight a nuclear war came from citations in certain Soviet military writing and also from the alleged massive Soviet civil defense program designed to protect the leadership, industry, and population in the event of war. The Carter administration never attempted to provide an effective counteranalysis to the Team B conclusions, except in regard to its findings on civil defense. More important, nothing more was heard about defense cuts. On the contrary, the defense budget was raised each year Carter was in office.

After Schlesinger had been fired in late 1975, he began corresponding with Eugene Rostow and Paul Nitze about the need to form a private national committee to influence public opinion about the dangers of détente and the need to increase our military power. At a luncheon at the Metropolitan Club in Washington in March 1976 it was agreed to form a Committee on the Present Danger. An all-out effort to organize the committee was mounted. After the election results were known, it was decided to go public. So, on November 11, 1976, a press conference was held in Washington. The Committee on the Present Danger was to be a bipartisan organization with Henry Fowler, former secretary of the treasury under Johnson; Lane Kirkland, now president of the AFL-CIO; and David Packard, former deputy secretary of defense under Nixon, as cochairmen. Actually the main leadership for the committee was to come from Paul Nitze, chairman of Policy Studies, and Eugene Rostow, the chairman of the Executive Committee. James Schlesinger would have been a leader in the committee had he not been made secretary of energy under Carter. The committee also included Richard

Allen, former national security adviser to Reagan, and Allen's associate Richard Pipes.

The committee announced that:

> our country is in a period of danger, and the danger is increasing. Unless decisive steps are taken to alert the nation, and to change the course of its policy, our economic and military capacity will become inadequate to assure peace with security. . . . The principal threat to our nation, to world peace, and to the cause of human freedom is the Soviet drive for dominance based upon an unparalleled military build-up. . . . If we continue to drift, we shall become second best to the Soviet Union in overall military strength, our alliances will weaken, our promising rapprochement with China could be reversed. Then we could find ourselves isolated in a hostile world, facing the unremitting pressures of Soviet policy backed by an overwhelming preponderance of power. Our national survival itself would be in peril, and we should face, one after another, bitter choices between war and acquiescence under pressure.

Except for the reference to China this could have been lifted from the Nitze-drafted NSC 68 of 1950 or the Gaither Report of 1957.

Jimmy Carter brought a strong team of SALT supporters into his administration, including Secretary of State Cyrus Vance, who knew about strategic weapons because he had been a deputy secretary of defense; Secretary of Defense Harold Brown, who had been a member of the U.S. SALT delegation; Paul Warnke, selected to be director of the Arms Control and Disarmament Agency and also chief SALT negotiator, who had been an assistant secretary of defense in charge of international security affairs; Leslie Gelb, who had worked for Warnke at Defense, chosen to be director of the Bureau of Political-Military Affairs in the State Department; and Marshall Shulman, adviser to Vance on Soviet affairs. Shulman had been a speech writer for Dean Acheson when he was secretary of state and was, for years, director of the Russian Institute of Columbia University.

Warnke was the most controversial of the group because he was an outspoken critic of excessive defense spending and gold-plated weapons systems. He had been a defense adviser to George McGovern when he ran for President in 1972. He was known in Washington as a very effective, tough-minded lawyer and expert on issues of national security. He was a law partner of Clark Clifford, who had been secretary of defense part of the time Warnke was at Defense. What disturbed the hawks most about Warnke was that he was a strong and persuasive advocate of genuine arms control. Instead of building more strategic weapons, he wanted to stop building and to cut back existing arsenals if he could get the Russians to agree.

So the Nitze-Jackson forces mounted a campaign to block Warnke's nomination and, if failing in that, to damage Warnke's public image and influence in the Carter administration. The hearings dragged on and on, with charges and countercharges becoming more strident each day. Jackson and his supporters worked together inside the Senate, while Nitze and the Committee on the Present Danger operated on the outside. They were joined by several right-wing groups, led by General Daniel Graham, called the Emergency Coalition Against Unilateral Disarmament, which included the American Conservative Union, the Conservative Caucus, the Committee for Survival of a Free Congress, and the American Security Council.

Warnke had been in the Defense Department when Nitze was deputy secretary of defense. They had had very different views on the American involvement in Vietnam. Nitze had thought the United States had to contain the Communist march everywhere; Warnke had not thought Vietnam was a good place to do it. Nitze wrote a letter to the chairman of the Senate Foreign Relations Committee in which he said that Warnke's abilities "at least with respect to defense matters do not include clarity or consistency of logic." When Nitze came before the Foreign Relations Committee to testify in person, he positively bristled as he characterized Warnke's views as "absolutely asinine, screwball, arbitrary and fictitious."

When the nomination came to the Senate floor, the hawks

won a great victory. Warnke was confirmed as SALT negotiator, but by a vote of only 58 to 40. Sixty-seven affirmative votes are needed to ratify a treaty. Senator Jackson had explained his campaign as "weakening Warnke as an international negotiator to the point of uselessness by holding the vote in his favor to sixty or less."[10] Jackson's aide Richard Perle was elated because he had masterminded the coordination of the anti-Warnke position papers in the Senate. According to his friend John Lehman, the "40 votes against Warnke—that was purely Richard."[11] Perle and Jackson considered the result of the Warnke battle a significant warning to President Carter which probably influenced his position on SALT.

Warnke was not confirmed until March 9, 1977. In the meantime, an even more serious disaster had been brewing. Senator Henry Jackson had been invited to the White House on several occasions to discuss SALT. He informed the President of his strong objections to SALT I and the Vladivostok accord. He was highly critical of the Kissinger negotiating record. Carter had been made aware by his advisers that it would be quite a coup if at the outset he could gain the support of Jackson for the administration's SALT program. After all, Jackson was a Democrat and had been the most influential critic of the Nixon-Kissinger negotiations. Therefore, Carter asked Jackson to put his suggestions for a new negotiating position in writing. Jackson was delighted and asked Richard Perle to draft a memorandum. The twenty-three-page policy paper, with a covering letter from Jackson, was delivered to Carter on February 15.

It advised dropping the Kissinger approach and attacking the Soviet ICBM throw-weight advantages. This meant reopening the issue of heavy ICBM's, including both the Soviet SS-18's and SS-19's. If the Soviets insisted on continuing to maintain heavy ICBM's, the United States should have the option of building a new, heavy ICBM of its own. The United States should insist that the Soviet Backfire bomber be classified as a strategic bomber and included in SALT. The United States should not agree to include the cruise missiles as strategic weapons. When Paul Warnke, who was not yet confirmed but was serving as a consultant, saw the paper, he rejected it as a "first-class polemic."[12]

Obviously the Jackson-Perle recommendations were extremely one-sided and nonnegotiable. But the fat was in the fire. From that point on it would be very difficult to retain Jackson's backing without incorporating at least some of his recommendations in the new SALT package. During the next several weeks Perle was seen lunching with key SALT officials at both the State and Defense departments. The policy direction had begun to shift dramatically away from the Vladivostok numbers and the subsequent Kissinger arrangements for dealing with cruise missiles and the Backfire bomber.

In addition to the prodétente officials already mentioned, Carter appointed Zbigniew Brzezinski, an anti-Soviet hawk of long standing, as his national security adviser. Brzezinski, executive director of the Trilateral Commission, had been instrumental in bringing Jimmy Carter into that organization. According to Carter, Brzezinski had served as his foreign policy mentor. So it was natural that when Carter ran for President, he made Brzezinski chairman of his committee to prepare foreign policy position papers.

As the complexities of drafting a new SALT position increased, the President decided to center the effort in the Special Coordinating Committee of the National Security Council, under Brzezinski's chairmanship. Brzezinski, who was a rival of Kissinger's, wanted to have his own imprint on the policy. He said that "Nixon, Ford and Kissinger had gone down a blind alley on the Soviet's turf and it was time to get back on our own." Brzezinski was less interested in concluding a deal with the Soviets than in demonstrating, in the first go-round, that the United States had a strong, tough negotiating stance. The President concurred.

Ironically it was William Hyland, the last holdover from Kissinger's NSC staff, who was asked by Brzezinski to prepare the draft negotiating proposal. Hyland, who knew the entire inside story of the SALT negotiations conducted by Henry Kissinger, was in an impossible bind. Nevertheless, he followed his instructions, reflecting the new policy guidelines that he had heard being developed by the Carter team. He developed a comprehensive proposal which provided for a cut in the Vladivostok numbers of 200 to 400 fewer strategic launchers, 120 to 220 fewer missiles with MIRV, a new category of land-based missiles with multiple warheads limited to 550, a cut in Soviet heavy missiles from 300 to 150, a limit on flight testing of ICBM's, a ban on mobile ICBM's and new ICBM's, while cruise missiles would be permitted up to a range of 2,500 kilometers.

Except for the Backfire bomber and possibly the ban on mobile ICBM's, which would have included the MX (only a gleam in the eye at the time), the whole package was clearly advantageous to the United States and disadvantageous to the Soviet Union. Months later Hyland admitted that he never had any illusion that the Soviets would accept the comprehensive proposal. At the time Secretary Vance insisted on having a second position based on Vladivostok. It was agreed that if the Soviets didn't accept the comprehensive proposal as a basis for talks, Vance could go back to the Vladivostok numbers, but with no controls on cruise missiles or the Backfire bomber. Those issues would be deferred until SALT III.

President Carter was enthusiastic about this dramatic new framework and decided to discuss the main points on national television in advance of Vance's trip to Moscow. The next day Senator Jackson, who had been fully briefed in advance, issued a press release enthusiastically endorsing the comprehensive proposal as "moving in the right direction—away from the folly of the Kissinger-Nixon-Ford approach."[13] Hawks all over Washington praised the new initiative as a move toward deep cuts which would mean arms control that contributed to U.S. security.

Vance, Warnke (who had barely moved into his new role), Gelb, and the others took off for Moscow to meet with Brezhnev and Gromyko. Of course, the talks were a fiasco. On the third day Brezhnev rejected the comprehensive proposal. He seemed particularly irritated at the recommendation that the Soviet SS-18's (heavy missiles) should be cut in half. He reminded Vance that he had agreed with Kissinger at Vladivostok to leave out the U.S. forward-based systems in Europe and

81

the French and British systems capable of striking the Soviet Union in part because Kissinger had agreed not to treat the Soviet heavies as a separate category. Brezhnev also rejected the second proposal based on the Vladivostok numbers because it deferred controls on cruise missiles. The Soviets had spent months negotiating a cruise missile formula and were content with the deal they had made with Kissinger.

The Moscow trip was an incredible disaster. When he got the details of the final meeting from Vance, Carter told the press that "if we feel the Soviets are not acting in good faith then I would be forced to consider a much more deep commitment to the development and deployment of additional weapons." Already Carter, influenced by Brzezinski, was moving up the slippery slope of arms buildup rather than arms reduction. He did not know what had hit him. In fairness to Carter it should be noted that he had been very badly briefed by his staff both on Jackson's true intentions and on the inequality of the package he was sending to Moscow.

But the damage had been done, very serious damage which lasts to this day. The highly publicized March 1977 comprehensive proposal had received glowing bipartisan praise. The public believes, as does much of Congress, that it was a serious attempt at genuine arms control. The proposal became a benchmark to judge future arms control efforts. Anything less would be attacked as something of a failure, a giving in to the Soviets. Even more damaging was the impression, left in the public mind, that the Soviets had rejected a proposal for deep cuts. This meant, it was claimed, that the Soviets were opposed to deep cuts in nuclear weapons and that therefore, the Soviets probably would not agree to substantial reductions at any time. The Soviets rejected the U.S. proposal, however, because it made deep cuts only in their ICBM's but did not make deep cuts in those systems where the United States has the advantage, such as strategic bombers and submarine missiles with multiple warheads. The Soviets have favored deep reductions in nuclear weapons for years, as long as the cuts are based on the principle of equality.

After the March debacle the ensuing months were used to try to repair the damage, essentially by returning to the

Vladivostok numbers and the negotiating positions already advanced by Kissinger. Speaking at the Notre Dame commencement on May 22, 1977, President Carter attempted to return to the tone of his campaign speeches:

> Being confident of our own future, we are now free of that inordinate fear of communism which once led us to embrace any dictator who joined us in our fear. For too many years we have been willing to adopt the flawed principles and tactics of our adversaries, sometimes abandoning our values for theirs. We fought fire with fire, never thinking that fire is better fought with water.
>
> . . . We have moved to engage the Soviet Union in a joint effort to halt the strategic arms race. That race is not only dangerous, it is morally deplorable. We must put an end to it. . . . Our goal is to be fair to both sides, to produce reciprocal stability, parity and security. We desire a freeze on further modernization and continuing substantial reductions of strategic weapons. We want a comprehensive ban on nuclear testing, a prohibition against chemical warfare, no attack capability against space satellites and arms limitations in the Indian Ocean. . . .
>
> I believe in détente with the Soviet Union. To me it means progress toward peace. But that progress must be both comprehensive and reciprocal. We cannot have accommodation in one part of the world and aggravation of conflicts in another.
>
> Nor should the effects of détente be limited to our two countries alone. We hope the Soviet leaders will join us in efforts to stop the spread of nuclear explosives and to reduce sales of conventional arms. We hope to persuade the Soviet Union that one country cannot impose its own social system upon another, either through direct military intervention or through the use of a client state's military force—as with the Cuban intervention in Angola.[14]

President Carter was developing the two themes that were to recur frequently during his four years: an advocacy of détente and reduction of nuclear arms combined with a ban on direct or indirect military intervention. Carter's call for a "freeze on further modernization and continuing substantial reductions of strategic weapons" along with "a comprehensive ban on nuclear testing" was exactly what Brezhnev was promoting. If achieved, it would have meant a reversal of the nuclear arms race. Why didn't it happen? There were two fundamental reasons.

First, the Soviets never accepted President Carter's call for reciprocal measures to ban military intervention. Quite the contrary, a few months after Carter's speech the Soviet Union began to airlift Cuban troops into Ethiopia to fight in the Ogaden desert. This was followed by the intervention in South Yemen, the Soviet-supported invasion of Cambodia by Vietnam, and the direct Soviet invasion of Afghanistan.

Secondly, the American hawks were opposed to a nuclear freeze and a comprehensive nuclear test ban. This would have made it impossible to produce and deploy new nuclear weapons systems. The hawks wanted to build the MX, the Trident II missiles, the cruise missiles, the Pershing II's, and the new strategic bombers. They believed in the chimera of nuclear superiority. So long as the Soviets were indulging in expansionism through the use of military power, it was not difficult for the American hawks to have their way.

The Committee on the Present Danger, the American Security Council, and other militarist organizations and think tanks hammered away on three major themes: the alleged huge buildup of Soviet military power to a point where it surpassed the United States; the alleged Soviet doctrine calling for fighting and winning nuclear wars; and the Soviet drive for world conquest. The Committee on the Present Danger, a small group of invited members, took the lead in providing the intellectual framework for the campaign, while the American Security Council was the operating arm.

The American Security Council, which has many retired high-ranking military and intelligence officers in its leadership, has a national membership of more than 230,000. As part of its political action organization, the American Security Council has formed the Coalition for Peace Through Strength, which is comprised of 232 senators and representatives, about 40 percent of the members of Congress. The coalition has endorsed a resolution calling for a "national strategy based on overall military and technological superiority over the Soviet Union." The American Security Council rates members of Congress on their voting records on selected issues of national security. In the 1980 election, eight out of ten senators given the lowest rating were defeated, and twenty-six representatives with so-called antidefense records were unseated.[15]

An important instrument for the political action of the American Security Council has been a series of films dramatizing the Soviet military threat. One film, *The Price of Peace and Freedom*, which features film clips from Soviet military maneuvers and statements from former U.S. and NATO military commanders, including former General Alexander Haig, has reportedly been seen by more than 50 million Americans on 200 local television stations. Typical of the film's message is an assertion by former Secretary of the Navy and current Reagan adviser William Middendorf: "Today we face a Soviet threat far greater than any other threat this nation has ever faced in its two hundred years of existence."

The combination of the campaign of the American hawks and aggressive Soviet adventures in the Third World made it progressively more difficult for the advocates of détente and arms control in the Carter administration. Zbigniew Brzezinski, who briefed the President on the major issues of foreign policy every day, was gaining influence with Carter. He had consistently pressed a harder line toward the USSR than had Vance and his State Department team. Brzezinski was concerned with the need for a balanced approach to the SALT negotiations while giving at least as high priority to issues of Soviet intervention in the Third World. He linked progress in SALT directly with better Soviet behavior. He sought ways to punish the Soviets for their aggression and was obviously delighted with the increasingly cordial relations developing with China. He made much, publicly and privately, of the visit to the United States of Vice Premier Teng Hsiaoping, which included a small dinner at Brzezinski's house for the Chinese leader.

RUSSIAN ROULETTE

One of the major flaws of the Carter administration was the President's failure to establish a unified foreign policy. Both Vance and Brzezinski were permitted to pursue obviously inconsistent, often contradictory policy lines. This lack of resolution became apparent in the President's speeches, which often reflected two points of view. The division was bad, too, in dealing with the Soviets. The Soviets were eager to exploit the dichotomy, portraying Brzezinski as the heavy and Vance and his assistants as the good guys.

This, in turn, led to exploitation by the American hawks, who looked to Brzezinski as their bastion in the Carter administration. The result was constant bureaucratic infighting conducted in an unusually adversarial and hostile atmosphere, even by Washington standards. The press was full of leaked stories presenting competing points of view. One of Brzezinski's most notorious outlets was Richard Burt, who covered national security stories for *The New York Times*. Burt, who came to the *Times* from a position as assistant director of the International Institute of Strategic Studies in London, was known on the Washington cocktail circuit as a hawk with well-established credentials as an opponent of SALT II and an advocate of big defense spending. Brzezinski was delighted to feed Burt stories advancing their mutual interests, which usually appeared on the front page of the most powerful paper in the United States.

By the fall of 1978, after only twenty months as director of the Arms Control and Disarmament Agency and as chief SALT negotiator, Paul Warnke found the situation so distasteful that he resigned. It was also said that Warnke wanted to be out of office well before the SALT II treaty was signed so that his presence would not impede Senate ratification of the treaty. Another major actor in the SALT II fight, Leslie Gelb, informed Secretary Vance and President Carter of his intention to resign as soon as the SALT II treaty was signed. Gelb's encounters with Brzezinski had been at least as bloody as those of Warnke.

On the night before his departure for Vienna to sign the treaty with Brezhnev, President Carter was given a preview of the forthcoming battle in the Senate. Scoop Jackson, in a speech before the Coalition for a Democratic Majority, said:

To enter a treaty which favors the Soviets as this one does on the ground that we will be in a worse position without it, is appeasement in its purest form. . . . Against overwhelming evidence of a continuing Soviet strategic and conventional military buildup, there has been a flow of official administration explanations, extenuations, excuses. It is all reminiscent of Great Britain in the 1930's, when one government pronouncement after another was issued to assure the British public that Hitler's Germany would never achieve military equality—let alone superiority. The failure to face reality today, like the failure to do so then—that is the mark of appeasement.[16]

Jackson's harsh attack was a forecast of things to come, demonstrating the deep division between the conservatives and the moderates in the Democratic Party and the almost certain defeat of Jimmy Carter in the coming election.

Shortly after the Vienna summit Richard Burt wrote a story about the shift of power in Brzezinski's direction. Unnamed officials said Brzezinski "was still bent on getting the State Department to conform to his views." They attributed the smoother relations to the departure from the government of two of his fiercest adversaries—Paul C. Warnke and Leslie H. Gelb. Both men said they were leaving for personal reasons, but a State Department official who worked with the two said Mr. Brzezinski had created an uncongenial atmosphere for them in policy debates. Other aides said Mr. Brzezinski had also been able to reduce the influence of Marshall Shulman, Mr. Vance's adviser on Soviet affairs. Indeed he had. During the last eighteen months of the Carter administration Shulman's advice seldom had much impact in White House decisions.

In an interview with Burt, Brzezinski said that he had focused on "pulling bureaucratic levers to make policy." He indicated that he had "prevailed on such critical issues as the deployment of the MX mobile missile and the handling of the Soviet-American summit meeting in Vienna." According to Burt:

Mr. Brzezinski's aides say his most important accomplishment has been to deflect State Department pressure for giving priority in American foreign policy to relations with the Soviet Union. They said that by pressing for the normalization of relations with China, and getting Mr. Carter to approve the [MX] mobile missile, Mr. Brzezinski had been able to insure that the meeting with Leonid Brezhnev in Vienna would be a low-key, mostly ceremonial affair.[17]

After a good July performance for the administration during the SALT II hearings before the Senate Foreign Relations Committee, everything went to pieces with the so-called discovery of the Soviet combat brigade in Cuba. It was Brzezinski who advised the President to take a hard line on the Soviet brigade, from which he later had to back down. It was Brzezinski, too, who pressed hardest for the NATO decision to deploy U.S. missiles in Europe capable of reaching Soviet targets. When Brezhnev gave his speech in Berlin announcing a decision to reduce unilaterally one Soviet division and 1,000 tanks from Germany, along with an offer to reduce unilaterally Soviet medium-range missiles in return for a startup of negotiations with the United States, it was Brzezinski who first dismissed the proposal in a statement to the press.

The Soviet invasion of Afghanistan brought all controversy about arms control to an end. Linkage was ascendant, and SALT II was dead. In the spring of 1980 Cyrus Vance resigned, ostensibly over his disagreement with the President about whether or not to attempt a military rescue operation to free the American hostages in Iran. But it was common knowledge that Vance, like Warnke and Gelb before him, felt that his effectiveness as secretary of state had come to an end. Zbigniew Brzezinski had decisively won the struggle for power. He now had his own people placed in key positions in State, Defense, the CIA, as well as the White House.

When Vance was succeeded by Senator Edmund Muskie, there was a great deal of fanfare about the senator's terrible temper and about how he didn't take kindly to end runs. It was agreed that Muskie, as secretary of state, would be his own man with the full backing of the President. But that was not to be. Two months earlier Brzezinski had begun rushing through a new strategic doctrine paper which was being prepared by a small group on his staff and a few Defense officials. Secretary Muskie had several meetings with Brzezinski during the days when the finishing touches were being put on the paper. On July 25 Muskie had breakfast with President Carter, Brzezinski, and Defense Secretary Harold Brown.[18] That was the day Carter put his signature to Presidential Directive 59, the new doctrine paper. Muskie ruefully informed the press afterward that he had never been consulted on the new policy position.

After the election of Ronald Reagan, Brzezinski gave an interview to *The New York Times* in which he was critical of the Vance priorities for SALT and the failure of the United States to respond to Moscow's military moves abroad. He blamed Vance's timidity on guilt among the Democrats about the misuse of power in Vietnam. He said that Vance, as a result, pursued a "do-gooder's agenda." Vance replied, in public, that Brzezinski's views were "hogwash." He said that Brzezinski put excessive weight "on the use of military power or bluff." He said: "I think it is of fundamental importance that there be only two spokesmen for the Government on matters relating to foreign policy: the President of the United States and the Secretary of State. Any other arrangement leads to confusion in the United States, the Congress and abroad."[19]

THE REAGAN HAWKS

Brzezinski has had the smile of a Cheshire cat as he has observed the unfolding national security positions of the Reagan administration since the 1981 inauguration. The new team insists on acquiring military superiority over the Soviet Union. The defense budget will be increased each year by 5 to 7 percent above inflation. Confrontation backed by military power is back in favor. Soviet behavior throughout the world will definitely be linked with arms control negotiation. The March 1977 SALT proposal is endorsed as a step in the right direction. The NATO decision of December 1979 to deploy U.S. ground-launched missiles in Europe has been pursued. And the strategic doctrine set forth in Presidential Directive 59 has been adopted. Democrats like Jackson, Nitze, Rostow, Brzezinski, and the neoconservatives are now directly linked with the Reagan forces, forming a coalition of conservative Democrats and conservative Republicans which, temporarily, represents a dominant foreign policy consensus in the United States.

Team B and the Committee on the Present Danger have moved into the seats of power in the new administration. Key national security positions, especially the policy-making positions, are now occupied by opponents of détente who want to build more weapons. The list includes: Secretary of State Alexander Haig, who resigned as NATO chief of staff and testified against the SALT II Treaty; Paul D. Wolfowitz, director of Policy Planning at State, who was a member of Team B; Richard Burt, director of the State Department Bureau of Politico-Military Affairs, who was Brzezinski's favorite journalist; Eugene Rostow, director of the Arms Control and Disarmament Agency, a leader of the Committee on the Present Danger; Edward Rowny, retired general, chief SALT negotiator, who resigned as the representative of the Joint Chiefs on the SALT II staff, so that he could testify against the treaty; Paul Nitze, chief of the U.S. delegation to the intermediate-range nuclear weapons negotiations in Geneva, who was a member of Team B and a leader of the Committee on the Present Danger; Richard Allen, until January 1982 national security adviser to the President, who was a leader of the Committee on the Present Danger; Richard Pipes, White House Soviet specialist on the NSC staff, who was chief of Team B and a leader of the Committee on the Present Danger; Fred Ikle, undersecretary of defense for policy and a member of the Committee on the Present Danger; Richard Perle, assistant secretary of defense in charge of arms control and Soviet affairs, who had been Senator Jackson's éminence grise and a member of the Committee on the Present Danger; John Lehman, secretary of the Navy and a member of the Committee on the Present Danger; William Casey, director of Central Intelligence and a member of the Committee on the Present Danger.

These are the men in the Reagan administration most responsible for strategic arms control. If there was ever a case of assigning foxes to guard the chicken coop, the Reagan team has done it better. These all are representatives of the cult of military superiority. Nuclear superiority and negotiated agreements to reduce nuclear weapons are incompatible concepts since real reductions will occur only when the two superpowers start from a base of relative equality or parity, such as exists today. Yet the entire Reagan team continues to argue that we must build up our nuclear power in order to negotiate from a position of strength. Such rhetoric may sound very patriotic and righteous, but if the policy is carried out, there will be no progress because the Soviets will never agree to a treaty which is less than equal.

The Committee on the Present Danger has taken control of American national security policy. A few months after the Reagan administration took office, a coalition of American organizations supporting strategic arms reduction wrote a letter to the White House raising policy questions about Soviet-U.S. strategic rivalry. They received a reply from a member of the National Security Council staff: "As you can imagine, I do not have time to respond adequately to the arguments and concerns you raise. I might suggest that you consult recent literature of the Committee on the Present Danger for a cogent presentation of the view of our situation that is the basis of *the fundamental approach of this Administration* [emphasis added]."[20] Essentially the approach is the same as that expressed in NSC-68 by Paul Nitze in 1950. It calls for a vast buildup of U.S. military power to contain the Soviet Union—a return to the cold war.

There is a difference, though, an ominous one, in the thinking of some of the Reagan strategists. This difference goes beyond the cold war to the requirement to fight and win a nuclear war. The theory is based on the findings of Team B that the Soviet Union is seeking nuclear superiority and is pursuing a doctrine of preparing to fight and win a nuclear war. Therefore, it is claimed the United States should counter with a move to gain strategic superiority and to fight and win a nuclear war. Richard Pipes, the White House expert on the Soviet Union and chairman of Team B, says:

91

The Soviet ruling elite regards conflict and violence as natural regulators of all human affairs; wars between nations, in its view, represent only a variant of wars between classes. . . . Soviet doctrine emphatically asserts that while an all-out nuclear war would indeed prove extremely destructive to both parties, its outcome would not be mutual suicide; the country better prepared for it and in possession of a superior strategy could win and emerge a viable society. . . .

. . . There is something innately destabilizing in the very fact that we consider nuclear war unfeasible and suicidal for both, and our chief adversary views it as feasible and winnable for himself.[21]

Pipes wants to resolve this dilemma by persuading Americans that nuclear war is not suicidal, that it is feasible and winnable.

One wonders why Pipes has waged such a campaign to prepare America for a nuclear war. Is it just prudent, facing of reality, or is there more to it? Pipes is an upper-class Polish Jew who escaped to the United States in 1940 just after the invasion of Poland. According to some of his graduate students at Harvard, "he hates Russia."[22] After he had been in his White House job only two months, he told the Reuters news agency that "there is no alternative to war with the Soviet Union if the Russians do not abandon communism." Apparently Pipes is prepared to risk nuclear war in order to attain his goal. It should be stressed that the White House press secretary disavowed Pipes's remarks as neither authorized nor an accurate reflection of policy.[23] However, the policy of the Reagan administration remains ambiguous on this point.

Colin Gray, a frequent consultant to the Reagan administration on strategic issues, has written extensively about the concept of nuclear war fighting advocated by the new national security team. He says:

Strategic flexibility, unless wedded to a plausible theory of how to win a war or at least insure an acceptable end to a war, does not offer the United States an adequate bargaining position before or during a conflict and is an invitation to defeat. Small preplanned strikes can only be of use if the United States enjoys strategic superiority—the ability to wage a nuclear war at any level of violence with a reasonable prospect of defeating the Soviet Union and of recovering sufficiently to insure a satisfactory post war world order. . . . Soviet leaders would be less impressed by American willingness to launch a limited nuclear strike than they would by a plausible American victory strategy. Such a theory would have to envisage the demise of the Soviet state. The United States should plan to defeat the Soviet Union and to do so at a cost that would not prohibit U.S. recovery. Washington should identify war aims that in the last resort would contemplate the destruction of Soviet political authority and the emergence of a post war world order compatible with Western values.[24]

This is a concoction of fantasies based on sheer madness. It is almost inconceivable that such thinking is at the heart of a very serious policy debate in Washington, which has not yet been resolved. But such is the case.

Chapter IV

Misestimating Soviet Power

The American hawks are now in power, more so than ever before, most of them having found nests in the Reagan national security apparatus. Almost without exception, they are cold warriors and advocates of military superiority over the Soviet Union. Through the years their assessment of Soviet power and intentions has had an important influence on U.S. foreign and defense policy. Their estimate of the Soviet threat has often exaggerated or distorted the facts. Sometimes the evidence has been presented to the public in a deceptive manner. Since the hawks will be making decisions during the next few years which may determine whether or not we survive, it is more important than ever to examine and understand their records.

In the late 1940's and early 1950's there was growing talk of a bomber gap, especially after the Soviets had detonated their first atomic bomb in 1949. The bomber scare continued through 1956, when President Eisenhower broke off arms limitation talks with the Soviet Union because he had been informed that any agreement at that time would give the Russians a strategic advantage. It was discovered, as our intelligence got better, that there had never been a bomber gap. In fact, the United States has always maintained a substantial lead over the Soviet Union in strategic bombers.

In 1957 the Soviets surprised the world when they

launched their first globe-orbiting Sputnik satellite. More ominous was the fact that the Soviets had also tested, successfully, their first intercontinental ballistic missile. The Sputnik provided evidence that such a missile could reach anywhere in the United States. Then came the Gaither Report with its warnings that the Soviet Union by 1959 or 1960 would have a sufficient number of missiles to coerce the United States. During the 1960 election campaign John Kennedy charged Vice President Nixon with having allowed the United States to become hostage to Soviet power. Soon after the election our intelligence cameras proved that there was no missile gap. In fact, the United States had deployed, in both Turkey and Italy, 105 intermediate-range missiles capable of reaching Soviet cities. These weapons, combined with B-52 strategic bombers and our beginning ICBM force, gave the United States a substantial advantage.

At the time of the Cuban missile crisis of 1962 it was generally acknowledged that the United States had an overwhelming lead in deliverable nuclear weapons. This continued to be true throughout the 1960's and into the 1970's, but then came the 1972 Moscow summit, which produced the SALT I interim agreement. Senator Jackson and other hawks immediately began ringing the alarm bells again. They claimed not only that SALT I was unequal but that it gave the Soviets important strategic advantages especially in throw-weight.

The agreement did allow the Soviets more ICBM's and more strategic submarines, but despite this apparent disparity in numbers, the SALT I agreement permitted the United States to maintain a commanding strategic lead. Unfortunately Kissinger and the Defense Department did a very poor job of explaining this to the public. The result was that most of the public accepted Jackson's criticism and applauded his insistence that no further inequalities be permitted in the future.

The Nixon administration should have answered Jackson with the following points: The SALT I interim agreement had a duration of only five years; it did not provide any controls over multiple warheads (MIRV) (we now know that the Soviets didn't deploy any multiple warheads on their missiles until 1975 and didn't have sub-launched MIRV until 1977); at the time SALT I was signed U.S. missiles with MIRV had three times as many warheads as were possessed by the Soviet Union; SALT I did not include strategic bombers; in 1972 the United States had 500 strategic bombers, while the Soviets had a nearly obsolete force of 140 strategic range planes; and the U.S. strategic bomber force carried 75 percent of the megatonnage of the U.S. strategic arsenal.[1]

Edward Luttwak, an opponent of SALT, wrote a revealing article in which he said: "Any competent analyses of the actual capabilities of Soviet and American intercontinental nuclear forces deployed at the time of the 1972 Moscow accords revealed that the latter were *far superior by every relevant measurement* [emphasis added]." But he also said there were political costs in publishing an agreement that seemed to give the Soviets numerical advantage:

> The force-level ceilings of the 1972 Moscow accords, by which the United States was portrayed as inferior in all published numbers, were a costly blow to American authority, already then much damaged by the incoherent pursuit of the Indochina war and the resulting domestic unrest.
> . . . [It] is not the recondite calculations of technical experts that count in the world political arena, but rather untaught perceptions of political leaders in which numerical indices loom large. . . . Prudent statecraft must therefore attend to the careful upkeep of military prestige as much as the maintenance of real military strength. Certainly no such prudence was exercised in 1972 when the world was quite suddenly informed that the Soviet Union had the right to deploy significantly greater forces than the United States.[2]

Now Luttwak is saying, almost gleefully it would seem, that SALT I, as it was misinterpreted by the public, "was a costly blow to American authority and prestige." Luttwak himself acknowledges that "U.S. strategic forces were superior by every relevant measure." So how did the public come to believe that SALT I left the United States in an inferior position? How did this misperception occur? Certainly not because of any claims by the Russians or interpretations from the Nixon administration. The false perceptions were developed and promoted by Senator Jackson, Richard Perle, and the other architects of the attack on SALT I.

When James Schlesinger was secretary of defense, he was troubled that there was not enough public support for large-scale expansion of the defense budget. He said: "Democracies are suffering from their traditional problem—they need an overt manifest threat in order to bring about appropriate allocation of resources within the society to maintain a defense establishment."[3] Since there was no obvious threat at the time, Schlesinger, Luttwak, and other advocates of big defense spending developed something called the perception theory.

The theory is a clever device with which to gain support for the defense budget because it seems to make sense. If our people, our allies, or our adversaries perceive that we are not powerful, even when we are, then our strength may not be sufficiently persuasive as a deterrent to aggression or political blackmail. A book by the Center for Strategic and International Studies at Georgetown University says:

> Political judgments are based on gross and unsophisticated perceptions. It is not the opinion of experts that matters, but rather the sometimes unscientific views of political leaders at home and abroad. . . . The perceptions that shape political evaluations and strategic plans are not fixed in the present; they are dynamic. A growing and innovative arsenal will be perceived as more powerful than one which is static—even if the latter retains an advantage in purely technical terms.[4]

In other words, even though the United States retains greater strategic strength, the USSR in the process of catching up will be perceived to be more powerful because its arsenal is growing more rapidly than that of the United States. The theory is carried even further with the warning that a perception of less rapid military growth in the United

States may lead our allies to be vulnerable to "Finlandiza-
tion." Finland, being on the Soviet border and confronted
with Soviet power, has been bullied into maintaining a neutral government which makes some political and economic
concessions to Soviet pressure. Our NATO allies might become vulnerable to similar coercion, it is claimed, if they
misperceive the military balance.

The answer to such a threat, according to the proponents
of the perception theory, is to build more and better weapons
so that it will be unmistakably clear to all that the United
States has more than matched Soviet power. The perception
theory thus becomes a version of Catch-22. American advocates of greater defense spending spread alarms about the
inadequacy of American power and the growing strength of
Soviet power. Misperceptions are created because in reality
the United States and its allies remain more powerful than
the USSR. Since misperceptions in the minds of misguided
politicians are the basis for political judgments, the result is
more defense spending.

An editorial in *Time* magazine in 1981, discussing the debate on U.S. missile vulnerability, noted that certain U.S.
experts had exacerbated the alarm. James Schlesinger
conceded to *Time:* "To an extent, this is a self-inflicted wound.
It would be better to go quietly about the business of fixing
the trouble. But one of the penalties of a democracy is that we
have to call attention to the problem in order to get the necessary remedies."[5]

Of course, there is another answer to the self-inflicted
wounds created by misperceptions. Since they have not been
inspired by Soviet propaganda or saber-rattling threats, but
rather by the exaggerations of American critics, how much
better it would be to tell the public the truth. During the
SALT negotiations it was argued by some that our bargaining
position might be weakened if we publicly described our real
strength. That is another one of those arguments that perpetuate misperceptions about reality. The best approach, in
a democracy, is for the government to present a fair and
accurate set of facts to the public and its Congress.

Just as misperceptions can be concocted, so can misunderstandings be inspired, especially in the complex and highly

technical information about weapons systems. After the Vladivostok summit further SALT progress was blocked because the Pentagon claimed that the Backfire bomber was a strategic intercontinental weapon and the Soviets claimed that it was not. It became apparent, through the years, that the Pentagon did not really consider the Backfire a strategic weapon. When first mentioned in the Defense Department's annual report to Congress, it was treated as a medium-range bomber. But then, when it was thrust into the SALT negotiations, it was listed in the report by Defense Secretary Rumsfeld as a strategic bomber.

When the Carter administration came into office, the next Pentagon report listed Backfire as medium-range. It was interesting to note that neither the comprehensive proposal nor the fallback proposal which Secretary Vance took to Moscow in March 1977 included the Backfire bomber. Yet Senator Jackson and the other hawks had applauded those positions because they were so clearly weighted to U.S. advantage.

The Backfire bomber is an intermediate-range (5,500 nautical miles) plane built for naval support and for targets in Europe and China. It could reach the United States only with a reduced bombload, flying slowly at high altitudes, which would make it vulnerable to detection and interception by U.S. air defenses. The USSR lacks tankers for inflight refueling of the Backfire, so on a one-way flight its only safe haven would be Cuba. In time of war it would not be difficult for the United States to destroy any planes that landed in Cuba. The main advantage of having manned bombers is their capability of being reused.

Why, then, would the Soviet Union employ intermediate-range bombers to attack the United States when it has an abundant supply of ICBMs and sub-launched missiles with ample payload and accuracy to destroy most of the targets in the United States for which they have been designed? The Backfire was not designed to hit such targets. The answer is obvious, as it has been from the outset. Nevertheless, the American hawks to this day still include the Backfire in the list of Soviet weapons which they claim seriously threaten the United States.

RUSSIAN ROULETTE

THE TEAM B CAPER

Of all the various maneuvers engineered by the American hawks, the Team B conclusions must be credited with having had the greatest impact, perhaps equal to the damage done by the Soviet military adventures in the Third World. The fact that the exercise occurred at all is a devastating commentary on the failure of the U.S. government at the time to be sensitive to the requirements of an effective intelligence system. American taxpayers contribute billions of dollars each year for the purpose of financing an intelligence system that should be the best in the world.

The CIA and the other intelligence arms of the U.S. government have made errors, sometimes very serious ones, but on balance we probably have the best intelligence available to any government. We have people with years of training and experience who are experts in their fields. The most important job they perform is the annual estimate of Soviet power and intentions. The decision to bring into the CIA from outside ten hawks, most of whom had had no intelligence experience, to review and challenge the work of the professionals was a travesty—especially because the views of the hard-liners were known in advance.

The leaking of the Team B findings to the media, with the confirmation by CIA Director George Bush that they had been adopted as the official estimate, was astounding. It represented playing politics with the American intelligence establishment. It was certain to reduce the morale, the prestige, and the effectiveness of the CIA professionals. Those responsible for our national intelligence estimates, in order to present a full and objective analysis, need to be independent of the policy makers and the politicians. No one could possibly have had any illusions about the objectivity of Team B.

The other damaging aspect of the Team B exercise was that the Carter administration permitted so much of the report to remain unchallenged. Undoubtedly this reflected inexperience and political timidity, but it also reflected the fact that Zbigniew Brzezinski and some of his like-minded associates found the Team B conclusions useful in promoting their own hawkish policies. Harold Brown, the secretary of defense, knew better, but except for the conclusions about civil defense, he failed to challenge the Team B assessment sufficiently.

It should be noted that Brown did, in several speeches, decry "simplistic comparisons of U.S. and Soviet military strengths." He did state that "the United States is the most powerful country in the world. The Soviet Union is not stronger militarily than the United States." He also said: "I believe those who mistakenly claim that the United States is weak or that the Soviet Union is strong enough to run all over us are not only playing fast and loose with the truth, they are playing fast and loose with U.S. security."[6]

That last is important. Certainly a defense budget which is based on inaccurate intelligence can be harmful. Our security can be damaged if our national economy becomes sick as a result of the inflationary pressures of excessive defense spending. Today we observe frantic attempts to balance the federal budget while, at the same time, rapidly increasing our defense budget. The main rationalization for the defense expansion is the findings of Team B and the Committee on the Present Danger.

Team B concluded that the Soviets intended to gain military and strategic superiority over the United States and would soon (this was 1976) achieve that goal. It also concluded that the Soviet Union has a different strategic doctrine from that of the United States and is preparing to fight and win a nuclear war. Team B rejected the view that the Soviets accept U.S. concepts of nuclear deterrence and mutual assured destruction. General Daniel Graham, one of the Team B panelists, said there had been "two catalytic factors" which influenced the team's conclusions.

One, he said, was the CIA estimate which recalculated the percentage of Soviet gross national product (GNP) expended on defense from 6 to 8 upward to 11 to 13. The other major factor was "the discovery of an important Soviet civil defense effort—very strong and unmistakable evidence that a big effort is on to protect people, industry, and to store food."[7] Team B concluded that the civil defense program was a clear indication of Soviet preparation to fight, survive, and win a nuclear war.

The Carter administration did reject the Team B assessment of the significance of Soviet civil defense. Appearing on national television, Secretary of Defense Brown said:

I don't think massive civil defense programs are going to succeed in protecting the population of countries that try it. I think that the Soviet civil defense program, although it probably is ten times as big as ours, would not prevent Soviet industry or a great fraction of the Soviet population from being destroyed in an all-out thermo-nuclear war.... If you target cities, they are not going to be saved by civil defense.[8]

A CIA estimate concluded that civil defense could not protect enough of the Soviet people and economy to maintain a viable society after an all-out nuclear attack. CIA Director Admiral Stansfield Turner said: "We do not believe that the existing preparations could prevent a general breakdown in the Soviet economy in the event of an American retaliatory strike.... We do not interpret the [civil defense program] as meaning that the Soviets are planning to initiate nuclear warfare."[9]

Colonel Donald L. Clark, U.S. Air Force (retired), who served as assistant air attaché at the U.S. Embassy in Moscow and on the joint staff of the Joint Chiefs of Staff, wrote:

The Soviet civil defense program is in reality a farce—a waste of money, time, and manpower. The overwhelming majority of the Soviet citizenry, who participate in it, recognize the program as a joke, and a typical example of bureaucratic mishmash. They mock the program and take advantage of it.... A Soviet doctor, now in the U.S., described his experience as the Civil Defense program director in his hospital as a farce. For example, in the basement of the hospital there were boxes and boxes of civil defense emergency supplies; but alas, not food, not clothing, not medical supplies—only World War II gas masks![10]

Speaking of the U.S. civil defense program, Dr. Howard Hiatt, dean of the Harvard School of Public Health, says: "If the civil defense budget were in my hands, I would spend all $120 million on morphine. Civil defense money is worse than wasted now. It misleads. It may let people believe they can escape in a nuclear war. They can't." Dr. Hiatt points out that in a nuclear war most of the doctors and medical facilities would be wiped out. Those that remained would be totally inadequate to care for the burn and radiation victims, who would die a slow, horrible death. He concludes that it is irresponsible to promote the illusion that civil defense can provide meaningful protection. The only answer, he says, is prevention of nuclear war.[11]

The greatest influence on U.S. public opinion, though, has not been the civil defense debate. It has been the assertion that the Soviets doubled their defense spending during the 1970's and have overtaken the United States. Most members of Congress believe this today. So, it seems, do most editorial writers. The CIA's revision has become part of the conventional wisdom of defense policy. A study published by the U.S. Air Force and prepared by the U.S. Strategic Institute said:

> Estimates prepared by the Central Intelligence Agency, as well as by U.S. academic economists, have been in error by as much as 100 percent. The CIA estimates were accepted without question until 1976, when they were acknowledged to be grossly in error and doubled. Economists have not yet recovered from the shock of that experience.

Similarly Richard Nixon, in his book *The Real War*, writes:

> In 1976 the CIA estimates of Russian military spending for 1970–1975 were doubled overnight as errors were discovered and corrected. . . . When the first concrete steps toward arms control were taken, American presidents were being supplied by the CIA with figures on Russian military spending that were only half of what the agency later decided spending had been. Thanks, in

part, to this intelligence blunder we will find ourselves looking down the nuclear barrel in the mid-1980s.

But Nixon, Team B, Congress, and the press have been tragically misinformed. While Team B's report of December 1976 remained classified, the CIA's own official report on Soviet defense spending of October 1976 had contradicted Team B's conclusions, not supported them. The true meaning of the October report has been missed. A gargantuan error has been allowed to stand uncorrected all these years. Here is the CIA's explanation for its change of estimates, published in the 1976 report:

The new estimate of the share of defense in the Soviet GNP is almost twice as high as the 6 to 8 percent previously estimated. This does not mean that the impact of defense programs on the Soviet economy has increased—only that our appreciation of this impact has changed. *It also implies that Soviet defense industries are far less efficient than formerly believed* [emphasis added].

So while the CIA increased its estimate of the percentage of Soviet GNP spent on defense from 6 to 8 percent to 11 to 13 percent, there had in fact been no doubling of the rate of actual defense spending. During the period between 1973 and 1976, as CIA analysts refined their methodology and obtained better intelligence, they made an important discovery. In assessing the cost of Soviet defense production, they had been crediting the Soviets with a degree of industrial efficiency close to that of the United States. What they discovered was that Soviet defense production, in fact, was not very efficient. Thus, the Soviet defense effort was absorbing a greater share of the GNP than previously believed. What should have been cause for jubilation became the inspiration for misguided alarm.

In truth, there have been no dramatic increases in Soviet defense spending during the entire decade. In its official estimate published in January 1980, the CIA concluded for the 1970–1979 period: "Estimated in constant dollars, Soviet defense activities increased at an average annual rate of 3 percent." In other words, the Soviets have indeed been increasing their defense budget each year at about the same rate as the United States and most of its NATO partners have raised their military spending during each of the past five years. The U.S. defense budgets for 1981 and 1982 call for an increase, in real terms, of about 7 percent.

Much has been made, also, of the 1981 CIA study which shows the total cost of Soviet defense activities for 1980 as 50 percent higher than the U.S. total in dollars and 30 percent higher in rubles. These figures have very little relation to reality because of the dubious methods used by the CIA. The CIA obtains the dollar cost of Soviet defense by estimating what it would cost the United States to pay for the Soviet defense establishment. The Soviets have 4.4 million people in their armed forces; the United States has 2.1 million. Here is how the CIA estimates the costs of Soviet military personnel:

> We obtain these manpower costs by applying U.S. factors for pay and allowances to our estimates of Soviet military manpower. Soviet military personnel performing duties similar to those of U.S. counterparts are assigned the *same rate of pay* as their counterparts [emphasis added].

But U.S. military personnel are all volunteers with relatively high levels of pay and allowances. The Soviet forces, on the other hand, are mainly conscripted and are paid about one-fifth the U.S. rate.

The CIA so far has not publicly confronted the obvious distortions caused by these discrepancies. Neither have Reagan and his advisers. (Similarly, when Reagan claims the USSR spends twice or three times as much as the United States on its strategic forces, he evidently relies on a similar formula by which Soviet costs for executive personnel, factory workers, research staff, computer technicians, etc. are calculated as if they were paid at relatively high U.S. salaries.)

It is surprising, moreover, that this highly misleading formula has not led the CIA to project even higher costs for

Soviet defense. The U.S. defense budget for fiscal year 1982 calls for more than 50 percent to be expended on manpower, whether for salaries, allowances, housing, training, medical needs, or other activities. (This does not include the $13.7 billion paid for military retirement.) If we estimate the cost of the Soviet forces—which comprise more than twice as many people as ours—at our own rates, we would expect that the Soviet defense budget would be 100 percent higher than ours. This would seem even more likely when one takes into account the inefficiency of Soviet defense industries, which all experts now agree produce weapons at a much higher cost than ours.[12]

We often hear that the Soviets are spending 11 or 12 percent of their GNP for defense while we are spending only 5½ percent of our GNP on defense. This does not mean that the Soviets are spending twice as much as we are. What is usually left out of the story is that our GNP is twice the size of the Soviet GNP. What it means is that the Soviet economy is subjected to twice as great a strain as the United States to maintain defense at current levels. Clearly the CIA's method of comparing costs is dangerously subject to misinterpretation and does not provide an adequate basis for either Congress or the public to weigh the defense balance.

It is true that the Soviet Union has been expanding its defense budget beyond inflation by about 3 percent each year for almost fifteen years, while the United States, immediately after Vietnam, had some declining years. Of course, before and during the Vietnam War U.S. defense spending was proportionately much greater. But the Soviets have been steadily catching up since their humiliation at the time of the 1962 missile crisis. However, there are some important facts to keep in mind while we evaluate the pace of the Soviet expansion.

Perhaps most important in considering relative military burdens are the Soviet costs related to China. The U.S. Defense Department says:

At least 22 percent of the increase in the Soviet defense budget during these years [1964–1977] has been attributed to the buildup in the Far East. . . . The high construction costs in Siberia suggest that the intelligence estimates may understate the cost of the Soviet buildup in the Far East substantially.

In addition, according to the Defense Department, the Soviets "station as much as 25 percent of their ground forces and tactical air power on their border with China."

The Soviet costs in connection with China come more sharply into focus when we observe that the Soviets have forty-four divisions facing China and thirty divisions facing NATO. Of the thirty divisions in Central Europe, four are standing guard in Hungary, five have remained in Czechoslovakia since the invasion of 1968, and two are in Poland. In other words, about twice as many divisions are committed to the China front as to the West German front.

Furthermore, the United States does not have to match the Soviet forces facing China. These forces are at the end of a long and tenuous line of communication that can be severed, in time of war, by missile strikes. They are not forces that can be readily transferred to combat in a European war. On the other hand, if it is argued that the U.S. defense budget should provide forces to counter the Soviet threat to China, then the Chinese defense budget should be included on our side—a total of $50 billion.

One of the longest-lasting worst-case myths perpetrated by the American hawks is the assertion that the Warsaw Pact has such overwhelming conventional superiority over NATO that Germany and the rest of Western Europe are threatened by a sudden blitzkrieg invasion by Soviet tank forces. This is one of the least likely scenarios imaginable. In the first place, the Soviets know as well as we do that a conventional war will soon become a nuclear war. They also know that their troops in Eastern Europe are living on quicksand. The Soviet divisions in Poland, Hungary, and Czechoslovakia stay in their barracks, out of sight, except when they are on maneuvers. Historically the Russians have been disliked, often hated, in these countries.

There have been anti-Soviet rebellions in all three of these

Warsaw Pact states. No Soviet marshal in his right mind would want to launch an offensive with such allies as partners. The Soviets have to anticipate that in the event of war there would be uprisings throughout Eastern Europe. The Soviets remember vividly the large-scale defections of Ukrainians and Georgians to the Germans during World War II.

There is always a remote possibility of unintended war in Central Europe, but it is much less likely today than in the late 1940's and 1950's. The several confrontations in Berlin and the pressure to reunify Germany made for potential conflict. But the *Ostpolitik* of Willy Brandt has greatly reduced the tensions in Berlin, and the recognition of East Germany as the German Democratic Republic has brought to an end the prospects for a reunified Germany. If the Russians had ever seriously contemplated an invasion of the Federal Republic of Germany, they probably would have done so when 550,000 American troops, and part of the U.S. fleet and Air Force, were tied down in Vietnam.

Americans often overlook the fact that the best troops in either NATO or the Warsaw Pact are the West Germans. They are drafted, well trained, and well equipped. There are 500,000 on active duty and another 1 million reserves ready for rapid call-up. Another fact not usually reported in Pentagon handouts is the much greater contribution made to defense spending by our NATO allies compared to that of the Soviet's Warsaw Pact allies. The International Institute of Strategic Studies reports that in 1979 the European members of NATO spent $76 billion for defense, and France, a non-NATO ally, spent $20 billion. The Warsaw Pact members other than the USSR spent $17 billion, or less than one-fifth of the defense outlay of our European allies.

It is important to place all the facts on the table when we evaluate NATO-Warsaw Pact strengths. For example, we are frequently informed that the Soviets have 50,000 tanks while the United States has 11,750 tanks. The United States did not give high priority to massive tank production because it believes that antitank weapons can be more effective. The United States currently has about 170,000 precision-guided antitank weapons, each capable of targeting a tank with extraordinary accuracy and blowing it up. The United States and its NATO allies have 17 million rounds of antitank munitions, including the latest antitank mines. American military leaders are unanimous in expressing the view that they would not consider trading the U.S. and NATO forces for the Soviet and Warsaw Pact forces.

As part of the evidence that the Soviets were achieving military superiority over the United States, Team B and its successor, the Committee on the Present Danger, have pointed to the "huge buildup of the Soviet Navy," which now has blue-water capabilities. ("Blue-water" means the high seas away from coastal waters. The Soviets do have a limited ocean-going navy.) In fact, this alleged Soviet naval superiority is used by the Reagan administration to justify an expansion of the U.S. Navy, by about one-third, to 600 naval vessels. It is true that the Soviets, starting from very little, have built a substantial fleet which outnumbers that of the United States, but it can't begin to compare with the U.S. Navy in terms of fighting power, control of the seas, or capacity to show the flag around the world.

The Soviets have a long coastline, and most of their fleet is made up of small coastal patrol boats and frigates. At the time of the Team B report, the Department of Defense claimed that the Soviet Union had built 205 large naval vessels between 1965 and 1976, as opposed to 165 built by the United States. But Senator Patrick Leahy of Vermont investigated the claim and found that most of the Soviet "major combatants were nothing more than small escort ships, and that, in fact, between 1961 and 1975 the United States had built 122 major surface combatants of more than 3,000 tons, while the Russians had built just 57."[13] The CIA estimate of Soviet defense spending for the ten-year period 1967–1977, which came out the year after the Team B report was leaked, had this to say about the Soviet Navy: "Spending for Navy and National Air Defense Forces grew more slowly than defense spending as a whole. As a result, the shares of investment and operating spending going to those forces were smaller in 1977 than in 1967."

In terms of tonnage and firepower, the navies of the Soviet

Union and its allies are about one-third those of the United States and its allies. The United States has thirteen giant aircraft carriers, while the Soviets have three relatively small aircraft carriers with only enough deck space for small planes capable of vertical takeoff. But the greatest advantage held by the United States is its long lead in antisubmarine warfare. The strategic submarines are unquestionably the most important weapons in the navies. The Soviet submarines are relatively noisy, and the United States has the capability to track them while at sea. This is one of the reasons the Soviets keep only about 10 percent of their strategic subs at sea. If war ever came, their lives might be very short.

The Soviet Navy faces substantial handicaps as a result of its geography. Former Navy Secretary W. Graham Claytor said:

> The Soviet Baltic fleet can be bottled up, in the event of hostilities, by mining the Danish straits. The Soviet Mediterranean squadron would lead an exciting but brief existence in the event of war and would have no way of getting out of the Mediterranean, the exits to which can easily be mined or blocked by submarines. Large portions of the Soviet Pacific fleet are based at Vladivostok on the Sea of Japan and can be bottled up by similarly closing the straits leading out into the Pacific.
>
> The only fleet having a semblance of access to the open oceans is the Northern fleet. And even that fleet has to travel all the way around Norway and fight its way through the Greenland-Iceland-United Kingdom gap into the Atlantic Ocean which the United States and its allies guard with aircraft and submarines.[14]

In other words, the United States and its allies hold a decisive advantage over the Soviet Navy. And the U.S. Congress is expending huge additional sums of the American taxpayers' money in response to misinformation about Soviet strengths.

Charles Duncan, Jr., deputy secretary of defense under Harold Brown, gave an unusually candid speech on the subject of distorted information. He said:

Why, you may ask, do some have the view that the Soviet Union has become the world's number one military power? The answer is that, to a large extent, we have created that image ourselves . . . in the understandable desire to reverse the antidefense mood and the propensity for reduced defense budgets of the early 1970's. . . .[15]

Now it is understandable that the Defense Department would want to influence public opinion about the dangers our nation faces, but the best way to do that is through an accurate presentation of the facts, not through exaggeration and misrepresentation. If the facts don't justify the spending, better not to spend. Expenditures based on distorted information are wasteful and harmful to the nation's economic health and security. Furthermore, too many false alarms lead in time to inadequate response in the event of real danger.

IS SOVIET STRATEGIC DOCTRINE DIFFERENT?

The exaggerations about Soviet military power have had costly and dangerous repercussions, but far more damaging was the adoption of the Team B conclusion that the Soviets have a different strategic doctrine from ours—the assertion that the Soviets are preparing to fight and win a nuclear war and that the Soviets believe in limited nuclear war. This conclusion has been instrumental in the U.S. move toward building an arsenal of counterforce weapons so that it would be in a position to fight and win a limited nuclear war.

In an attempt to preempt the Republicans, Zbigniew Brzezinski and Harold Brown rushed through Presidential Directive 59, which was signed by Jimmy Carter on July 25, 1980, just before the Democratic National Convention. PD 59 provided a rationalization for limited nuclear warfare and the weapons needed to fight such a war. In a speech explaining the reasons for PD 59, Harold Brown claimed that the policy and the programs needed to implement it were required because the Soviets believe a nuclear war is winnable:

111

The Soviet leadership appears to contemplate at least the possibility of a relatively prolonged exchange if a war comes, and in some circles at least, they seem to take seriously the possibility of victory in such a war. We cannot afford to ignore these views—even if we think differently, as I do. We need to have, and we do have, a posture—both forces and doctrine—that makes it clear to the Soviets, and to the world, that any notion of victory in nuclear war is unrealistic.[16]

Shortly thereafter, during a campaign speech, Ronald Reagan said:

The Soviet Union does believe that a nuclear war is possible, is survivable and is winnable by them. They have the nuclear edge today to attack our silos, our nuclear weapons, and still have enough left that if we retaliate in any way with, let's say, some surviving submarine missiles or something, that they can attack our industrial centers and our population. And it has been estimated by military intelligence that the casualties in such a war would be ten to one in favor of the Soviet Union.

Clearly Reagan and Brown had accepted the views of General Graham, Richard Pipes, and the other members of Team B.

Shortly after the Team B findings had been publicized, General Graham testified before a subcommittee of the Senate Foreign Relations Committee. He said:

Today the Soviets are pursuing their military programs with such vigor and purposiveness that one cannot readily escape these conclusions—the Soviet leadership continues to believe Lenin's admonition that the capitalists will lash out in their death throes in one final big war, i.e., war is inevitable and that it will be "won" by the USSR.[17]

General Graham is seriously mistaken. The avoidance of nuclear war has been basic to Soviet doctrine since 1956, when party chairman Nikita Khrushchev assessed the possible consequences of nuclear war and reversed the Lenin doctrine that war between capitalist states and socialist states is inevitable.[18]

Richard Pipes, the chairman of Team B, has written extensively about how Soviet doctrine differs from U.S. doctrine on nuclear war. He has analyzed some of the published writing of former Soviet Defense Minister Marshal Andrei Grechko. Marshal Grechko didn't say it, but Pipes claims that his views can be summarized thus:

[An] industrial strike in the United States, the explosion of a terrorist bomb in Belfast or Jerusalem, the massacre by Rhodesian guerrillas on a white farmstead, differ from nuclear war between the Soviet Union and the United States only in degree, not in kind. Such conflicts are inherent in the stage of human development which precedes the final abolition of classes.

Pipes goes on to say:

In addition *(though we have no solid evidence to this effect)*, it seems likely that Soviet strategies reject the mutual-deterrence theory on several technical grounds of a kind that have been advanced by American critics of this theory [emphasis added]:
1. Mutual deterrence postulates a certain finality about weapons technology: it does not allow for further scientific breakthroughs. . . .
2. Mutual deterrence constitutes "passive defense" which usually leads to defeat. It threatens punishment to the aggressor after he has struck, which may or may not deter him from striking. . . .
3. The threat of a second strike, which underpins the mutual-deterrence doctrine, may prove ineffectual. The side that has suffered the destruction of the bulk of its nuclear forces in a surprise strike may find that it has so little deterrent left and the enemy so much, that the cost of striking back would be exposing its own cities to total destruction by the enemy's third strike. The result could be a paralysis of will, and capitulation instead of a second strike.

113

RUSSIAN ROULETTE

It should be carefully noted that these are the views of Americans who don't like the theory of assured destruction. Pipes has no evidence, but he thinks the Soviets must think this way, too.

Pipes thinks the logic of this probable Soviet position demands a policy based on preemptive nuclear strikes:

> Soviet theorists draw an insistent, though to an outside observer very fuzzy, distinction between "preventive" and "preemptive" attacks. They claim that the Soviet Union will never start a war—i.e., it will never attack—but, once it had concluded that an attack upon it was imminent, it would not hesitate to preempt. They argue that historical experience indicates outbreaks of hostilities are generally preceded by prolonged diplomatic crises and military preparations which signal to an alert command an imminent threat and the need to act.

But the Soviets argue no such thing. They make a very clear distinction between first strike, which they reject, and launch under attack.

Pipes's attempt to make sense out of his view that the Soviets are getting ready to launch a nuclear war strains the reader's credulity even more when he concludes that:

> the USSR could absorb the loss of 30 million of its people and be no worse off, in terms of human casualties, than it had been at the conclusion of World War II. In other words all of the USSR's multimillion cities could be destroyed without trace or survivors, and provided that its essential cadres have been saved, it would emerge less hurt in terms of casualties than it was in 1945.[19]

Alexander Solzhenitsyn, who reviles the Soviets, nevertheless loves Russia and would hate to see 30 million or even 1 million Russians killed. In a 1980 article in *Foreign Affairs* he observed that Pipes's selective use of evidence "affects me in much the same way as I imagine Rostropovich would feel if he had to listen to a wolf playing a cello." Inasmuch as Pipes, General Graham, and the other members of Team B have had

114

such influence on American policy, it is worth taking a more exacting look at the evidence.

Soviet and U.S. leaders have never talked about launching a first strike to win a nuclear war, nor have the leaders of either country threatened such a strike for coercive political purposes. President Brezhnev has explicitly rejected the concept of limited nuclear war. "I am convinced," he has said, "that even one nuclear bomb dropped by one side over the other would result in general nuclear exchange—a nuclear holocaust not only for our two nations, but for the entire world. . . . The starting of a nuclear war would spell annihilation for the aggressor himself."[20]

Commenting on Presidential Directive 59 in an interview with *The New York Times* on August 25, 1980, General Mikhail A. Milshtein, a Soviet expert on nuclear strategy, said:

> Our doctrine is that we will never use nuclear weapons unless an aggressor uses them first. . . . We believe nuclear war will bring no advantage to anyone and may even lead to the end of civilization. . . . Our doctrine regards nuclear weapons as something that must never be used. They are not an instrument for waging war in any rational sense. . . . What is new now, it seems to me, is that the possibility of waging nuclear war has been accepted on the very highest levels of the American Government. . . . The main danger is erosion of the concept that nuclear weapons cannot be used.

Now Pipes and other hawks may argue that the public statements of Brezhnev and Soviet officials like General Milshtein merely represent political propaganda and do not reflect the real policy of the Soviet regime. But there is, fortunately, abundant evidence from internal Soviet classified documents and the confidential journal of the Soviet General Staff, *Military Thought,* which demonstrates that the Politburo and Soviet military leaders have adopted the concepts of mutual deterrence and mutual assured retaliation. Even before the SALT talks started, top Soviet generals were writing articles in their military journals which rejected the validity of first strike and nuclear war fighting.

RUSSIAN ROULETTE

In November 1967 Nikolai I. Krylov, commander in chief of the Strategic Missile Forces, wrote:

> Under contemporary circumstances, with the existence of a system for detecting missile launches, an attempt by an aggressor to inflict a surprise preemptive strike cannot give him a decisive advantage for the achievement of victory in war, and moreover will not save him from great destruction and human losses.

In a 1968 article Marshal Krylov said: "Everyone knows that in contemporary conditions in an armed conflict of adversaries comparatively equal in power (in number and especially in quality of weapons) an immediate retaliatory strike of enormous destructive power is inevitable."

In May 1969 General of the Army Semyon P. Ivanov, commandant of the Military Academy of the General Staff, wrote: "With the existing level of development of nuclear missile weapons and their reliable cover below ground and under water it is impossible in practice to destroy them completely, and consequently it is impossible to prevent an annihilating retaliatory strike."

At the first meeting of the U.S. and Soviet SALT delegations in Helsinki in November 1969, according to U.S. Ambassador Gerard Smith, both sides stated that mutual deterrence was the underpinning of strategic arms limitation. The Soviet delegation submitted a written position which had been cleared at the highest political and military levels in Moscow:

> Even in the event that one of the sides were the first to be subjected to attack, it would undoubtedly retain the ability to inflict a retaliatory strike of crushing power. Thus, evidently, we all agree that war between our two countries would be disastrous for both sides. And it would be tantamount to suicide for the ones who decided to start such a war.

Either Pipes had not done his homework, or he was dissembling when he claimed that only the United States considers nuclear war to be suicidal.

Misestimating Soviet Power

Throughout the SALT negotiations the Soviets have rejected the quest for nuclear superiority, on the part of either side, and have stressed the importance of parity and equality as a basis for making real cuts in nuclear weapons.

In January 1978 Marshal Viktor Kulikov, who had been chief of staff of the Soviet forces, wrote: "The Soviet state, effectively looking after its defense, is not seeking to achieve military superiority over the other side, but at the same time it cannot permit the approximate balance which has taken shape between the USSR and the US to be upset, to the disadvantage of our security."

These writings by Soviet military commanders were for their fellow military officers, not for general public consumption, and therefore clearly reflect the internal view of Soviet military doctrine.

Richard Pipes and other members of Team B continually refer to the fact that Lenin adopted the doctrine of Clausewitz that war is "a continuation of political relations." But Colonel Ye Rybkin, the leading ideologist at the Lenin Military-Political Academy, has refuted Lenin and concluded: Rejection of nuclear war . . . is dictated by the new realities of the era. . . . [There] is an objective need to end the arms race. . . . [The] quantity of nuclear weapons has reached such a level that a further increase would in practice make no change—a sufficient quantity of arms has been amassed to destroy everything alive on earth several times over.

Boris Dmitriyev, a civilian commentator, wrote an analysis of the Clausewitz doctrine for *Izvestia* in which he concluded that in a nuclear age "War can only be the continuation of madness." And of course, any war between the Soviet Union and the United States would be exactly that—madness. The USSR does not believe in limited nuclear war. The Soviets have made it abundantly clear that if they are ever attacked with nuclear weapons, they will respond with all the nuclear power at their disposal. This is why the recently perfected U.S. theories of limited nuclear war and counterforce weapons make no sense at all. They are based on a false assessment of Soviet policy and intentions.

Raymond Garthoff, an American authority on Soviet military doctrine, has written:

The record indicates that the Soviet political and military leadership accepts a strategic nuclear balance between the Soviet Union and the United States as a fact, and as the probable and desirable prospect for the foreseeable future. They are pursuing extensive military programs to ensure that they do not fail to maintain their side of the balance, which they see as in some jeopardy, given planned American programs. They seek to stabilize and to maintain mutual deterrence. In Marxist-Leninist eyes, military power is not and should not be the driving element in world politics. With "imperialist" military power held in check, the decisive social-economic forces of history would determine the future of the world.[21]

Soviet generals have always asserted that if they are attacked with nuclear weapons, they will fight back and ultimately win the war. The same is true of U.S. generals who are frequently engaged in so-called war games where the battles are waged on computers and other mechanical equipment. The United States usually wins such "games." In a nuclear age, when both sides have enough weapons assuredly to destroy each other, it is pathetic to see military men going through the motions of trying to fight and win a nuclear war, which they know is impossible. And in fact, all the evidence indicates that they both believe in mutual deterrence, that neither side will strike the other with nuclear weapons unless it has been attacked and that neither side believes that nuclear war is a feasible option for obtaining political objectives. The only sane policy, therefore, is to get on with the business of reducing nuclear weapons on an equal basis.

The real debate is with those who hold desperately to the view that weapons, especially nuclear weapons, should continue to have political meaning. They constantly refer to the need to have sufficient power to force the Soviet Union to back down, without bluffing, as was claimed to be the case in 1962, when the Soviets withdrew their missiles from Cuba. They insist that the United States should restore its nuclear superiority. On the other side are those who accept the fact that since the Soviets have achieved nuclear parity, they will never again accept anything else. The best course, therefore, is to accept reality, end the strategic arms race, and cut back the existing nuclear arsenals to a much lower level. Those who believe in strategic stability also reject the argument of the American hawks that more weapons need to be built to strengthen the bargaining position in future negotiations. That is merely a rationalization for a continuing arms race.

Chapter V

Avoiding Nuclear War in Europe

Europe is on the threshold of dramatic change, the full dimensions of which are only beginning to be comprehended. After World War II a series of political and military arrangements provided relative stability in Europe, lasting for thirty-five years. It is now clear, however, that the postwar political alliances and the policy concepts upon which they were based are being subjected to such severe challenge that they cannot survive much longer in their present form. Soviet domination of Eastern Europe and U.S. domination of Western Europe have been a perverse and unnatural consequence of the war. Now the people of Europe have set in motion the process of revision.

NATO and the Warsaw Pact are clearly in transition. Events in Poland are only the most dramatic manifestations of the meaninglessness of the Warsaw Pact. Throughout Eastern Europe there is mounting evidence of important change. The mass rallies throughout Western Europe supporting nuclear disarmament are symptomatic of the dynamic political action that is sweeping most of Europe. It is time for the Soviet Union and the United States to start focusing on the implications of this change. What it means is that in time both powers should withdraw their military forces, both nuclear and conventional. This is essential for the political health of Europe and the avoidance of World War III.

In order to have perspective on what is occurring, it is worth recalling the major elements that shaped the policies, on both sides, after World War II. The central issue was the containment of Germany, which had been responsible for launching two world wars in a period of twenty years. Today, especially in the United States, it is often forgotten that Germany was the focus of concern. The Soviet Union had been partially occupied and partially destroyed by the Germans, who were responsible for 30 million dead and severely wounded Russians. The Soviets were determined that Germany should never again obtain the power to threaten their survival.

After the war the main political problems in Europe stemmed from the fact that Germany was divided, occupied in the East by the Soviet Union and in the West by the United States, Britain, and France, and that the former capital, Berlin, was an island in the East occupied by all four powers. For several years the Soviets attempted to promote a solution based on a reunified Germany which would remain forever neutral and disarmed. They had in mind a treaty similar to what was eventually negotiated in Austria. The Soviet proposal was rejected; instead, the Western powers formed NATO, which later included the Federal Republic of Germany. The Soviets responded with the Warsaw Pact and consolidated their occupation of most of Eastern Europe. Ever since, they have given priority to the maintenance of secure military supply lines from the Soviet Union to eastern Germany, where they have maintained twenty divisions of the Red Army.

In the West a creative and constructive approach toward curbing the reemergence of German nationalism was pursued. West Germany was embraced in a partnership. The Marshall Plan and NATO cemented the Atlantic alliance. French leaders like Jean Monnet and Robert Schuman were instrumental in leading the way to the Coal and Steel Community and the European Economic Community (Common Market). The German economy became part of the broader European economy. Charles de Gaulle and Konrad Adenauer strengthened the political alliance between France and Germany. The United States, Britain, and France continued to maintain troops in Germany.

As the cold war developed during the fifties, emphasis was placed on the containment of the Soviet Union, especially by the United States. The United States was pursuing the policy of liberation in Eastern Europe, and there was talk of possible Soviet military action. There were several incidents in Berlin. Tactical nuclear weapons were placed in Germany. The West Germans were not allowed to have nuclear weapons, but they did have a veto on the use of some of them through the two-key system, which restrains either government from the ability to launch independently. Tensions ebbed and flowed throughout the cold war, heightened by events such as the Soviet invasion of Hungary, the construction of the Berlin Wall, and the invasion of Czechoslovakia.

Through the years West Germany gradually rearmed within the NATO framework to the present level of 500,000 troops and a large reserve force subject to rapid call-up. The United States, from the beginning of NATO, had provided a nuclear umbrella for the security of Europe with a pledge to attack the Soviet Union with nuclear weapons if the Soviets ever invaded Western Europe. The presence of the American troops in Germany provided insurance that the United States would act.

Then, from 1969 to 1972, came détente with the *Ostpolitik* of Willy Brandt. This provided for a nonaggression pact between the Federal Republic of Germany and the Soviet Union, diplomatic relations with Poland and Czechoslovakia, the four-power agreement on Berlin, and, most important of all, West German recognition of East Germany as a separate state (within a single German nation). The West German Constitution still calls for the ultimate reunification of Germany. *Ostpolitik,* combined with the Nixon-Brezhnev summit of 1972 in Moscow, reduced East-West tensions substantially. Any lingering fears of a Soviet invasion of West Germany virtually disappeared.

For some time Mike Mansfield of Montana, the Senate Democratic majority leader, had been pressing for a large reduction of U.S. troops in Germany. By 1973 it looked as though the Mansfield Resolution might be adopted in the Senate. The Soviets became alarmed and called for diplomatic negotiations to discuss troop reductions in Europe. This resulted in the mutual and balanced force reduction (MBFR) talks which have been going on in Vienna ever since. The reason the Soviets were alarmed was that they knew that if U.S. troops left Germany, they would be replaced by German troops. This in turn might lead to growing German nationalism. In the MBFR talks the Soviets have insisted on not only balanced reductions of forces of U.S. and Soviet forces but also, most important from their standpoint, reductions in German forces. An impasse has resulted in the negotiations, with both sides contriving highly technical reasons to block progress.

Instead of being reduced, U.S. forces have been augmented and strengthened. The U.S. contribution to NATO is more than $80 billion a year. In order to rationalize spending this huge sum, there has been a return to the warnings of an imminent Soviet blitzkrieg with the tanks of the Red Army sweeping across the plains of northern Germany. Throughout the cold war there has been no evidence that the Soviets were willing by such action to risk launching World War III and a probable nuclear holocaust. Since *Ostpolitik* and especially since the political revolution in Poland, the blitzkrieg scenario has been preposterous. Even so, it is still given respectful attention by most members of Congress when it is trotted out each year at budget time by the Pentagon.

THE THEATER NUCLEAR WEAPON FIASCO

One of the products of the Soviet tank blitzkrieg scenario was the neutron bomb uproar. American research and development had discovered that the enhanced radiation of neutron bombs would be very effective for killing the personnel inside Soviet tanks. Of course, antitank precision-guided missiles, which are nonnuclear, are just as effective, and the United States already has 170,000 of them in Germany. Nevertheless, the Carter administration decided to press ahead to deploy neutron weapons in Europe. The decision inspired political resistance all over Europe, with greatest sensitivity welling up in West Germany, where the neutron bomb would be used. But German Chancellor Helmut Schmidt was subjected to intense U.S. pressure, and he reluctantly agreed to permit the deployment of the neutron weapons on German soil.

Schmidt was understandably troubled by U.S. tactics. Some of his advisers and some American strategic weapon experts, who were in Bonn at the time, told him that he could not rely on President Carter for support of German security. One of the Americans was Fred Ikle, the present undersecretary of defense for policy. Schmidt was persuaded to speak out. In October 1977 he delivered a major address at the International Institute for Strategic Studies in London.

Schmidt developed a new theme which challenged the thirty-year-old reliance of Western Europe on the U.S. nuclear umbrella. He noted that the SALT II treaty had established strategic parity between the United States and the USSR. At the same time he observed that the Soviets were increasing their nuclear strength in Europe by modernizing their intermediate-range ballistic missile force through the deployment of the SS-20's. Schmidt said it was essential for the West to respond by rectifying the nuclear balance in Europe.

The Pentagon and the strategic thinkers who advocate a U.S. limited war-fighting capability were delighted. The Schmidt speech provided the impetus for planning the deployment of U.S. missiles in Europe capable of hitting targets in the Soviet Union with great accuracy. The NATO High Level Group (HLG) was assigned the task of developing a program to counter the Soviet SS-20's. In mid-1978 the HLG recommended that NATO should have long-range nuclear weapons in the European theater which could strike at the Soviet Union. It was argued that this action would fill in the "missing rung on the ladder of escalation so that NATO would be in a position to respond to any selective use of Soviet nuclear weapons against Western Europe by striking Soviet territory without resorting to U.S. central systems. This capability according to war-fighting theory would deny the Soviet Union any potential advantage of 'escalation control.' "[1]

This was the beginning of the most inept, poorly conceived plan ever devised for the NATO alliance, and there have been some very bad ones, including the so-called multilateral force. By late 1978 Chancellor Schmidt had begun to realize that the NATO plan could have destructive political consequences. By the West Germans' agreeing to deploy on their soil nuclear missiles capable of attacking Soviet territory, the whole fabric of the *Ostpolitik* or détente might be threatened.

Détente was very popular in the Federal Republic. There was a greater feeling of peace than at any time since World War II. West German exports to the Warsaw Pact countries had tripled in a decade, exceeding $8 billion, and trade with East Germany, which is counted separately, had reached $5.6 billion. In addition, 250,000 ethnic Germans had been repatriated from the Soviet Union and Eastern Europe. Eight million trips are made each year by West Germans to visit friends and relatives in East Germany, and 50,000 phone calls to the East are made every day. Before 1970 there were none. Berlin has remained tranquil for a decade. The era has been marked recently by increased business investment.[2]

Opposition began to mount among those Germans most apprehensive about jeopardizing the continuing benefits of détente. Chancellor Schmidt, therefore, announced that Germany would not agree to the deployment of new long-range theater nuclear weapons unless other NATO members on the European continent took them also. He was referring to Belgium, Holland, and Italy, where some tactical nuclear weapons are deployed. Norway and Denmark have renounced the deployment of any nuclear weapons on their soil, and Greece and Turkey were considered too unstable. Schmidt also endorsed the view of those who argued that no new deployment should occur without an attempt to stop the buildup of European-based missiles through arms control negotiations with the Soviets.

By February 1979 U.S. planners, fearing another embarrassing episode similar to the neutron bomb controversy, from which President Carter had backed away, agreed to the creation of a NATO Special Group to work out useful arms control approaches to the issues created by the Soviet modernization of its medium-range missiles. By summer the Special Group and the HLG were drafting an integrated plan calling for arms control measures as well as deployment of missiles in Germany, the United Kingdom, Italy, Belgium, and Holland. As already noted, the weapons chosen—the Pershing II ballistic missile and ground-launched cruise missiles—were most unfortunate from the standpoint of arms control.

The ground-launched and sea-launched cruise missiles were the subject of great controversy during the SALT II negotiations. No solution was reached, but they were put under temporary control in a protocol to the treaty lasting until December 31, 1981. The "Joint Statement of Principles for Subsequent Negotiations," signed by Presidents Carter and Brezhnev at the same time the SALT treaty was signed, June 18, 1979, specified that the parties would pursue in SALT III "resolution of the issues included in the Protocol to the Treaty." An important reason for concern about deployment of any ground-launched or sea-launched cruise missiles was, and is, the virtual impossibility of verifying the numbers and locations of such missiles by existing means of intelligence. For this reason opponents of arms control are eager to have the weapons deployed.

The Pershing II ballistic missile is even more dangerous than the cruise missile because its great accuracy, combined with its capability to destroy Soviet command and control systems in six minutes, will force the Soviets to adopt a policy of launch on warning which will increase the probability of accidental nuclear war. The risks inherent in adopting these two weapons systems were never adequately thought through, from either a political or a military standpoint. Most of the planning was done by Zbigniew Brzezinski and his associates, who were advocates of concepts of limited nuclear war fighting.

However, as the discussion spread from the military experts and strategic planners to the politicians, the press, and the public, the controversy began to grow, especially in the Netherlands, Denmark, and Norway. Many observers in

Europe stressed the importance of moving ahead with the SALT process to deep cuts and qualitative controls not only in strategic weapons but also in the European nuclear weapons. They wanted to emphasize cutbacks through negotiation with the Soviets rather than military buildup. Klaus de Vries of the Netherlands, representing the North Atlantic Assembly's Military Committee, said: "I want to endorse the criticism voiced by several observers that not only are the levels too high, but that the [SALT II] Treaty does too little in checking the momentum of armaments development."[3]

In Brussels on September 1, 1979, Henry Kissinger gave a speech which shook the very foundations of NATO with reverberations that are still being felt. Kissinger said:

> No one disputes any longer that in the 1980's, and perhaps even today, but surely in the 80's—the United States will no longer be in a strategic position to reduce a Soviet counterblow against the United States to tolerable levels. . . . Our European allies should not keep asking us to multiply strategic assurances that we cannot possibly mean or if we do mean, we should not want to execute because if we execute, we risk the destruction of civilization. . . .
>
> We must face the fact that it is absurd to base the strategy of the West on the credibility of the threat of mutual suicide. . . . [If] there is no theater nuclear establishment on the continent of Europe, we are writing the script for selective blackmail in which our allies will be threatened and we will be forced into a decision where we can respond only with a strategy that has no military purpose, but only a population destruction purpose.[4]

The New York Times reported that:

> in an attempt to gain support for the proposed NATO missile force Mr. Kissinger called for an immediate effort to build up American nuclear power in and around Europe. He said that the United States had to develop the capability to wage small-scale nuclear wars as well as all-out strategic conflicts. For the most part, American nuclear policy has been based on the assumption that the

ability to destroy Soviet cities would be enough to deter a nuclear threat against NATO. But Mr. Kissinger suggested that without the ability to carry out pinpoint nuclear attacks against the Soviet Union and its allies the United States might not be able to resist Soviet military pressure on Western Europe in the near future.[5]

Kissinger's speech undermined the credibility of continuing European reliance on the U.S. nuclear umbrella. His hypothesis that the United States could not protect Europe any longer with its strategic forces for fear of nuclear holocaust, but could give protection by basing U.S. missiles in Europe with a "capability to wage small-scale nuclear wars," was inconsistent on two counts. Clearly the Soviet Union would not spare the territory of the United States if it were attacked by U.S. missiles based in Europe. The Soviet Union would make no distinction between a U.S. missile from South Dakota and one from Germany. Furthermore, the Soviet Union has made it very clear that if the United States launches a nuclear attack, there will be no such thing as "a small-scale nuclear war." Not only was Kissinger eroding the political fabric of NATO and the continuing security guarantee of the United States, but he was also compounding the fears of those Europeans who believe that the United States is willing to risk a limited nuclear war in Europe.

A week after the Kissinger speech McGeorge Bundy, former national security adviser to Presidents Kennedy and Johnson, gave a speech in Switzerland which was on the mark. He said:

For many years NATO's most truly strategic weapons have been the assigned American submarines, and they in turn have always been only as reliable as the American guarantee. There is no way of changing this reality by new deployments of long-range weapons on land and no reasons for Americans to press that mode on their allies. Nor is the basic guarantee best measured by comparing the numbers of long-range American-controlled weapons in NATO alone against SS-20's and Backfires. Remembering that this strategic world is ineluctably bipolar, we must recognize that in any moment of serious stress neither Washington nor Moscow is at all likely to regard such American weapons as separately usable or a clearly limited kind of force. Any American-controlled weapons that can reach the Soviet Union will almost surely be all alike to them both.

It follows that the strategic protection of Europe is as strong or as weak as the American strategic guarantee, no matter what American weapons are deployed under NATO. (I do not here exclude a useful contribution from the existence of British and French weapons, but that is not a major variable in the current debate, however one estimates it.) And I believe the effectiveness of this American guarantee is likely to be just as great in the future as in the past. It has worked, after all, through thirty years, and, as we have seen, twenty of those years have been a time of underlying parity in mutual destructive power.

The enduring effectiveness of the American guarantee has not depended on strategic superiority. It has depended instead on two great facts: the visible deployment of major American military forces in Europe, and the very evident risk that any large-scale engagement between Soviet and American forces would rapidly and uncontrollably become general, nuclear and disastrous. . . . My conclusion, then, is that marginal changes in strategic numbers are no threat to the American strategic guarantee in NATO. That guarantee rests not on numbers of warheads but on an engagement that poses a wholly unacceptable and innately unpredictable risk to the other side.[6]

Unfortunately the alarmist rhetoric of Kissinger received far more attention in the European press than the balanced wisdom of Bundy. Moreover, the Kissinger remarks, instead of contributing to the resolve and unity of NATO, had raised doubts and strengthened dissent. In the meantime, U.S. pressure on the NATO allies mounted.

On October 6, 1979, President Brezhnev gave an address in East Berlin, announcing that the Soviet Union would unilaterally dismantle an unspecified number of its medium-range missiles in Europe if NATO would agree to forgo its decision to deploy new missiles in Europe and would enter into immediate negotiations with the Soviet Union.

The Soviet initiative did have some impact in Europe but was clearly not succulent enough to break up the NATO consensus. If Brezhnev had offered then what he offered months later—to freeze all further deployment of SS-20's in return for negotiation—he might have achieved important results. The Brezhnev speech did strengthen the hand of those in NATO who were maintaining that a firm decision to deploy the weapons would benefit the West in future negotiations.

As the moment for decision approached, the doubts began to grow, especially among the smaller NATO countries. The governments of Holland, Belgium, and Denmark all had fragile coalitions which might come apart in the face of popular pressure. Since NATO operates on the principle of unanimity, it was essential that all members endorse the decision. During the week before the NATO meeting the prime ministers of Norway and the Netherlands and the foreign minister of Denmark flew to Washington to seek the assurance of President Carter that he was firmly committed to negotiating an agreement with the Russians. At the last minute Denmark proposed to NATO a six-month delay in the deployment decision to ascertain whether the Soviets would agree to dismantle enough SS-20's to make missiles for NATO unnecessary. The Dutch suggested separation of the production and deployment decisions with postponement of the decision to deploy until potential progress in arms control negotiations had been ascertained.

On December 12, 1979, the NATO ministers met in Brussels and, after seven hours of complex, sometimes contentious discussion, agreed to adopt the two-track decision of deployment and arms control. The agreement provided that all 108 of the Pershing II missiles would be deployed in Germany and that the 464 ground-launched cruise missiles would be deployed as follows: Germany, 24 launchers with 96 missiles (4 missiles to a launcher); the United Kingdom, 40 launchers with 160 missiles; Italy, 28 launchers with 112 missiles; Belgium, 12 launchers with 48 missiles; and the same for the Netherlands.

The NATO ministers also agreed that 1,000 U.S. tactical nuclear warheads (of the 7,000 deployed) would be withdrawn from Europe as soon as feasible. (That withdrawal was completed in 1980.) The ministers stressed the importance of arms control as a contribution to NATO security and East-West stability. They welcomed the contribution of the SALT II treaty toward achieving those objectives. They agreed that long-range theater nuclear weapon systems should be included in the next round of U.S.-Soviet talks: "Limitations on U.S. and Soviet long-range theater nuclear systems should be negotiated bilaterally in the SALT III framework in a step-by-step approach." They also agreed that the limitations should be based on the principles of equality and adequate verification. They created a special high-level consultative body within the alliance to support the U.S. negotiating effort.[7]

The Netherlands and Belgian governments both submitted reservations to the decision. The Netherlands, while agreeing to the two-track proposal, said that it would not be able to announce a final decision on deployment of new missiles on Dutch territory for at least a year. The Belgians postponed a decision for six months, saying their decision would depend on arms control negotiations. If the negotiations should fail, the Belgians said, they would move ahead with deployment. As it happened, the anticipated negotiations did not commence. Shortly after the NATO decision the Soviets began sending troops into Afghanistan. For the next ten months U.S.-Soviet diplomatic relations were in the deep freeze.

Preliminary talks between the United States and the Soviet Union on the limitation of medium-range nuclear arms in Europe did not begin until October 27, 1980, eight days before the defeat of President Carter in the U.S. election. The Geneva talks lasted for about a month, but because of the lame-duck nature of the U.S. delegation, they were doomed to merely going through the motions. The U.S. wanted to talk only about the Soviet SS-20's, including those facing China, and the Soviet Backfire bombers. The Soviets insisted on talking about U.S. so-called forward-based systems, including American planes based in Europe capable of carrying nuclear weapons to Soviet targets, as well as planes on carriers in the Mediterranean which are known to carry nuclear weapons. As anticipated, these talks achieved nothing.

When the Reagan administration took office in January 1981, the hawks moved into power. They had rejected the terms of the SALT II treaty and proclaimed that it made no sense for the United States to return to the negotiating table until the necessary decisions were made to build a new round of strategic weapons so that the United States could bargain from a position of strength. Priority was given to planning the new defense budget, which over a five-year period would cost more than $1.5 trillion. Combined with the huge expansion in defense spending was a hostile, anti-Soviet stance adopted by President Reagan, Secretary of State Haig, and other members of the national security team. The Soviets were accused of cheating and lying and fomenting an international conspiracy of terrorism. At no time since the height of the cold war, when John Foster Dulles talked of nuclear brinkmanship, had the anti-Soviet rhetoric in Washington been so provocative. The chill which had existed since the Soviet invasion of Afghanistan was intensified. Serious diplomacy was at a standstill.

The Reagan administration announced its determination to move ahead with plans to install new land-based missiles in Europe beginning at the end of 1983. However, the European members of NATO were facing growing political opposition because there was so little indication that the new team in Washington would seriously move ahead with the arms control negotiations called for in the NATO decision. When the NATO ministers met in Rome in early May 1981, this issue was high on the agenda. There was agreement to move toward negotiations but, even so, the final communiqué gave priority to arms buildup. It said:

> . . . The modernizing of NATO's Long Range Theater Nuclear Forces is more essential than ever and offers the only realistic basis for parallel Theater Nuclear Forces

arms control. Since the December 1979 decision Soviet threats and efforts to divide the allies have only strengthened their resolve to take steps necessary to maintain deterrence, redress the imbalance in Long-Range Theater Nuclear Forces and insure their security.[8]

It was agreed that Secretary of State Alexander Haig would meet with Soviet Foreign Minister Andrei Gromyko at the September meeting of the United Nations to set a date for renewing negotiations before the end of the year. The negotiations would rely on an "updated threat assessment and a study of functional requirements for NATO Theater Nuclear Forces."

THE EUROPEAN NUCLEAR DISARMAMENT MOVEMENT

Within a month of the December 1979 NATO decision a peace movement began to spread throughout Europe. Organizations emerged in the Netherlands, West Germany, Norway, Denmark, and the United Kingdom. An umbrella organization, called the Campaign for European Nuclear Disarmament (END), was created. By the fall of 1980 membership was growing rapidly. In Hamburg, 100,000 turned out for an antinuclear rally, 75,000 in Amsterdam, and 70,000 marched to Trafalgar Square in London.

But it wasn't until 1981, after the Reagan administration had moved into Washington, that the antinuclear movement reached massive proportions with significant political importance. In October and November more than 250,000 marched on Bonn, another 250,000 marched through London to assemble at Hyde Park, 300,000 marched in Amsterdam, and another 200,000 in Rome. These crowds were three times the size that had marched the year before. Clearly the movement had the sort of momentum which forced politicians to pay attention. In the Netherlands the movement was so powerful that no political party could support a decision to deploy U.S. cruise missiles and remain in power. None of the parties in the coalition formed by Prime Minister Andreas van Agt in

September 1981 favored installing the new missiles. As a result, the Dutch probably will never accept the proposal that they base forty-eight cruise missiles on their soil.

Jan-Miendt Faber, the head of the Interchurch Peace Council, the largest Dutch antinuclear organization, with 200,000 members, says: "We are not unilateral disarmers. We do not want to seriously upset the balance that now exists. Only public pressure on East and West can begin to achieve balanced disarming."[9] The Dutch peace movement is broadly representative, including not only church groups but members of the States-General and military people, some of them high-ranking and on active duty. Many soldiers and sailors in uniform can be seen marching in the antinuclear demonstrations.

The movement in Belgium is not as large and well organized as the one in Holland, but it, too, has political clout. In May 1981 the Belgian coalition government announced that it would not make a final decision on whether to accept the U.S. cruise missiles on its territory until the end of 1982. Norway and Denmark have been opposed to nuclear weapons on their soil for some time, but they were participants in the NATO decision. A growing number of politicians in those countries are raising questions about the merits of that decision. In Italy the coalition government, despite the large Italian Communist Party, still maintains that it will accept the cruise missiles. In the fall of 1981 there were large demonstrations, for the first time, in Rome, Florence, and also Sicily, where the missiles will be based.

In Germany there is a strong pacifist movement led by the Protestant Church. The church's national congress, held in Hamburg in June 1981, was attended by 150,000 who were vociferous in their opposition to any of the NATO missiles on German territory. The German movement also includes a large environmental group and all of the intellectual left. Opposition to the NATO decision has grown each month in Chancellor Helmut Schmidt's Social Democratic Party, in which more than half the members are opposed to accepting the U.S. missiles. Willy Brandt, chairman of the SPD, has made it clear that he opposes the missiles unless the Soviets turn down serious negotiation. By a wide margin the party's youth and women's branches are opposed to the missiles. The youth organization of the Free Democratic Party of Foreign Minister Hans-Dietrich Genscher has voted to urge West Germany to abandon the NATO decision on the ground that the program represents only the interests of the United States.

A recent poll in West Germany of young people aged sixteen to twenty-nine "showed that 56 percent want to avoid war at all costs even if it means that the Soviet Union would take over Western Europe. Within the same age group, if the choice is between life under Communism or fighting a war, only 25 percent say that democracy is worth defending."[10]

The most rapid growth has occurred in Britain, where the Campaign for Nuclear Disarmament (CND) has become a powerful political force in less than two years. Bruce Kent, a Roman Catholic priest, who served as a tank officer in the British military, is the secretary-general of the CND. Kent says he believes in unilateral nuclear disarmament for Britain because the British nuclear force is neither independent nor credible. E. P. Thompson, the intellectual guru of the movement and one of the leaders of European Nuclear Disarmament, says his campaign

> has as an objective the creation of an expanding zone freed from nuclear weapons and bases. It aims to expel these weapons from the soil and waters of both East and West Europe, and to press the missiles, in the first place, back to the Urals and to the Atlantic Ocean.
>
> The tactics of the campaign will be both national and international. In the national context, each peace movement will proceed directly to contest the nuclear weapons deployed by its own state, or by NATO or Warsaw Pact obligations upon its own soil. Its actions will not be qualified by any notion of diplomatic bargaining. Its opposition to the use of nuclear weapons by its own state will be absolute. Its demands upon its own state will be unilateral.[11]

The left wing of the British Labor Party has adopted the unilateralist position. The Labor Party opposes the deployment of U.S. cruise missiles in Britain. Michael Foot, the party leader, has pledged that if Conservative Prime Minister Margaret Thatcher accepts the missiles, he will send them back to the United States as soon as he returns to power.

The Social Democratic Party in coalition with the Liberal Party has taken the lead and seems a likely winner in the next British election. David Owen, one of the top Social Democrats and foreign minister in the last Labor government, is not a unilateralist but is a critic of the NATO decision. He is a strong supporter of the SALT process and believes that levels of nuclear weapons should be sharply reduced through negotiation. He does not support the view that new nuclear weapons are needed, in either Europe or the United States.

The breadth of British opinion favoring serious attempts to control nuclear weapons, and opposed to political linkage, was demonstrated by Edward Heath, a Conservative party leader and British prime minister from 1970 to 1974. He said:

> Europe's stake in détente extends to the sphere of arms control. This reduces uncertainty in both East and West about the strategies and military options of each side, and it helps to limit weapons systems that are highly destabilizing to the military balance. . . . [The] West should pursue a two-pronged strategy embracing both détente and deterrence.[12]

All Europe, from left to right, is on a different course from Washington. The unilateralists have broken through the trauma of psychic numbness. Most people are well aware of the constant peril of the nuclear bomb, but because they feel impotent to do anything, they push it out of their thoughts. But the unilateralists, who believe their survival and that of their children are at stake, have decided to act. In the process incredible energy has been released. Through political action they intend to change governments and policies to block the further deployment of nuclear weapons in their countries.

Some unilateralists demand the elimination of all nuclear weapons from their nations.

In Britain, by referendum and council action, more than 120 cities—including some of the biggest, such as Birmingham and Manchester—have declared themselves nuclear-free zones. They oppose the deployment of any nuclear weapons or the shipment of any nuclear weapons or materials through their territory. They oppose any government civil defense programs because they give the illusion that nuclear wars can be fought. These nuclear-free zones have no standing in law, but they have tremendous political and psychological significance because they express the popular will.

The position of the British, German, and Italian governments continues to support multilateralism based on arms control negotiation. British Foreign Minister Lord Carrington has asserted several times that continuing SALT progress is indispensable to the security of the United Kingdom. Politicians throughout Europe have been unable to ignore growing resistance to nuclear weapons in Europe. Polls taken at the end of 1981 showed that a majority of those polled in Britain, Germany, and Holland were opposed to any new nuclear weapons.

Most of the rest of Europe was opposed, too. All Scandinavia had long opposed nuclear weapons on its soil. Austria and Yugoslavia were nonaligned and opposed. The election of Andreas Papandreou in Greece gave power to the long-standing opposition in that country. Papandreou has announced that he will remove U.S. nuclear weapons from Greece. He has also pledged to attempt to form a Balkan nuclear-free zone, including Rumania, Bulgaria, Yugoslavia, and Greece. Leaders of all those governments have indicated their approval of the idea.

Perhaps most remarkable is the developing indication throughout Eastern Europe of a desire for a nuclear-free Europe. Members of Solidarity in Poland have given their strong support. But the Soviet Union has been feeling pressure from several sources, not just from Poland. In Bucharest, Rumania, more than 300,000 people marched demanding that both the United States and the Soviet Union cut back their nuclear weapons. Rumanian Communist Party Chief Nicolae Ceausescu has demanded that the Soviets dismantle their SS-20 missiles in return for a real cutback in the West.

When a Soviet submarine, reportedly armed with nuclear weapons, ran aground inside Swedish territorial waters, all Scandinavia was enraged. Negotiations had been proceeding to create a Nordic nuclear-free zone, but the Soviet submarine brought all such plans to a halt.

In East Germany five regional Lutheran Church organizations held all-day meetings demanding an end to militarization. Speaker after speaker condemned the buildup in East-West tensions and education that brands fellow human beings as enemies.[13] A group of East and West Germans wrote an open letter to Soviet President Brezhnev urging the demilitarization and neutralization of both East and West Germany to ease tensions and to make additional nuclear arms in Europe unnecessary. The letter was signed by four members of the West German parliament, one of whom said: "This is the first time the citizens of both Germanies have spoken with one tongue to one of the superpowers." The letter ended by asking for the withdrawal of Soviet and NATO "occupation troops from both parts of Germany."[14]

The antinuclear movement has even penetrated the Soviet Union. In 1981 the Campaign for Nuclear Disarmament sign, CND, in Cyrillic, was seen painted on walls in Moscow and Leningrad, and students, including some children of Central Committee members, were observed wearing CND buttons. Marshal Nikolai V. Ogarkov, the Soviet chief of the General Staff of the armed forces, wrote in the Communist party journal *Kommunist:*

> Over a period of 36 peaceful years two new generations of people have in fact grown up having no knowledge derived from personal experience of what war is. . . . Questions of the struggle for peace are sometimes interpreted not from class positions, but somewhat simplistically: any kind of peace is good, any kind of war is bad.[15]

Ogarkov's complaint is similar to that made by hawks in Washington. The young Russians have their own version of "Better Red Than Dead." Perhaps "Better Alive Than Dead."

WHY HAS IT HAPPENED?

Why is Europe filled with so much anxiety about the growing possibility of nuclear war? After all, the Continent has been vulnerable to attack from Soviet nuclear weapons since the late fifties. Soviet strategic weapons could obliterate European cities—as could the early medium-range nuclear weapons, the SS-4's and SS-5's. The latter are city busters with much larger warheads than the SS-20's, which have three smaller warheads. But Europeans have not been alarmed about the possibility of Soviet aggression. In fact, the *Ostpolitik*, which relaxed tensions in Germany and Central Europe beginning in the late sixties, combined with continuing progress in nuclear arms control in SALT I and SALT II and backed up by the American security commitment to NATO, contributed to reassuring Europeans about their safety.

This all began to erode with Henry Kissinger's speech indicating that Europe could no longer rely on the nuclear umbrella of the United States. Since the Soviets had achieved strategic nuclear parity with the United States, and a medium-range advantage with the installation of the longer-range, more accurate SS-20's, the NATO allies were vulnerable to selective blackmail, or so it was claimed. In order to avert such blackmail, Kissinger contended, the United States needed to be able to wage small-scale limited nuclear war in Europe because no U.S. President would any longer risk an all-out strategic exchange with the Soviet Union. The NATO decision to deploy U.S. nuclear missiles in Europe capable of striking targets in the Soviet Union was rationalized as the best means for answering the dilemma posed by Kissinger.

This was followed in the summer of 1980 by Presidential Directive 59, setting forth a new official American doctrine for fighting limited nuclear wars. Then came the Reagan election, with the American hawks ascendant; a rejection of

SALT II; a call for the most gargantuan military program in history—all combined with the most bellicose, anti-Soviet rhetoric since the height of the cold war. Europeans rapidly focused on the implications of these developments for their own security. Here was a new U.S. administration, opposed to serious arms control negotiation, employing confrontational rhetoric, and advocating a doctrine of limited nuclear warfare.

Now the 572 nuclear missiles to be deployed in Europe, under the NATO decision, were to be 100 percent owned and controlled by the United States. The European states would be providing only the real estate. Any decision to launch the weapons would be made by President Reagan and his advisers. Under these circumstances it is not difficult to understand why the anxiety level in Europe had increased so rapidly and why Europeans were voicing their determined opposition to these U.S. weapons.

For some time the term "flexible response" had been used to describe NATO military options, but in the public mind it had been associated with deterrence. The terms "war fighting" and "limited nuclear wars" were something else. Brigadier General Niles J. Fulwyler, commanding general of the U.S. Army Nuclear and Chemical Agency, appeared on a CBS-TV documentary about U.S. military power which was widely shown in Europe during the summer of 1981. He said:

> What we're really talking about here is an attempt to have limited-use nuclear weapons, and we want to ensure that our adversary understands that in a case like this it would be a restrained use and for specific targets, for specific time frames. . . . I feel that it's very important at least to be able to try to have the limited use of nuclear war and have that option rather than when we cross that threshold to go straight to general nuclear release, which is everything.[16]

Since the 1950's the United States has been assigning various types of battlefield tactical nuclear weapons to Europe.

It was cheaper to deter the Red Army with small nuclear weapons than with an expansion of NATO's conventional forces. The concept of flexible response was developed in the 1960's, when defense planners talked about a ladder of escalation beginning with conventional weapons and moving to tactical weapons, to medium-range weapons, and finally to strategic weapons if the Soviets had not been deterred at one of the earlier stages. These scenarios were always nonsensical but were seldom challenged during the years that the United States maintained undisputed strategic superiority. The doctrine never should have been granted credibility, but today, as John Barry of the *Times* (London) asserts, "the people of Western Europe, lacking a kamikaze tradition, will think it too risky to retain."

Since Europeans have a growing awareness of this risk, they were astounded to read that President Reagan had told a group of newspaper editors that he could see where there could be a nuclear exchange in Europe without such a conflict's escalating into all-out nuclear war between the superpowers. When this provoked a storm of protest in Europe, the State Department issued a statement: "The President's remarks are completely consistent with the Alliance's long-standing strategy of a flexible response in Europe." Of course, this was correct, but the reaffirmation of a very dubious policy was not reassuring to Europeans.

A few weeks later, in October 1981, Secretary of State Alexander Haig told a congressional committee that NATO had a long-standing contingency plan to fire a nuclear warning shot if the Soviets were giving indication of aggressive action. The next day Secretary of Defense Caspar Weinberger denied that there was any such contingency plan and said that it would be inappropriate to contemplate one. Nevertheless, Haig, who had been in command of NATO forces, clearly knew the facts, and Weinberger, a man with no military experience, clearly did not.

When asked to clarify these issues of limited use of nuclear weapons at his press conference, President Reagan said that he had been asked:

[Is] it possible to ever use a nuclear weapon without this spreading automatically to the exchange of the strategic weapons from nation to nation? And I gave what I thought was something that was possible, that the grave difference between theater nuclear weapons—the artillery shells and so forth that both sides have—that I could see where both sides could still be deterred from going into the exchange of strategic weapons if there had been battlefield weapons troop-to-troop exchanged there.

On the question of the nuclear warning shot the President said: "Oh. Well, that, there seems to be some confusion as to whether that is still a part of NATO strategy or not. And so far I've had no answer to that."[17]

The President's views on limited nuclear war were not shared in Europe. Shortly before his death in 1979, British Admiral of the Fleet Lord Mountbatten, chief of the Defense Staff from 1959 to 1965, wrote:

The belief that nuclear weapons could be used in field warfare without triggering an all-out nuclear exchange leading to the final holocaust is more and more incredible. I cannot accept the reasons for the belief that any class of nuclear weapons can be categorized in terms of their tactical or strategic purposes. In all sincerity, as a military man I can see no use for any nuclear weapons which would not end in escalation that no one can conceive.[18]

Admiral of the Fleet Lord Hill-Norton, who was chief of the British Defense Staff from 1971 to 1973, says that he knows "of no informed observer who believes that warfighting with nuclear weapons is credible."[19] Field Marshal Lord Carver, who was the next chief of staff, said: "It is not a concept which any sensible, responsible military person now holds that you would fight a war in Europe with tactical or theater nuclear weapons and thus avoid a strategic nuclear exchange."[20]

According to the International Institute of Strategic Studies in London, the United States and the Soviet Union would not be able to wage a limited nuclear war in Europe or anywhere else. Its paper concludes: "There can really be no possibility of controlling nuclear war. . . . Nuclear weapons are simply too powerful and have too many disparate effects, not all of which are predictable to be used in precise and discriminatory fashion." One of the reasons nuclear war cannot be limited or controlled, the study points out, is that "command systems and communications, including satellites, are so vulnerable to destruction or manipulation."[21]

Not only do British and German nuclear strategists consider limited nuclear war to be fantasy, but so do the Soviets. For years the Soviets have been very clear that they have no illusions about keeping nuclear wars small or limited. In an interview with *Der Spiegel* magazine in West Germany, President Brezhnev said there can be no such thing as limited nuclear war:

> If a nuclear war breaks out, whether it be in Europe or in any other place, it would inevitably and unavoidably assume a worldwide character. Such is the logic of the war itself and the character of present-day armaments and international relations. One should clearly see and understand it. So those who possibly hope to set fire to the nuclear powder keg, while themselves sitting snugly aside, should not entertain any illusions.[22]

By the time Caspar Weinberger completed his participation in the NATO defense ministers' meeting at Gleneagles, Scotland, in October 1981, it was clear to him that something had to be done about holding together the NATO alliance. The antinuclear movement was much more than an expression of pacifism by a noisy minority; it was a powerful and growing political force representing clear majority opinion in several NATO countries. Furthermore, U.S. strategic doctrine and U.S. arguments about the political and military relevance of the new weapons were under severe challenge from respected European experts. So, when the other defense ministers unanimously pressed the United States to accept the zero-based option for the forthcoming talks with the Soviets, he reluctantly agreed. This meant that the United States would attempt to negotiate an agreement in which the Soviets would cut their medium-range missiles to zero in return for no deployment of medium-range missiles by NATO.

A few weeks later in his *Der Spiegel* interview Brezhnev rejected the zero-option idea:

> . . . Rather peculiar preliminary conditions are being formulated: U.S. forward-based means should not be mentioned, nuclear weapons of the United States' allies in NATO should not be included in any balance, the scope of the talks should be limited to Soviet medium-range missiles, which should be dismantled in return for U.S. missiles planned to be deployed in Europe. . . . Those in the United States who are advancing these sorts of proposals apparently themselves do not expect for a second that the Soviet Union might agree to them. . . . They are designing in advance the deadlock of the talks so as to say: Look, the USSR has no regard for the West's opinion, so the United States can do nothing but deploy the missiles.[23]

Despite Brezhnev's rejection of the zero-based option, President Reagan decided to adopt it as the centerpiece of his approach to the Geneva negotiations. He made his positions public before the National Press Club, with simultaneous television and radio coverage in Europe. The tactic was similar to that of Jimmy Carter when he publicized his negotiating positions in advance of the Moscow talks in March 1977. The Reagan speech was clearly a propaganda effort focused on Europe rather than on the Soviet Union.

The President said:

> The United States is prepared to cancel its deployment of Pershing II and ground-launched missiles if the Soviets will dismantle their SS-20, SS-4, and SS-5 missiles. . . . Now we intend to negotiate in good faith and go to Geneva willing to listen and consider the proposals of our Soviet counterparts. . . . The second proposal that I've made to President Brezhnev concerns strategic

weapons. . . . [We] will seek to negotiate substantial reductions in nuclear arms which would result in levels that are equal and verifiable. Our approach with verification will be to emphasize openness and creativity rather than secrecy and suspicion which have undermined confidence in arms control in the past. . . . And let us see how far we can go in achieving truly substantial reductions in our strategic arsenals. To symbolize this fundamental change in direction we will call these negotiations START—Strategic Arms Reduction Talks.

The third proposal I've made to the Soviet Union is that we act to achieve equality at lower levels of conventional forces in Europe. Finally, we must reduce the risks of surprise attack and the chance of war arising out of uncertainty or miscalculation. I am renewing our proposal for a conference to develop effective measures that would reduce these dangers. . . . All of these proposals are based on the same fair-minded principles: substantial, militarily significant reductions in forces, equal ceilings for similar types of forces and adequate provisions for verification. . . . I believe that the time is right to move forward on arms control and the resolution of critical regional disputes at the conference table. Nothing will have a higher priority for me and for the American people over the coming months and years.[24]

The most significant aspect of the President's speech was its change of tone from the previous rhetoric of anti-Soviet hostility to a more balanced emphasis on the importance of reducing the threat of nuclear weapons through negotiation. The most important substantive part of the speech was the President's recognition of the importance of getting back to SALT or START, as he calls it, with emphasis on substantial reductions in numbers based on the principle of equality. But there was clear evidence that the Reagan administration had not thought through a realistic position on strategic weapons. The President said that "we can make proposals for genuinely serious reductions but only if we take the time to prepare carefully."

His remarks about a new approach to verification based on "openness . . . rather than secrecy and suspicion" had ominous implications for serious arms control. The Soviet Union is not open. It is totalitarian, and thus, secrecy pervades the system, less so than in the past, but extensively. In a series of background briefings for several newspapers Eugene Rostow, the director of the Arms Control and Disarmament Agency, said that the Reagan administration would insist on having on-site inspection to verify compliance with the terms of arms control agreements. Clearly that is the only means for verifying highly mobile weapons such as ground-launched cruise missiles. Moreover, the Soviets, because they are a closed society, would almost certainly reject the necessary large-scale inspection by foreign representatives on their territory.

Thus, the new verification approach is a nonstarter. It implies a lack of serious intent. The beauty of the SALT I and SALT II treaties was that they were not based on trust. Both sides agreed that their national means of intelligence were adequate to monitor the other side's compliance with the terms of the treaty, to ensure that there was no cheating. The answer is obvious—freeze nuclear weapons at present levels and start cutting to lower levels. Don't build new weapons such as ground-launched cruise missiles which cannot be adequately monitored by existing means of intelligence. But the Reagan administration is still giving priority to the deployment of nonverifiable weapons. Until this is reversed, the good intentions expressed in the Reagan speech will be merely cosmetic.

Starting nuclear talks with the Russians on European medium-range nuclear weapons was a clear case of the cart before the horse. The only reason it was done was to assuage European public opinion because the talks were called for as part of the unfortunate NATO agreement. There was never any possibility of reaching agreement on medium-range nuclear weapons except in the context of an agreement which also included strategic weapons. That is why the NATO communiqué stated that the negotiations must be in the framework of Salt III, assuming as they did at the time that the SALT II treaty would be ratified.

President Reagan revealed that he understood this, in part, when he said that there was no point in talking about medium-range missiles only in Europe. As he pointed out, SS-20 missiles deployed east of the Urals have the range to strike every major city in Europe, and SS-20's facing China in Siberia, because they are mobile, can be moved to locations where they can hit European targets. But what President Reagan didn't reveal, making the whole medium-range missile debate academic, is the fact that all Soviet strategic weapons, with a slight change in trajectory, can also destroy European cities. In other words, an agreement to ban SS-20's would not make Europe safer, unless the strategic weapons were banned, too.

The same is also true on the NATO side. The most powerful weapons assigned to the NATO command are the U.S. Poseidon submarines which have enough MIRV'd missiles to destroy all major Soviet cities. The Poseidons are strategic weapons. There is no need for any more NATO missiles unless there is an intention to adopt a policy of nuclear war fighting. This point is well made by Michael Howard of Oxford, one of Britain's foremost military analysts:

> The belief of some strategic analysts that the Russians can only be deterred from attacking us by the installation of precisely matching systems—"ground-launched missiles must be matched by ground-launched missiles"—is politically naïve to the point of absurdity. The United States is "coupled" to Europe not by one delivery system rather than another, but by a vast web of military installations and personnel, to say nothing of the innumerable economic, social and financial links that tie us together into a single coherent system. To satisfy those pedantic analysts who require still further guarantees, the Americans, whose patience seems inexhaustible, have already allocated to NATO a submarine-based nuclear force of immense destructive power.
>
> If all this is insufficient to deter the Soviet Union from a course that they are, in any case, likely to contemplate only in the very direst of extremities, what difference will be made by the installation of Pershings and cruise missiles, particularly if these remain under sole American control?[25]

Howard is answering the Conservative Party proponents of the NATO decision, but his remarks are applicable to all supporters. The decision was a disaster.

Furthermore, one of the real dangers of giving priority to the NATO decision by emphasizing talks on medium-range missiles in Geneva is that the antinuclear movement in Europe may succeed in blocking the deployment of the missiles. Obviously the Soviets are willing to go through the motions in Geneva in hopes that exactly such a result will occur. They would achieve a major political objective without making a single concession in the nuclear arms talks. The consequences for the Atlantic alliance would be devastating.

The only sensible course is for the United States to move rapidly to broad, all-inclusive talks with the Soviet Union covering all nuclear weapons. These should include long-range, medium-range, and tactical nuclear weapons. The goal should be to dismantle as many as possible on an equal basis, with emphasis on eliminating counterforce weapons and banning the testing and deployment of any new nuclear weapons. The trouble is that the Reagan administration is continuing to give priority to building new weapons for NATO rather than to arms control measures that would eliminate the need for such weapons. If it continues on this course much longer, it will achieve neither missile deployment in Europe nor arms control.

Chapter VI

A Proposal for a Negotiated Solution

The superpowers are on a collision course which, if not checked, will lead to mutual destruction and world disaster. U.S.-Soviet relations have steadily declined since 1975, but the consequences of the impasse are far more dangerous today because both sides have, since the 1950's, built arsenals of almost incomprehensible destructive power. As the arms race, especially the nuclear arms race, continues, the risk of unintentional or accidental war leading to holocaust becomes far too great. The central issue for both the United States and the Soviet Union is survival.

In order to survive, both sides will have to acknowledge the reality that neither side can any longer assert its national will through military coercion of the other. Again, Clausewitz and Lenin are irrelevant; they have been overtaken by military technology. War can no longer be an extension of politics in a nuclear era when both superpowers have approximately equal nuclear power. There can never again be military superiority of one superpower over the other. The mindless effort to achieve such superiority moves each side closer to the hair trigger. Control of the weapons systems has become so complex that in time of crisis, accidental launch is a growing risk.

Neither side has yet fully comprehended the implications of this reality. It means that both the United States and the Soviet Union will have to jettison certain concepts about

149

themselves and each other. As Henry Kissinger used to say this means a new conceptual framework. It means a negotiated accommodation which provides for the survival of both nations. In order to succeed, it requires both political and military restraint. The SALT process failed because there was no political agreement.

What does this mean for the United States? It means not only recognition but acceptance of the fact that the Soviet Union has military power approximately equal to our own. It means that the continuing arms race reduces security. It means that the containment policy of the 1950's is dead. We can never again be the world's policeman, nor can the Soviet Union for that matter. The economic resources and technology of the United States and its allies are substantial, but not large enough to contain the Soviet Union throughout the world by military force. It means a new approach to competition with the USSR.

What does this mean for the Soviet Union? It means giving up any remaining illusions of a world of Communist states dominated by Moscow. It means indefinite coexistence with states which have different economic and political systems. It means that the Soviet Union will give up, along with the United States, any further attempts to advance its influence in the world through the use of combat military force. It means a new approach to competition with the United States.

During the cold war the United States tried to contain communism with military power, and for the most part it was successful. It sent combat forces into Korea, Lebanon, the Dominican Republic, and Vietnam. It also engaged in numerous covert paramilitary operations in various parts of the world. But the Vietnam War brought such military intervention to an end; after Vietnam the overwhelming sentiment in the United States was opposed to direct or indirect interventionism. The American people wanted an end to the cold war, so they welcomed the end of military confrontation and embraced the U.S.-Soviet détente negotiated by Nixon and Kissinger. This embrace of détente extended throughout the country, with majority support from both political parties, as could be observed in the landslide reelection of Richard Nixon in 1972.

As we have noted, détente was a fragile concept in the United States. Instead of growing stronger, it gradually declined as a result of the continuing Soviet military buildup and especially because of Soviet military adventures in the Third World. There had always been opponents of détente in the United States, but in the period 1970–1975 they were a distinct minority. Today they are a dominant majority. The United States is preparing once again for cold war confrontationism, with new military bases, a rapid deployment force, covert operations in Afghanistan and elsewhere, and a huge increase in the military budget. The hawks in Moscow have rejuvenated the hawks in Washington, and vice versa.

If we are to survive, we must return to the negotiating table. Détente should be restored, but this time we need to negotiate a much clearer understanding, on both sides, of what we mean by it. The most difficult task of such a negotiation will be to establish workable ground rules for the inevitable competition which will continue to exist. Both sides recognize that because the two systems are so different, there will always be competition. The Soviets say the two systems represent alternative models of social and economic development. There is essentially no problem about social and economic competition. The problem comes from military competition.

The Russians understand about survival. They have been invaded many times during their long history, and during World War II 30 million of their people were killed or severely wounded. Pearl Harbor represents the only invasion of the territory of the United States. The Soviets have demonstrated unmistakably their desire to control and drastically to reduce the numbers of nuclear weapons. They sometimes use the term "military" détente because they emphasize the importance of SALT and the need to reduce the dangers of military confrontation. Certainly the control of nuclear weapons is one of the priorities of détente, but the other indispensable priority is a mutual understanding of how to manage the continuing competition between the two super-powers.

There is a basic difference of doctrine that requires resolution. This is well illustrated by a speech at the beginning of 1981 by Soviet Foreign Minister Andrei Gromyko:

> Proletarian internationalism as a fundamental principle of Soviet foreign policy means that this policy consistently upholds the basic interests of world socialism, of the forces of the international communist working class and national liberation movements. As for peaceful coexistence [the Soviet term for détente] it represents a specific form of class struggle, a peaceful competition, precluding any use of military strength, between two opposite socioeconomic systems—socialism and capitalism.[1]

In other words, there is a distinction between peaceful coexistence and proletarian internationalism. In détente (peaceful coexistence) the competition is to be peaceful without using military strength, but proletarian internationalism permits "upholding" the basic interest of national liberation movements, sometimes presumably with Soviet military strength. Explaining the Leninist policy of peaceful coexistence as distinguished from class struggle, Viktor Kortunov, a Soviet ideologist, said: "No one can put a freeze on the world socio-political development on the pretext of détente. International agreements cannot alter the laws of class struggle."[2]

In an article in *Foreign Affairs* in the summer of 1981 Henry Trofimenko said the United States, in exchange for a SALT agreement, was trying to get the Soviet Union to accept the status quo in the Third World. Soviet leaders, he said, have always made clear their intention "to support the struggle of [Third World] peoples for their social and national liberation." But he added that "a Soviet military presence is not the main component of aid and support with respect to developing countries."[3] Yet this clearly means that a military presence is considered to be an acceptable element of such assistance.

This distinction which the Soviets make between "proletarian internationalism" and "peaceful coexistence" goes to the very heart of the breakdown in U.S.-Soviet relations. This is an issue which requires priority attention at the negotiating table by the leaders of the United States and the USSR. It is undoubtedly the main reason for the collapse of the "Basic Principles of Relations Between the USSR and USA" signed at the Moscow summit in 1972. It is interesting to recall that the "Basic Principles" were promoted at the initiative of the Soviet Union. They contained twelve principles of conduct—including peaceful coexistence, mutual restraint, noninterference in the internal affairs of the other, and rejection of attempts to gain unilateral advantage at the expense of the other. But while Nixon and Kissinger interpreted peaceful coexistence to mean restraint, especially in the use of military power, anywhere in the world, the Soviets interpreted it to mean peaceful coexistence in the direct relations between the superpowers.

Secretary of State Alexander Haig was Kissinger's deputy on the National Security Council staff at the 1972 Moscow meeting, and he took part in the drafting of the "Basic Principles." Shortly after Haig became secretary of state, he said that "all new Soviet-American agreements including arms control, trade and financial credits will be held up until there is a new understanding on the limits of Moscow's activities throughout the world." In an interview with Haig, James Reston of *The New York Times* reported:

In his view, it is important to try to reach agreement on what he calls "the norms of international behavior." That is to say, he thinks a serious attempt must be made to establish rules that would outlaw the use of military force, either directly or indirectly, to achieve political ends anywhere in the world.

He does not oppose what has been called "competitive coexistence" between Moscow and Washington for influ-

153

ence in third countries, but he is against an arms limitation agreement that sanctions or tolerates direct military
intervention by the Red Army as in Afghanistan, or by
Cuban mercenaries, financed and supplied by the Soviet
Union, in Africa, Latin America or elsewhere.[4]

The issue, of course, is the direct or indirect use of Soviet
or proxy combat forces to intervene in Third World disputes.
It is abundantly clear that the distinction the Soviets have
tried to make on this matter was not accepted in 1972 and
cannot ever be accepted by the United States as a basis for
peaceful coexistence or détente. Furthermore, if the Soviets
continue to insist on the right to intervene with combat forces
in Third World disputes, it will be politically impossible for
the United States to negotiate treaties for nuclear disarmament. The U.S. Senate would simply not ratify treaties under
such circumstances.

The United States has always relied on its nuclear power to
deter superior Soviet conventional forces. If the Soviet Union
continued to intervene with combat forces in the Third
World, it would be a virtual political impossibility for any
United States President to promote measures of nuclear disarmament, no matter how meritorious they might be; opponents
of nuclear disarmament would always win the argument.
Thus, there are only two realistic alternatives: to negotiate a
genuine détente which encompasses both military interventionism and nuclear disarmament or to continue the present
course of risky adventurism and an even more risky arms
race, leading almost certainly to the ultimate catastrophe.

Seen in those terms, the requirement for a negotiated settlement becomes undeniably compelling. As Haig says, the
United States does not oppose competitive coexistence. But it
does oppose the advance of Soviet power and influence
through the use of combat forces. The U.S. response to such
military intervention will be military confrontation, in one
form or another. That is the course we are on today. Soviet
interventionism has brought serious arms control negotiations to a halt. What is needed to break this impasse are
simultaneous negotiations on two tracks.

A Proposal for a Negotiated Solution

On one track would be negotiations concerning the issues of interventionism; on the other, negotiations concerning measures for reducing the dangers of nuclear war. This two-track approach is essential because the nature of each negotiation is so different; negotiators will require very different expert knowledge of political, military, and technical matters. Furthermore, both sets of negotiations deal with substance that ought to be clearly separated rather than linked. The successful negotiation of an agreement which reduces the threat of nuclear war is clearly in the mutual interest of both powers. The same can be said for an agreement that reduces the possibility of confrontation between the superpowers in the Third World. Both negotiations should move ahead simultaneously with the goal of bringing them independently to a successful conclusion at a summit meeting.

The Reagan administration would have to compromise on its present course, which calls for rearmament before serious arms control negotiation and for resolution of the issues of Soviet interventionism before arms control agreements can be reached. This is referred to as linkage. The Soviet Union would have to compromise, too, by giving up its doctrinal position which insists on a distinction between superpower peaceful coexistence and Third World military interventionism. Such compromise by both powers is indispensable if negotiated progress is to be made. The simultaneous two-track negotiating formula is also indispensable because any attempt to move only on one track is doomed to failure, as experience has demonstrated.

What this approach means is that both powers will have, for the first time, a clear grasp of the means for avoiding war. At the Moscow summit in 1972 the "Basic Principles of Relations" were almost an afterthought negotiated on the spot. The 1979 Vienna summit where Brezhnev and Carter signed SALT II had no formal agenda item dealing with interventionism. At the meeting, as already noted, Carter told Brezhnev that the use of Soviet military power in the Third World, either directly or by proxy, was unacceptable. Brezhnev, just as firmly, replied that the Soviet Union would continue to

155

give assistance to liberation movements. All this should be resolved, in advance, through negotiation.

A THIRD WORLD MILITARY
NONINTERVENTION PACT

Quite clearly the Soviet Union was taken by surprise at the repercussions inspired by its invasion of Afghanistan, especially in the United States. The United States is moving rapidly to expand its entire military arsenal, its clandestine assets, and its military bases. The failure of SALT and the increasing militarism in the United States have generated serious concern in the Kremlin. President Brezhnev and his top expert on the United States, Georgy Arbatov, both have called for reciprocal restraint. That is an excellent principle upon which to base future U.S.-Soviet competition, but it needs to be spelled out. What does reciprocal restraint mean?

The dimensions of competition also need to be spelled out. What can be tolerated, what cannot be tolerated? Clearly such things as trade, economic assistance, scientific and cultural exchange programs, and information programs, including propaganda, are tolerable aspects of competition. Military assistance programs, including training of military personnel and the provision of military advisers, are probably inevitable. (Both powers have already agreed that they would not provide nuclear weapons to Third World states.) Political and psychological covert operations, while undesirable, are likely to continue for some time to come. Espionage and the various forms of technological intelligence gathering will certainly continue.

The most unacceptable form of competition is direct intervention with combat forces, such as occurred in Vietnam and Afghanistan. Another form of unacceptable intervention is by third-party proxy forces or by covert paramilitary or so-called volunteer forces. Clearly unacceptable, too, is the provision of encouragement and military assistance for one state to attack another.

The principles of military noninterventionism are spelled out in the United Nations Charter, the Helsinki accords, and the "Basic Principles" of U.S.-Soviet relations, but they have been too ambiguous, too subject to differing interpretations, to prevent the present impasse. Something more precise needs to be negotiated if nuclear war is to be avoided. In the process both sides will, of necessity, have to reach some understanding on the most pressing political issues which could provoke direct U.S.-Soviet confrontation.

Perhaps the best approach to the first stage of a U.S.-Soviet military nonintervention pact would be to establish parameters by the realities of power as established by the last great war. World War II brought the United States into Western Europe, the Pacific, and Northeast Asia, including Japan and South Korea. That war also brought the Soviet Union into Eastern Europe. The Soviet Union has remained essentially the same, in terms of political geography, as has North America. South and Central America have traditionally been protected from external invasion by the United States and, more formally, by the Organization of American States—except for Cuba.

In terms of power, the major developments after World War II were the emergence of the United States and the Soviet Union as superpowers both armed with nuclear weapons capable of destroying each other and the disintegration of the European and Japanese empires. The collapse of the British, French, Dutch, Belgian, and Portuguese empires and the defeat of Japan created a power vacuum in most of Africa, the Middle East, Southwest Asia, the Indian subcontinent, and Southeast Asia. Most of the cold war competition between the United States and the Soviet Union has occurred in this Third World power vacuum.

With the Portuguese withdrawal from Mozambique and Angola, the last of the prewar colonial empires ceased to exist. Many new states have emerged, and some old states continue to have very fragile governments. The best way to prevent superpower competition in that area from triggering a nuclear war would be the negotiation of a military nonintervention pact covering the specified territory—i.e., the Middle East, all Africa except South Africa, Southwest Asia, the Indian subcontinent, and Southeast Asia. The nation of

South Africa is left out because there is no power vacuum there.

A military nonintervention pact in this Third World area would have to be based on the principle of equality. While recognizing that competition between the two powers would continue, it would place a ban on all forms of external intervention with combat forces in the designated Third World area. This ban would include any direct intervention by the Soviet Union or the United States with combat forces, the indirect intervention by third-party proxy combat forces, and intervention with covert paramilitary or volunteer forces. The ban on combat forces would be comprehensive, prohibiting intervention with such forces even if a Third World state in the area should request such assistance. It would also prohibit the establishment of military, naval, or air bases for the use of either superpower.

This pact would apply to the future, but consideration should also be given to extending the agreement to existing circumstances which are in clear violation of the terms. This would mean that the United States would give up certain existing bases and planned bases, as well as any plans for use of the rapid deployment force in the area, and certain covert military operations. The Soviets would withdraw from Afghanistan and would use their influence to persuade the Cubans to withdraw from Angola, Ethiopia, and South Yemen. The Soviets would give up their naval base in Aden.

There are numerous questions that come to mind about the feasibility of such a military nonintervention pact, but they all can be answered in the affirmative if the two powers decide to move for survival by establishing genuine détente, genuine relaxation of tensions through negotiated agreements. One of the first questions that occurs to Americans is: What about Israel? What if Israel were attacked by a state like Syria, or Libya, or Iraq or all of them together? The United States would continue to give Israel the military supplies it wants, but it would not send in its own combat forces. Ever since the time of David Ben-Gurion the Israelis have insisted on fighting their own wars; they do not want U.S. troops. Now that Israel and Egypt have reached a settlement, it is generally agreed that no combination of other Arab states could seriously threaten the security of Israel so long as the United States continues to make available the necessary military assistance.

The Soviets might ask what about Israel's frequent air strikes and incursions into Lebanon. Isn't Israel a proxy state of the United States? The answer is no. The United States condemns such Israeli aggression, just as it condemns Palestinian raids into Israel. If the United States and USSR sign a military nonaggression pact, it will behoove the United States to establish more clearly the ground rules for using U.S. military supplies for truly defensive purposes, only in the event of aggression. The distinction between prevention and preemption may be difficult to make, but it should be less difficult in an atmosphere where both superpowers are seriously attempting to relax tensions. In fact, the negotiation of a military nonintervention pact could lead to greater U.S.-Soviet cooperation in reaching a solution of the long-festering Palestinian problem.

And what about the Vietnamese invasion of Cambodia? The Soviet Union not only gives financial assistance and arms to Vietnam but has openly encouraged and supported the invasion of Cambodia. Such support of military aggression would be clearly inconsistent with the terms of a military nonintervention pact. If the Soviets signed such a pact, they would be expected to use their good offices to influence Vietnam not to pursue aggressive action, just as the United States would be expected to restrain Israel from aggressive acts.

And what about China? What if China decided again to punish the Soviets' Vietnamese ally? The Soviet Union has reason to worry about possible Chinese aggression, as the past record demonstrates. But if the Soviet Union found itself confronted by Chinese aggression requiring military action, such action would not occur in the Third World territory covered by the pact. It would be most improbable that the Soviet Union would send its troops to Vietnam, or elsewhere in the Third World, in order to fight with China. If war comes between the Soviet Union and China, it will undoubtedly occur directly across the Sino-Soviet border, where the Soviets have forty-five divisions backed up by planes and missiles and a direct line of supply.

From the Soviet standpoint, one of the possibly advantageous aspects of a U.S.-Soviet pact leading to real détente would be a change in U.S.-China relations. The United States would be more even-handed in its treatment of both the Soviet Union and China and less interested in seeing China's military power strengthened. In fact, if China should engage again in military action in the Third World, the United States could be expected to join the Soviet Union in condemning any Chinese aggression.

In a similar manner, a U.S.-Soviet military nonintervention pact could lead to greater cooperation with respect to goals in South Africa. The two powers could use their joint efforts toward a political settlement in Namibia. Obviously the United States would like to see more progress toward ending apartheid in South Africa, preferably without growing violence and war among Africans. But if war comes, it will be far better that it come without the involvement, on opposite sides, of U.S. and Soviet military personnel or proxy forces.

Other questions that are certain to be raised include revolutions and uprisings in Central and Latin America. Isn't this part of the Third World in the sense of including poor, underdeveloped countries? The Latin American states certainly have a history of struggle for freedom from colonialism, but their Spanish, French, British, and Portuguese colonial experience, with the exception of a few states in the Caribbean, ended long ago. For the most part they are members of the Organization of American States with deeply held opposition to external intervention in their national or hemispheric affairs. Nevertheless, there are revolutionary struggles in Latin America which the Soviets call part of the liberation movement.

However, the Soviets would never risk sending their combat forces into a Latin American dispute or civil war, even if requested to do so. Nor is it likely that Cuban combat forces will be sent into such disputes. This would trigger action by most of the OAS members, including a possible naval blockade of Cuba, such as occurred during the Cuban missile crisis. The Soviets may make a claim that Latin America should be included, but such a demand is not very substantial in view of the geography, the history, and the long-established presence of U.S. power.

Of course, there is also the question of Poland. But Poland is not a Third World state and does not fit the terms of the military nonintervention pact. In accordance with the Warsaw Pact, if the Polish government requests military assistance, there is no question that the other Warsaw Pact members, especially the Soviets, will grant such assistance. The United States and the other NATO members have made their position unmistakably clear with respect to Soviet military intervention in Poland. But clearly Eastern Europe does not meet the criteria established for a U.S.-Soviet military nonintervention pact in the Third World.

Critics of attempting to negotiate a Third World military nonintervention pact with the Soviets claim that it is naïve and illusory because the Soviet hawks will never give up their dream of world domination, with military force if necessary. After all, it is claimed, the Soviet Constitution provides that the Soviet Union is committed to supporting liberation struggles. But the Soviet Union has not defined the word "support." Under the terms of the pact the USSR could continue to provide support to liberation movements through all means except the intervention of external combat forces. In this sense Soviet doctrine would have to become explicit rather than ambiguous.

But the potential benefits to Moscow would be enormous. The pact would provide a broad framework for the Soviets to save face in Afghanistan, where they are bogged down in an expensive and unwinnable struggle for political and military control. Since the pact covers the entire specified Third World area, with equal obligations for both superpowers, the Soviets could justify withdrawal of their troops because they would receive something in return. Of course, the pact would mean that U.S. covert support for the Afghan resistance would end as Soviet troops were withdrawn.

161

RUSSIAN ROULETTE

The Soviets would benefit from the commitment of the United States to keep its combat forces out of the area, just as much as the United States would benefit from a Soviet commitment. One of the most important benefits would be the virtual elimination of a direct U.S.-Soviet military confrontation in the Third World. The avoidance of such confrontation has been a key tenet of Soviet policy. Yet it has been generally agreed during the last decade that the tinder box for World War III is more likely to be an explosion in the Middle East or the Persian Gulf than in Central Europe.

Moreover, the pact would permit the successful negotiation of a solid nuclear disarmament agreement for weapons in the United States, the Soviet Union, and Europe. The U.S. Senate would almost certainly ratify an agreement providing for deep cuts in nuclear arms if the pact were also mutually adopted. This would significantly strengthen the security of both superpowers and would eventually save both governments hundreds of billions of dollars.

The achievement of genuine détente would probably have other important benefits for the Soviet Union and the United States. The various exchange programs would bloom again. Hostile propaganda would be curbed by both sides. The Jackson-Vanik amendment would probably be replaced, permitting the achievement of a trade agreement which grants the Soviet Union most favored nation status and access to credits from the Export-Import Bank. Undoubtedly, as trade expanded, U.S. export restrictions would become more flexible, permitting the Soviets to obtain some important items of U.S. technology that have been blocked by recent U.S. export controls.

The resistance to this new conceptual framework for peaceful coexistence would probably be as great from the American hawks as from the Soviet hawks. Most American hawks are opposed to U.S.-Soviet détente, even of the genuine variety described here. Some American hawks believe that the United States should prepare for an ultimate showdown with the Soviet Union, even if it means nuclear war. Some American hawks believe that there can never be peace in the world until the Soviet system has been replaced by revolution, internal collapse, or external force. Fortunately this view is held by a small minority of Americans.

But there will certainly be strong and powerful resistance from the military-industrial complex to the agreements described here. There is so much power and financial profit at stake that it will vigorously oppose détente. However, the advantages to the United States would be just as enormous as those to the Soviet Union. Most important of all would be the contribution to U.S. national security in terms of both decreasing the threat of war and increasing the strength of our national economy.

The pact would considerably reduce tensions in the Persian Gulf and provide a basis for the United States, the USSR, and the gulf states to reach an agreement guaranteeing the sea-lanes and access of Persian Gulf oil to the commercial market. This would be vital to Europe, Japan, and the United States and perhaps advantageous, in time, also to the Soviet Union. The pact, because it would ease military tensions, should contribute to the prospects for reaching negotiated settlement of many of the disputes that continue to boil in the Third World.

The pact will be welcomed by almost all the Third World nations because they want the superpowers to stay out. Most of them have condemned U.S. and Soviet military adventures in the Third World. The Third World nations have, almost unanimously, supported resolutions at the United Nations calling for an end to the arms race. Third World states justifiably believe that the massive U.S.-Soviet military spending deprives them of their share of the world's wealth. They hope that both the United States and the Soviet Union will significantly increase their loans and grants of economic assistance to the Third World.

Probably the only nation which would vigorously oppose a U.S.-Soviet military nonintervention pact is China. China opposes U.S.-Soviet détente and encourages hostility between the two giants. It would like to see the two powers destroy each other, leaving China to pick up the pieces. It opposes arms control agreements and peaceful coexistence because it fears that may lead the Soviets to move their military forces from west to east, thus increasing the Soviet threat to China's security. Clearly China's interests and concerns must be taken into consideration by the United States, but they are not grounds for blocking U.S.-Soviet détente.

As noted, the Reagan administration, especially in the person of Secretary of State Haig, has talked about establishing more exacting principles for U.S.-Soviet behavior in the Third World. But rhetoric and demands for restraint will not be enough. What is needed is a comprehensive mutual commitment banning the intervention of combat forces in the Third World. Once the two sides agree to negotiate on these terms, the process, despite some strong opposition, is likely to be dynamic. There are so many obvious and important advantages to both powers, and most public opinion will give such a U.S.-Soviet pact a resounding endorsement.

NUCLEAR DISARMAMENT

President Reagan has asserted many times during the campaign and since arriving at the White House that he is prepared to sit down with the Russians and negotiate deep cuts in nuclear weapons to the point where neither side threatens the survival of the other. But Reagan has been hoodwinked by his advisers, who have informed him that the Soviet Union is not prepared to make deep cuts. As evidence they cite the Soviet rejection of the "comprehensive proposal" which Cyrus Vance took to Moscow in 1977. David Aaron, who was deputy to Brzezinski on the NSC staff, characterized the U.S. proposal this way: "We would be giving up future draft choices in exchange for cuts in their [the Soviets'] starting line-up."[5] Reagan believes that the Soviets won't consider deep cuts until the United States has built another round of strategic nuclear weapons so that it can negotiate from strength.

The theory of building nuclear bargaining chips so that we can negotiate from strength is a nonsensical hoax. To the extent it is believed, it becomes a wonderful rationalization for perpetuating the arms race. The Soviets are no more likely to negotiate from a position of inferiority than we are. In order to cut nuclear arsenals, it is essential that both sides believe that there is parity or relative equality. If one side builds a new system and obtains an advantage, the other side will respond with a countermove. The only meaningful time to negotiate about new nuclear systems is *before* they have been deployed, not after.

The Soviet Union has been on record for several years as espousing deep cuts so long as they are based on the principle of equality and undiminished security. In a memorandum to the United Nations General Assembly in 1976, Soviet Foreign Minister Gromyko said:

> The arms race in the nuclear age is fraught with a far more serious threat to the life of the peoples than at any time in the past. . . . One modern nuclear warhead has a destructive power exceeding that of all explosives used by the states in the Second World War. . . . In a situation in which nuclear weapons pose the greatest danger to mankind, complete nuclear disarmament becomes the most important measure. . . . The first thing necessary for this purpose is to stop the arms race, that is, to stop manufacturing nuclear weapons, equipping the armed forces of States with them, developing new models and types of such weapons. At the same time, or immediately after that, reductions in the stockpiles of nuclear weapons should commence, with the transfer of nuclear materials thus released to peaceful sectors of the economy. The ultimate goal of the reduction should be the complete elimination of all types of nuclear weapons— strategic and tactical, offensive and defensive. Along with the reduction of stockpiles of nuclear charges, warheads and bombs, there should be a reduction of their means of delivery.[6]

When Jimmy Carter and Leonid Brezhnev signed the SALT II treaty in Vienna on June 18, 1979, it included a "Joint Statement of Principles and Basic Guidelines for Subsequent Negotiations on the Limitation of Strategic Arms." The guidelines set forth among others, the following two objectives:

1. Significant and substantial reductions in the numbers of strategic offensive arms.

2. Qualitative limitations on strategic offensive arms, including restrictions on the development, testing, and deployment of new types of strategic offensive arms and on modernization of existing strategic offensive arms.

Clearly the Soviets are prepared to negotiate not only deep cuts in numbers of strategic nuclear weapons but also controls over new types of nuclear weapons and improvements in existing systems.

At the sixty-third anniversary of the Soviet Revolution, November 6, 1981, Nikolai Tikhonov, chairman of the Council of Ministers of the USSR, said: "We believe that there are no international problems that could not be solved through negotiations with reasonable consideration of mutual interests. The Soviet Union is prepared to reach an understanding on the reduction or ban of any weapon, above all, nuclear, and on the prevention of the manufacture of new types and systems of weapons of mass annihilation."[7]

U.S. public opinion has been seriously misinformed about Soviet intentions. The public thinks that the Soviet Union believes that limited nuclear wars are feasible and winnable. It thinks that the Soviets rejected a genuine offer to negotiate deep cuts in nuclear weapons in March 1977. It thinks that the Soviet Union has no intention of restraining its military buildup, especially its strategic expansion, until it has achieved significant superiority over the United States. Therefore, the U.S. public supports a giant increase in our defense budget to build the necessary weapons and forces to counter growing Soviet power.

As demonstrated in the previous chapters, the Soviet threat has been exaggerated and misinterpreted, especially with respect to Soviet military intentions. However, very real Soviet military aggression in the Third World has made it possible to present a persuasive case that the Soviets intend to use their growing military power for expansionism and, if confronted, it is claimed, to fight and win a nuclear war. This perception would be reversed by the successful negotiation of a military nonintervention pact. But while the nonintervention pact is being negotiated, a nuclear reduction treaty should also be negotiated simultaneously, on a separate track.

President Reagan says he wants to call the next round of talks START (strategic arms reduction talks) instead of SALT (strategic arms limitation talks). Unfortunately all the evidence, on the basis of Reagan administration decisions so far, indicates that START is a cosmetic maneuver. Instead of planning to reduce strategic arms, the administration has announced decisions to continue the arms race and to build several different strategic counterforce weapons.

The main barrier to strategic arms control has been the American hawks, who oppose the concept of nuclear equality. Until recently the United States has maintained nuclear superiority. The American hawks want to restore that superiority, but that is an unrealistic and very dangerous course. The sane approach would be to negotiate a treaty which would reduce and control nuclear weapons systems to a point where neither power threatened the survival of the other, where neither side could gain any conceivable advantage by striking first in a surprise attack.

The Soviets are eager to reach such an agreement so long as it is based on the principle of parity or equality. The painstaking negotiations expended on SALT I and SALT II, over a period of ten years, have established the facts. Though the technology—the size and numbers of launchers and warheads in the two nuclear arsenals—is very different, both sides agreed that their forces are essentially equal. The thoroughness with which the issues were covered during previous negotiations should facilitate the next round. In fact, if the two sides are committed to reaching an agreement on deep cuts, they should be able to reach settlement on a treaty in not more than two years.

There should be four priority goals in the next round of negotiation: (1) to eliminate the threat of counterforce; (2) to cut the number of launchers and warheads to a level which preserves nuclear deterrence but reduces the danger of accidental or unintentional nuclear war; (3) to freeze nuclear systems at an agreed level and ban the development, testing, or deployment of any new nuclear weapons; and (4) to authorize only those weapons systems that can be verified by existing means of intelligence.

How could these goals be achieved? Counterforce weapons are the most dangerous because they are powerful and accurate enough to destroy some of the other side's nuclear weapons and command and control systems. They are dangerous because they can cause the opponent to adopt a policy of launch on warning to use his weapons before they are destroyed. This is called "use 'em or lose 'em." Launch on warning substantially increases the risk of accidental or unintended launch. The systems which are most vulnerable to counterforce today are the land-based ballistic missiles (ICBM's), the command and control systems (both human and electronic), and bombers which can't get into the air in time or submarines that are caught at their bases.

Today the Soviet counterforce weapons that have been deployed are the SS-18's and SS-19's. These large missiles carry enough warheads with sufficient accuracy and explosive power to destroy U.S. land-based missiles in their hardened silos. Theoretically, when the Soviets had deployed enough of these warheads, they would be capable of destroying the entire U.S. ICBM force, if the U.S. missiles were not launched on warning. This is the so-called window of vulnerability, which may exist by 1983 or 1984 if not checked by arms control negotiation.

The United States has been adding Mark 12A warheads to its Minuteman III missiles, which have sufficient weight and accuracy to be used as counterforce weapons. In addition, it intends to deploy Pershing II ballistic missiles in Germany by early 1984. These are counterforce weapons. Other counterforce weapons planned for the U.S. arsenal are the MX missile, scheduled for deployment between 1986 and 1988, and the Trident II sub-launched missile, which should be available by 1990.

The best way to deal with the counterforce threat on both sides is to eliminate it. In the March proposals of 1977 the U.S. Joint Chiefs of Staff estimated that the Soviet counterforce threat could be contained if the Soviets would agree to limit their ICBM force with multiple warheads (MIRVs) to 550 (this is the number of MIRV'd Minuteman III's which the United States has deployed). The Soviets were also asked to limit their SS-18's to 150 because the SS-18 carries ten warheads. In order really to diminish the threat of Soviet counterforce, it probably would be desirable to cut the Soviet ICBM force with multiple warheads to 350 and the number of SS-18's to 100. Since 75 percent of the Soviet strategic force is in ICBMs, this would be quite a concession.

Only 25 percent of the U.S. strategic force is made up of ICBMs, so in order to match the Soviet concession, the United States would have to make cuts where it has the advantage—in bombers armed with air-launched cruise missiles and in strategic submarines carrying MIRV'd missiles. The Soviets have more strategic submarines than the United States, but because their MIRV technology has lagged, they have only a fraction of the sub-launched warheads possessed by the United States. What this formula would accomplish would be not only a curbing of the counterforce threat but also a substantial reduction in the strategic nuclear arsenals of both sides. A 350 limit on ICBMs with MIRVs would mean that the United States would cut its Minuteman III force with Mark 12A warheads by 200. It would also cut its strategic submarine force and its strategic bomber force carrying air-launched cruise missiles in some mix which would provide a total of warheads for the United States equal to the total of Soviet warheads.

When the agreed total was set, both sides would freeze their forces at that figure, with a ban on the development, testing, or deployment of any new nuclear weapons. This would mean that the Soviets would not deploy their next round of nuclear weapons and the United States would discontinue the MX missile, the Trident II missile, the Pershing II, and the ground-launched cruise missiles scheduled for Europe. Even with those cuts, both sides would have more than ample deterrent forces, but the threat of war fighting and counterforce would have been removed.

There are two approaches to the problem of obsolescence. The best would be to retire the weapons on an equal basis when they become obsolete. For example, when the fifty-four

Titan II missiles became obsolete, as will soon be the case, they would not be replaced. The Soviets would retire an equal number of missiles at the same time—for example, SS-11's. Both the Titan II and the SS-11 are un-MIRV'd missiles. If this approach were pursued by careful negotiation and maintained through the years, by 2020 the strategic nuclear forces of both sides would have been virtually eliminated by attrition and obsolescence. If this approach is not acceptable, another method would be to replace existing weapons, upon obsolescence, by similar or identical weapons. In any case, there should not be modernization with new types of weapons.

Speaking of modernization leads to the very thorny problem of the SS-20's, the Soviet replacement for the medium-range SS-4's and SS-5's. There are approximately 250 deployed, about a third facing China and the rest aimed at targets in Western Europe. The SS-20's are mobile, carrying three MIRV'd warheads. Their mobility poses a problem for adequate verification. A possible solution would be for the Soviets to dismantle all their SS-20's located in the Ural Mountains, both east and west. In return the United States would not deploy the 572 missiles slated for Europe and would withdraw the Poseidon submarines assigned to NATO, which carry 450 warheads.

This would leave the Soviets with some aging, single-shot SS-4's and SS-5's, some fighter-bombers capable of carrying nuclear weapons, and the growing, modern Backfire bomber fleet. The United States would continue to have the FB-111's based in England and fighter-bombers on aircraft carriers, both of which are capable of carrying nuclear bombs to Soviet targets. Also, the independent British and French nuclear forces would continue to have a limited capability of reaching Soviet targets. Ideally all these weapons systems should be reduced. However, they don't have sufficient importance to alter the U.S.-Soviet strategic balance. It would be fine if the British, French, and Chinese would join the talks, but the last two have so far shown stubborn resistance to including their nuclear forces in the negotiations.

The question of the SS-20's facing China is difficult, but if the Chinese continue to reject negotiation, the Soviets will insist on keeping them. Perhaps this should be accepted in return for the Soviets' dropping the issue of the separate French and British nuclear systems. If the entire negotiating package described in this chapter is carried to fruition and genuine détente becomes a reality, it is not inconceivable that before the end of the century NATO and the Soviet Union will agree to eliminate all nuclear weapons from Europe whether they be tactical, medium-range, or bomber-carried.

Another very important element in demonstrating the commitment of the superpowers to reverse the nuclear arms race would be the signing of a comprehensive nuclear test ban. The Soviets are prepared to sign such a treaty tomorrow. After years of haggling about adequacy of verification measures, an important breakthrough was made in 1978. The Soviet Union accepted, in principle, new procedures for verification proposed by the United States and Britain. Each of the three nations would agree to the construction on their territory of stations capable of monitoring seismic waves. Those data would be encrypted in such a way that they couldn't be tampered with and transmitted to the two other signatory countries. The Soviet Union also agreed to human on-site inspection in particular circumstances when the data transmitted by the seismic stations needed to be supplemented.[8]

The great advantage of a comprehensive test ban is that it provides conclusive evidence that both sides have decided to give up the nuclear arms race. What is the point of building expensive new nuclear weapons if you can't test them? How do you know whether they will work? The United States is blocking the comprehensive test ban treaty because it wants to build a whole series of new weapons systems and wants to test the nuclear warheads and neutron bombs. The best approach, though, is to negotiate deep cuts and controls, including the control of the comprehensive test ban.

There are many variations, of course, on what has been said here. Perhaps they should be tried so long as they accomplish the objectives of deep cuts and better security in a fairly short negotiating span. When he accepted the Einstein Peace Prize, George Kennan gave a moving speech dealing with the subject of survival. He proposed a 50 percent cut, across the board, of the nuclear arsenals of the two superpowers:

> a reduction affecting in equal measure all forms of the weapon, strategic, medium range, and tactical, as well as all means of their delivery—all this to be implemented at once without further wrangling among the experts, and to be subject to such national means of verification as now lie at the disposal of the two powers. . . . Whatever the precise results of such a reduction, there would still be plenty of overkill left—so much so that if the first operation were successful, I would like to see a second one put in hand to rid us of at least two-thirds of what would be left.[9]

After the speech Soviet Ambassador Dobrynin congratulated Kennan and said such a reduction would be possible if the two countries would talk. The sooner the better, he said. Kennan's proposal is appealing for its simplicity, especially the business about implementation "without further wrangling among the experts." Unfortunately the experts, probably experts on both sides, will destroy the meaning and the sanity of what Kennan says. The only way the Kennan proposal will be implemented would be by a summit meeting between Reagan and Brezhnev at which they both announced their intention of going ahead with a 50 percent reduction.

In 1980 Andrei Sakharov, the father of the Soviet hydrogen bomb and the greatest Soviet dissident, wrote a "Letter from Exile" to *The New York Times*. He said:

> Despite all that has happened, I feel that the questions of war and peace and disarmament are so crucial that they must be given absolute priority even in the most difficult circumstances. It is imperative that all possible means be used to solve these questions and to lay the groundwork for further progress. Most urgent of all are steps to avert a nuclear war, which is the greatest peril confronting the modern world.

Chapter VII

A Soviet Commentary

AUTHOR'S NOTE: Most of this chapter is written, at my invitation, by Georgy Arbatov, who is the leading expert in the Soviet Union on U.S. affairs. Mr. Arbatov is a member of the Central Committee of the Soviet Communist Party and is the director of the Institute of U.S. and Canadian Studies of the Academy of Sciences of the USSR. He is a personal adviser on U.S. affairs to President Leonid Brezhnev and appears frequently in the Communist Party paper Pravda *and on Soviet television, interpreting major policies of the United States. He has written several books and pamphlets about Soviet-American relations and has frequently lectured and appeared on television in the United States. The last part of this chapter presents the author's reply to Mr. Arbatov.*

The author of this book asked me to write a chapter containing a critique and an assessment of his analysis. I could not fail to accept. Fully aware of the modesty of my efforts, as well as of Mr. Cox's (I hope he will excuse me for these words), I still believe that now it would be inadmissible to forgo even the slightest opportunity to try to dispel the fog of misperceptions and illusions about the arms race and nuclear war, which are probably the most formidable challenges humanity has ever faced in the course of its history.

Arthur Cox has written a frightening book. It is especially frightening for the reason that it deals not with political ghosts, not with apocalyptic visions of an uncertain future, but with things utterly and unmistakably real. Quite properly he opens his book with a description of a false nuclear alarm that occurred in the United States recently. It was one of those alarms which make so frightfully real the haunting specter of an accidental war. This episode, as I have understood the idea of Mr. Cox, underscores the fact that even the present situation, if unchanged, is fraught with the threat of a nuclear holocaust. And if we have already become accustomed to living with the atom bomb, it is a bad and dangerous habit because even without a sinister intention on either side it all may someday end with a big bang.

I tend to share these ideas of the author. I also agree with his warning that present trends in the arms race, in strategic thinking and policies, tend to make, as they develop, a nuclear war not only possible but probable and, under certain circumstances, even inevitable. It all depends on how much time is going to be wasted. Arthur Cox is undoubtedly right in reminding us again and again that we still have a chance to avoid the threat.

I would not add much to the reasons he is citing in favor of prompt and resolute actions to curb the arms race, reverse it, and get back to détente. I think he is absolutely right in pointing out the danger of a self-starting nuclear fire inherent in the very existence of the accumulated stockpiles of arms, not to mention those yet to be produced. It is all the more so, considering the present state of certain minds—I mean, some fashionable trends in strategic thinking in the United States and some other countries, for instance, the notion of a winnable nuclear war and the limited nuclear war concept. And these are not just ideas, for they are supported with new weapons systems (or is it vice versa, and the ideas are put forward to justify the systems?).

I could say much more. I don't think that the fact that we have been able to survive the first thirty-five years of the nuclear era should give us grounds for great optimism. I think our survival has been due to sheer luck no less than to good statesmanship, a luck which one must never stretch too far. Moreover, this sheer luck and even statesmanship will be less reliable in the future, since the introduction of new destabilizing weapons systems will complicate matters even further. The situation will get worse also owing to the appearance of more actors in international relations (and in international conflicts), including nuclear actors because the present state of affairs, if unchanged, will make nuclear proliferation inevitable. This will aggravate matters further because quite a few of these new nuclear actors, for various reasons, may not have an adequate sense of responsibility and/or an understanding of the complexity of the world situation (yes, I have China in mind, but not only China). Under these circumstances it will be even more difficult to ward off conflicts and crises in the future or manage them once they have started.

We should also keep in mind that the world is facing growing difficulties with natural resources. This alone could be a powerful incentive for détente and greater cooperation which could provide for more prudent utilization of, and even help us increase, the earth's riches. But given the present mood in Washington and some other NATO capitals, the resources problem can prompt adventures of the classical imperialist and colonial type on their part. This trend is increasingly apparent in the U.S. policies, specifically in the American efforts to expand NATO's functions under the pretext of having to guard access to resources.

One more point comes to mind. The future with respect to chances of avoiding a nuclear war looks much less promising to me personally when I contemplate the recent political transformations in the U.S.A. They have confirmed me, a student of America for many years, in the belief that some of American political ways, modes of thinking, and traditions may make the prospects of civilization's survival in the nuclear era look very fragile indeed.

I have in mind the recent turn in American politics which was more than a turn toward conservatism (or neoconservatism, for that matter) or toward assuming a tough posture. Considering the shape and scale of the shift, it looks as if the most extremist views have triumphed among American policy makers, and attempts are made to formulate on the basis of those views and enforce, regardless of all realities of our time, the most extremist policies. It is hard for me to believe that this will last long (especially when one considers the intellectual level and degree of experience of many of those now elevated to the positions of power in Washington), but while it does last, it may cause a lot of trouble to the whole world, America included. Frankly speaking, I was somewhat surprised at the ease with which the U.S. political mechanism allowed all this to happen. It had been assumed that this mechanism tends to frustrate political extremism and encourage more or less middle-of-the-road tendencies.

I think I know what kind of response I should expect from the author. Actually he has already given it in the second chapter: The Soviet Union is to blame for this—specifically, its "involvement, either indirect or direct, in intervention with external combat forces in Angola, Ethiopia, South Yemen, and Afghanistan, combined with continuing support for the Vietnamese invasion of Cambodia." It was this, writes Arthur Cox, that "insured the political victory of cold warriors and confrontationists in the United States." To prove his point, as the reader will recall, he indulges in near mysticism, a kind of political spiritualism which Kremlinological antics always remind me of. In arguing with Mr. Cox, I will put this part aside, since nothing mysterious or supernatural has happened in the Kremlin in recent years. These years are rather characterized by a "business as usual" approach.

I would not like to dwell too much on the author's interpretation of specific events that took place in the countries he is citing. But let me make a few observations.

Speaking of Angola, it is a fact of life that Cuban troops and Soviet military supplies began pouring not into a vacuum, not into a serene country, but into an Angola torn by strife, victimized by the interference of Portuguese mercenaries and South African troops, of the CIA, of Peking, which was supporting its clients in Angola with money, advisers, and arms. And Ethiopia? The need to help it with foreign troops and supplies would have never arisen had it not been attacked by Somalia, which claimed the Ethiopian province of Ogaden. But could Somalia have started the war, if it had not been led (or misled) to expect help from the United States and some other countries? And this encouragement of Somali claims was in its turn motivated by the intention to deprive the Soviet Union of an access to Berbera and other Somali ports in the Indian Ocean.

I have even more to say about Afghanistan, where an undeclared war instigated from abroad started long before the arrival of the Soviet military contingent. I could discuss Cambodia, too.* But a detailed discussion of all those events would go far beyond the bounds of one chapter. All I wanted to do at this place was inform the American reader that we have our own viewpoint, as well as grounds to blame the United States for much of the difficulties the world is facing.

We could have a protracted argument with Arthur Cox on who was right and who was wrong in Angola, Ethiopia, or Afghanistan. But I think we can approach the problem in a broader context. What would have happened if the Soviet Union and its friends had behaved differently in each of the cases cited by Mr. Cox? What if we had not heeded the MPLA's request and let the CIA, Peking, and South Africa install there a regime to their own liking? Or if we had allowed the dismemberment or, perhaps, even liquidation of Ethiopia, the oldest independent state in Africa? What if we had permitted, for the first time in many decades, a regime in Afghanistan that would have been hostile to the USSR and that, acting on orders from Washington and Peking, would have turned that country into still another outpost of anti-Soviet activities? Would all that have helped détente or not?

If we are to follow the author's logic, détente would have benefited. Yet I am convinced that it would have been only damaged since the appetites of those who favor applying constant pressures on the USSR would have been whetted. Mr.

*The position of the United States and of the West on Cambodia strike me as the top of hypocrisy and the double standard. Two very similar events happened almost simultaneously: Ruthless, bloodthirsty dictators were overthrown and ousted from their countries as a result of combined efforts by domestic opposition groups (based partially inside the country, partially in emigration) and the troops of a neighbor country. I mean Pol Pot of Cambodia and Idi Amin of Uganda. Amin's overthrow was loudly applauded in the West, while the deposed Pol Pot, whom Washington itself had labeled the worst violator of human rights in the world while he had been in power, was immediately taken under Western protection, his sins forgotten, and Vietnam received punishment for helping Cambodia throw him out.

Cox himself talks of the sobering effect the American defeat in Vietnam had on Washington. Why does he believe, then, that easy victories in Angola, the Horn of Africa, and Southwest Asia would not have had the opposite effect? The hawks follow their own logic. Having gained quite a few commanding heights in Washington, they are placing great emphasis on Soviet "weak spots," which, as their line of thinking goes, make it imperative for the United States to step up pressure on the Soviet Union in expectation that it will eventually give in. "This is no time to capitulate to the Soviet Union, which is now facing very serious trouble," says Eugene Rostow, the Arms Control and Disarmament Agency director. What is meant by "capitulation" here is a U.S. consent to deal with the Soviet Union on an equal basis. Talk about "serious trouble" facing my country is what we have heard since 1917, and many times it has turned out to be a dangerous self-deception of the West. But let us even skip over this item and try to understand the implications of his statement. Its meaning is that the United States in its turn would agree to détente only under pressure. If there is no such pressure, then the United States will pursue the policies of escalating tensions and continuing the arms race.

Citing one of my articles, the author charges me with a failure to realize that the majority of Americans regard the "Soviet adventures" in the Third World to be "the very essence of cold war behavior—the opposite of détente and relaxation of tensions."

I cannot claim that I always understand Americans correctly. This is a tremendously difficult job indeed. I would not argue about perceptions either. All I can say is that perceptions do not form by themselves but very often are to a great degree molded by powerful and skillful manipulators. And not always do they reflect eternal truth and wisdom (after all, for millennia people believed that the sun rotated around the earth). But Mr. Cox is right in one respect, although in a different way—all the cases he cites have to do with the cold war, its heritage, vestiges, and philosophy.

I think it is an obvious fact that a certain political background and certain political frame of thinking led to the use of military force, exacerbating a conflict and "spilling it over" the national frontiers. According to this frame of thinking, causes and effects of any event should be viewed from a perspective of global military confrontation between the USSR and the United States, East and West. And this indeed is the very essence of the cold war approach, and it is absolutely contrary to détente and relaxation of tensions.

Mr. Cox has not seen fit to reproduce some other arguments often used in the West to explain the deterioration in East-West relations in recent years. And judging by what he says in his book, it was not the result of a simple omission. He obviously does not share the view, now so widespread in Washington, that the alleged Soviet military "superiority" changed the military balance in such a way that the West became vulnerable to the "Soviet threat." On the contrary, the author has made a lot of what I think are sound and realistic points with regard to the military balance.

I would like to say just one thing in this connection. Fantastic allegations about the "Soviet military buildup" and "military superiority" apparently constitute the biggest and most dangerous lie of our time. It is the biggest lie not only because it is often based on exaggerations, false figures, and pure concoctions but also because it ignores some major politicogeographic realities, the most important of them being the fact that the Soviet Union under present circumstances has to regard as its potential adversaries not only the United States but also the NATO allies of the United States, Japan, and China.

As soon as one includes this factor in the equation, the picture becomes radically different. Even those Americans who are endowed with the most fertile imagination in this field prove incapable, however hard they try, to ascribe to us a military budget, or a force strength, or weapons arsenals that would go beyond what our potential adversaries have, taken together. Here are a couple of examples.

According to the annual publication of the International Institute of Strategic Studies in London, *The Military Balance 1981–82*—which, by the way, incredibly overrates our defense spending—the ratio of the Warsaw Treaty Organization and the NATO budgets is 1:1.5 in favor of NATO ($164.7 billion to $241 billion, correspondingly). If one brings Japan and China into the picture, the correlation will be at least 1:2. Similar gaps in the numbers of troops, nuclear warheads, and naval vessels are even bigger.

But the lie about the Soviet "military superiority" and "military threat" is not just the biggest but also the most dangerous lie of our time. It is the most dangerous, for at present it is virtually the only rationale for the arms race. This lie is also dangerous because it poisons the political atmosphere and sows fears, hostility, and distrust among Americans and Westerners in general toward the Soviet Union—as well as distrust among our people toward the United States and the West, for they know in Moscow that they know in Washington just what the real situation is. Thus, since this real situation is so rudely and persistently distorted, the motives can be only sinister. Is it not logical to assume so?

But all these are precisely the *intended* results of the "Soviet threat" campaign. Its instigators are well aware of the real situation, and it does not suit them not because the Soviet Union is on the edge of becoming the dominating military force in today's world, but because the United States has lost its own former status of dominance and because it desperately wants to restore it.

So the increase of tensions, the undermining of détente, and the regression back to cold war were in my opinion not caused by the events Arthur Cox mentions. Quite the opposite is the case. History cannot be "replayed," of course. But I am strongly convinced that if détente had been given a real chance, if it had been pursued more vigorously, if we had been more persistent in overcoming the remnants of the cold war, we might have succeeded in avoiding its resurgence. Many events of the last five to six years might have taken a different shape. Some crises would have not taken place at all; others could have been managed by political means. This refers to Angola, Ethiopia, Afghanistan, and Cambodia. This refers to other crisis situations which Mr. Cox does not mention but which may yet flare up and cause serious conflicts.

A Soviet Commentary

The Middle East and the Persian Gulf, South Africa, and Central America are regions where possibilities of such developments can't be excluded.

I have one more objection to Mr. Cox's premise that the events in the above-mentioned countries are the cause of the sharp exacerbation of tensions in the world and of the increased danger of nuclear war.

I do not wish to minimize the importance of each of those events, even less their cumulative effect. But no matter how these events are interpreted, they do not relieve a great power possessing an enormous might of the responsibility to work for the prevention of nuclear holocaust.

I am not saying this because I intend to throw the ball over to the other side and respond to a charge with a counter-charge. I think what is involved here is much more serious: how the powers bearing the main burden of keeping peace view various events and how they behave in the world arena.

To prevent a nuclear war, to safeguard civilization are a formidable task, indeed. It involves much more than a lack of a desire to start war. It takes an active posture and energetic efforts to build a lasting structure of peace. To have this kind of peace, it is necessary to restructure in a fundamental way the existing system of international relations. This restructuring would involve ending the arms race, establishing an atmosphere of trust, expanding the dialogue, and promoting just and mutually beneficial cooperation around the world. The most difficult aspect of this undertaking is that we must start solving these problems without delay and try to solve them simultaneously. We should work on them right now, under the present circumstances, despite the continuing arguments and misunderstandings, when one side does not like quite a few things the other side is doing. It would be utterly senseless to wait for an aseptic, sterile situation, for some ideal conditions. These would not come by themselves, and when they are established, no further pleas for peace and understanding will be necessary. That's why I reject as groundless any attempt to explain, much less to justify, dangerous behavior of either of the two states, no matter what extraneous events are used to rationalize such behavior. To see the cause of irresponsible policies of a great power in somebody who irritates or displeases it means to justify irresponsibility.

According to the official American explanations of its new-found "hard line," the United States was provoked to adopt it. But if the Soviet Union had followed a similar approach, it would have had many more reasons to be provoked to take a cold war path. Does not the U.S. military and political collusion with China, which involves augmenting the Chinese war machine and cooperation in intelligence gathering, pose a greater danger to Soviet security than Angola, Cambodia, or Afghanistan to the security of the United States? I could draw up a whole list of our claims to America: Egypt, the torpedoing of the 1977 joint declaration on the Middle East. And Chile. And the foiling of the SALT II treaty, of course. And the American failure to carry out the terms of the trade agreement signed by our two governments. I could go further, but the point is that the Soviet Union has not considered them all sufficient ground for renouncing the policy of détente, dropping our intention to normalize relations with the United States, to attempt to end the arms race.

We may recall, incidentally, that détente was not initiated in exceptionally favorable circumstances: The Vietnam War was raging; half a million GIs were fighting in Indochina, while we were aiding Vietnam. And—let's not shut our eyes to that—many an American boy was killed with Soviet weapons. And some Soviet boys were killed by American bombs in Hanoi and Haiphong, including those days in May 1972, when the United States resumed the bombing of North Vietnam and mined its ports on the eve of the first Soviet-American summit meeting.

Were we and Americans right in starting negotiations in that tense and strained atmosphere, in not forgoing the summit? Looking back, one can state with certainty, yes, we both were right, in spite of the fact that both sides (and, if it comes to that, especially we) had ample reason to indulge in biblical wrath and cancel the dialogue.

No, real responsibility for the current deterioration of the world situation lies not with the Soviet Union, which allegedly provoked some influential Americans to get tough,

A Soviet Commentary

but with those influential Americans who simply longed to be provoked and were desperately searching for a pretext. This book confirms it to an extent—the author devotes considerable space to the activities of those powerful forces in the United States which from the very beginning wanted to put an end to détente, to frustrate the initiated process of arms limitation, and to return to the policies of confrontation. Mr. Cox provides an interesting, detailed, and expert analysis of the activities of these forces. And those pages of the book leave an impression of something akin to an organized conspiracy against détente, disarmament, and peace. This is precisely why I was surprised to see Arthur Cox somehow relieving them of their blame and criticizing instead the Soviet Union, concentrating on events in Angola, Ethiopia, Afghanistan, and Cambodia.

I am anticipating the author's reaction. He may say (and, probably, will) that when talking about the events in these countries, he meant their effect not on the American hawks but on the American public, the voters who voted into offices the proponents of the arms race and confrontation.

Well, if Arthur Cox meant to say that all those events were resourcefully and aptly manipulated by the opponents of détente to deceive and brainwash the public, whip up the hysteria and chauvinism, it would be perfectly all right with me.* This is true beyond any doubt. And many other events were manipulated exactly along the same lines: the American hostages' ordeal in Iran; almost all Soviet defense programs; declarations by the so-called dissidents and the visa problems. And quite often propaganda campaigns of this kind were generated without a semblance of a real event to back them up; the book tells us, for instance, how the "missile gap" myth was created in the late fifties and early sixties.

This is the heart of the matter. History shows us that campaigns will be started irrespective of the Soviet "behavior" (I should not be understood to believe that against this background the USSR may do whatever it pleases). We will not

*I would just like to add that the outcome of the 1980 election was strongly influenced also by the condition of the economy and by the domestic situation in general.

satisfy the hawks, the extreme right, no matter what we do, short of one thing—if we ceased to exist, disappeared as a society from the face of the earth (hints of this kind are rather transparent in some of the pronouncements of several high-positioned officials of the administration, e.g., Richard Pipes).

This does not surprise me and my colleagues. Ever since the Russian Revolution of 1917 we in the Soviet Union have become accustomed to unabated hatred and to unwillingness to accept our existence as a fact of life and, moreover, to recognize our right to be the way we are. What worries me is something else. Up until now this kind of attitude, much compromised, rejected by history, has not been discarded by some American politicians who are still able, despite the numerous lessons of history, to deceive so many Americans—among other things, on cardinal issues of vital importance to their own survival as a nation.

Yes, adequate, correct perceptions of the Soviet Union, of its goals and intentions, and of its role in the world are of vital importance for the survival of the United States, as well as the question of what kind of policy toward the USSR suits the United States national interests best. For a time highly placed Americans tried to deny it, placing Soviet-American relations rather low on their list of political priorities. One might think that the present American leaders proceed in their foreign policy from other, more realistic assumptions, for have they not put the East-West axis at the center of their world view? Well, they indeed have. But in a peculiar form—a form of the "Soviet threat" or, as more respectable Americans put it, the "Soviet challenge," which is again declared to be the number one problem in U.S. foreign policy.

But does that reflect an understanding by the administration of the importance of Soviet-American relations for the United States? Most emphatically not, for Washington—as of now—is attempting to gain not from improvement of these relations but from undermining them single-mindedly and ostentatiously. The American leadership is apparently trying to generate the energy which the U.S. foreign policy is lacking in Europe, Middle East, Asia, Africa, Latin America by means of heightening tensions between the two largest world powers.

A Soviet Commentary

A new anti-Soviet crusade not only will fail to promote American interests but will expose them to greater dangers than ever before. America not only will fail to make new friends along this road but will make more adversaries among those who live better and breathe more freely in a multipolar world without wars than in the atmosphere of crusades. Along this road America, plunging into the abyss of an unbridled arms race, not only will fail to strengthen its economy but may ruin it. Above all, is it too difficult to imagine what all this may lead to if the United States, one of the two major nuclear powers in the world, conducts its relations with the other power in the manner of a trigger-happy cowboy from a western movie?

With this I would like to conclude my comments on the causes of the complex and dangerous world situation that has emerged. I am not so self-assured to believe that this shuts off the argument on this question. The argument will go on, no doubt. But is it not better to leave it to historians and move on to a more pressing question: What is to be done next? What can we do to avoid the mortal threat hanging over us all—to prevent a nuclear war, stop the arms race, revive the process of building a healthy, good-neighborly relationship between the United States and the USSR and stabilize the international system?

An obvious accomplishment of Mr. Cox's book is that it deals with this question extensively. His main suggestions fill a whole chapter titled "A Proposal for a Negotiated Solution."

This chapter contains a few points I utterly disagree with, particularly the one I have dealt with above—the author's view of the causes of international tension and intensification of the arms race. Some passing remarks on the Soviet attitudes toward nuclear war, peaceful coexistence, and proletarian internationalism or on Lenin's concept of the relation between war and policy, attest to Arthur Cox's insufficiently deep knowledge of these issues. Sometimes he repeats hearsay and others' misjudgments.

But I would rather not overload my discussion of the author's ideas with critical statements. I certainly agree with him on the main thing: We need a broad, far-reaching agreement between the United States and the USSR on a diverse spectrum of international problems, on arms limitation issues in particular. We need to take measures to improve radically relations between our two countries because the present situation is fraught with the danger of a catastrophe, a threat to the very existence of our two countries and all humanity.

I would say more: These ideas of Mr. Cox are shared not only by myself personally. If they were to be embodied in U.S. foreign policy, they would find an active favorable response in the Soviet Union and, I am sure, would open the way to far-reaching agreements. And this is more than a mere supposition. I am making this conclusion on the basis of the foreign policy platform worked out by the Twenty-sixth Congress of the Communist Party of the Soviet Union and of a whole series of new proposals put forward by Leonid Brezhnev in his recent speeches.

I could agree to many other specific statements by Mr. Cox, for instance, his view that "in order to survive, both sides will have to acknowledge the reality that neither side can any longer assert its national will through military coercion of the other."* Or his statement "There can never again be military superiority of one superpower over the other." And—most important—when he postulates "If we are to survive, we must return to the negotiating table."

I would add: And the more problems, mutual disagreements, and dissatisfactions we have, the more expedient we should be in pursuing such a course. But we should be doing this fully recognizing that we are embarking on a very difficult trail.

An effort to provide for security and survival through rearmament is a much simpler undertaking. Nothing is simpler than to adopt the posture of a 100 percent tough patriot who hates the enemy so much he won't even talk to him. What you

---

*And this does not contradict any of Lenin's statements. He referred several times to Clausewitz's notion that war is a continuation of political relations by other means. But the idea expressed alongside was one and the same: that the character and causes of war should not be mystified, that they stem from the policies causing a particular war. If a policy was imperialist, such would be a war (he meant, specifically, World War I). An attempt to use such quotes to ascribe a militaristic outlook to Lenin is distortion and a fraud.

do is just pour more millions of dollars into the military budget and adopt new arms programs.

This logic is invitingly simple. But life repudiated it a long time ago. The trouble with it is that led by this logic, you are bound to perpetuate the arms race and in this way undermine your own security. Just as futile are attempts to reach exclusively by a military buildup a "safe" and "just" balance of military power. You should not forget that the other side does its own accounting—and in its own way, not yours—and estimates you and your intentions, the correlation of forces, and your military buildup. And it will be acting to regain parity on the basis of its own calculations and estimates. This is how the mechanism of the arms race works.

It is along this road that the world has been seeking security in vain for centuries. This road has become especially dangerous in a nuclear era.

It is dangerous even if the efforts allegedly aimed at "parity through arms buildup" are not motivated by an intention to seek superiority. If we are to speak of what is going on now, the situation resulting from U.S. policy looks, I am sorry to say, different.

That's why there is no alternative to negotiations, even though this is a difficult road, requiring fresh approaches to many old problems, enormous patience, wisdom, self-discipline, and a keen sense of responsibility.

Being a realist, I certainly would not argue that one can so easily, on one nice morning, throw away all armaments, and forget about armies, weapons, and defense. But realism based on past experience, particularly the experience of a nuclear era, tells that efforts to seek security exclusively through building up armies and weaponry are no less utopian.

It is, of course, encouraging to see that Arthur Cox is just one of many people who have come to recognize this truth, that it looks now even as if the Reagan administration is coming to recognize it, at least rhetorically. Time will tell how serious and constructive are Washington's intentions to seek negotiation of an arms control (more than that, arms reduction) agreement.

But let me get back to Arthur Cox's suggestions. He believes that one should work on two agreements simultaneously. One is political ("ground rules for the inevitable competition" between the two countries) including "issues of interventionism." The other is military (limitation and reduction of arms—i.e., "measures for reducing the dangers of nuclear war").

I do not see why such negotiations and agreements should be impossible or undesirable. But I would like to make a few observations on the practical aspect of this idea.

Why the author puts negotiations and agreements on political issues first is absolutely clear. This stems directly from his understanding of the causes of the turn from détente toward a cold war. And although I utterly disagree with Mr. Cox on the latter issue, the dialogue itself on the principles of relations, on approaches to the central issues of foreign policy, would be desirable in my opinion (and if this dialogue were to produce a new agreement, so much the better).

It would be desirable because the existing agreements and documents might be (as the author says) not specific enough. What is troublesome, from our viewpoint, is that the Reagan administration, as did the Carter administration earlier, adopted a very ambiguous stand with regard to these documents. I am, for one, not certain whether the administration considers them* binding documents or not.

I am not going to raise anew the issue of succession in the United States, even though the situation in this regard in the United States is thoroughly bad, making negotiations and even overall relations with the United States ever more difficult. But I would like to say that it might be useful to get a clear picture of what the new U.S. leadership actually considers to be the foundation of its relations with the Soviet Union in terms of principles, agreements, and accepted rules of conduct.

Mr. Cox says the political negotiations will be the most difficult. I don't think this is true, for negotiations on disarma-

---

*I have in mind not only the expired or nonratified SALT agreement, but also such documents as the "Basic Principles of Relations Between the USSR and the USA," the agreement on prevention of nuclear war, and the Helsinki Final Act (with all its four baskets, of course).

ment will be, if anything, no easier. But I can't fail to take up more extensively the question of my attitude toward the ideas the author puts forward in support of his thesis.

In his opinion, the basic differences in the doctrines are the main thing preventing a common understanding of the "rules of the competition." More specifically, he means the interpretation of the principle of peaceful coexistence of countries with different social systems. Still more specifically, Mr. Cox is implying that there is a contradiction between the principle of peaceful coexistence, on the one hand, and the principle of proletarian internationalism, on the other.

The author's arguments in this regard—may he forgive me for saying that—sound rather scholastic. And the quotations he cites from the Soviet sources prove nothing apart from the fact that the Soviet Union recognizes and highly values both these principles.

But all arguments advanced by Mr. Cox lack one essential element: He does not address the question of what forms of assistance to national liberation movements abroad are justifiable, according to our political theory—or doctrine, as the author calls it. The heart of the matter is that the Marxist-Leninist theory rejects the idea of "exporting revolutions"—i.e., promoting them through military intervention. And this is not just theory because this problem has on a number of occasions been in the focus of ideological and political struggle among Communists. As a result of those struggles, the views of Trotskyites, the ultraleftists who advocated "revolutionary wars," were repudiated.

By the same token, we oppose the "export of counterrevolution"—i.e., attempts to do away with social and national liberation movements with the help of military interventions from abroad. It is quite appropriate to mention this because in practically all cases cited by Mr. Cox such attempts at intervention did take place, prompting us, along with a number of other socialist states, to provide assistance to respective movements and governments.

I am saying this to dispel the author's apprehension about possible problems to be encountered if we are to try to reach agreement on the main political issues because this would demand of the Soviet Union a repudiation of "its doctrinal position which insists on a distinction between superpower peaceful coexistence and Third World military interventionism." No, renouncing military interventions in other countries or the use or threat of force in international relations in no way contradicts either the doctrine or the interests and political aims of the Soviet Union. But this renouncing should be shared by the United States and other powers. We have seen many instances of military meddling in the affairs of other countries by the United States, China, Israel, South Africa, France, and others. There should be no doubt, either, that the Soviet Union will support an agreement to liquidate military bases of all countries on foreign territories.

I believe that the author's attempt to limit the sphere of such an agreement to the Third World—especially considering his very peculiar definition of it—and the number of participants to the Soviet Union and the United States only weakens his proposal and renders its realization more problematic. And I don't think Mr. Cox should have ignored the importance for this agreement—or any other agreement for that matter—of bilateral Soviet-American relations and East-West relations in general, the importance of reinstating a normal, healthy political atmosphere. And here I have to get back to what seems to be my principal disagreement with Arthur Cox.

He believes that the aforementioned events in the Third World and the actions of the Soviet Union in connection with those events caused the sharp deterioration in Soviet-American relations and resulted in the undermining of détente. I don't agree with this assessment, for I see the causes of the changes in U.S. policies, in the activization of the opponents of détente in the U.S. and in some other countries. I also believe that many of those events would never have happened, had Soviet-American relations not deteriorated and had the arms limitation negotiations been more successful. I believe that in future, too, the state of Soviet-American relations and East-West relations will influence events in the Third World and especially international implications of these events and the general political climate around the world much more profoundly than the events in the Third World will affect the relations between the powers bearing the major responsibility for preventing the nuclear war.

Now, to the second proposal by Mr. Cox—his idea of parallel negotiations to reduce nuclear weapons. The Soviet Union is strongly devoted to such negotiations and agreements, provided they are based on the principles of equality and equal security. I can only side with him when he says that "the main barrier to strategic"—I would add, "and not only strategic but arms control in general"—"has been the American hawks, who oppose the concept of nuclear equality."

With regard to the "four priority goals" outlined by Mr. Cox—i.e., the most pressing issues to be negotiated, I think all of them to be important enough to deserve the closest attention at the talks. It is obvious, though, that these issues are viewed from an American perspective, and the proposed solutions are geared to American interests and concerns first and foremost, sometimes at the Soviet expense.

I am not sure if I have a right to reproach Mr. Cox for this. This kind of approach is likely to be only natural, since the American strategic community is very vocal and has imposed its frame of reference not only on American specialists but on some specialists outside the United States, even on unbiased analysts. The problem of counterforce capabilities might be illustrative in this regard.

I would like to touch upon just one aspect of that problem which has in my view not been adequately discussed. All the talk of counterforce capabilities and first-strike concepts has largely been based on a model created in the United States. According to this model, the ICBM is a weapon suitable for a counterforce strike or even a first strike, while the function of SLBMs (submarine-launched ballistic missiles) and bombers (or a portion of them) is to deal a second, retaliatory strike in response to the adversary's first strike.

It should be noted, however, that this model born in the 1960's was not so much a result of good and accurate calculations as a rationale, a justification (postdated to an extent) of the strategic forces built in the United States. In its details the model reflected the characteristics of the American geostrategic situation, as well as the outcomes of fierce infighting between the U.S. Army, Navy, and Air Force.

But it is hardly justifiable to accept this American model as an absolute truth. The USSR has a different history, a different geostrategic situation, different weapons systems and armed force structures. And if these natural differences exist, this does not mean that the USSR is betting on counterforce or planning a first strike. It can be argued plausibly that ICBMs do match SLBMs as a deterrent. Communications with them are more reliable; attacking them would mean attacking the adversary's territory and thus would be no different, or at least less different, from starting an all-out war (which can't escape the notice of the side planning a preventive strike). In case they ever become vulnerable, there is always a countermeasure: launch on warning and under attack. It can never be ruled out by the side planning a counterforce attack, which apparently serves to reinforce the deterrent. SLBMs and bombers can likewise be evaluated differently from the way Americans do it. If, for instance, a conflict starts as a conventional rather than a nuclear war, easier than to attack ICBMs would be an attempt to sink at the earliest stage as many submarines armed with strategic missiles as possible—especially when one considers that it could be done without nuclear strikes at the adversary's territory. Or what can prevent airplanes from taking off (as planned, by the way) and letting the adversary guess where they are—whether hiding from the attack or already deployed at the firing line for the launching of highly accurate cruise missiles? (In this scenario, I follow American, not Soviet, strategic concepts. We are against "first strike" and "limited nuclear war" doctrines, considering them not only morally wrong but also utterly false and utopian.)

In short, many false or dubious premises dominate American thinking on these issues, and American ideas on the subject can't be accepted on trust.

I would limit myself to these remarks on the problem of counterforce, leaving all discussions on specific numbers and systems to experts who would conduct negotiations.

The three other issues touched upon by Arthur Cox are

undoubtedly important and should become subjects of negotiations and agreements. But I think the list could be extended to include other, no less important problems. One of them would be: What shall we do with agreements negotiated within the SALT I and SALT II framework? Our point of view is that we should keep all their positive elements, all that remains essential should be preserved and legalized in some way. The dubious situation when these agreements seem to be there and at the same time not to be there should be cleared up.

I would introduce yet another very important issue. I mean an agreement on the prevention of the arms race in outer space. This would be easier to do now than tomorrow or the day after. And the problem is very grave indeed. If this genie is let out of the bottle, neither side will win, while everybody's loss would be enormous.

Mr. Cox's arguments about SS-20 are to a degree outdated. The respective negotiations are already under way, and some of the ideas discussed at those talks are, in my opinion, more realistic and at the same time radical.

I would like to conclude by returning to the political aspect. Each specific agreement, unquestionably, serves to improve the general climate, to make the political relations more stable and political attitudes more realistic, clear, and conducive to a firmer peace and to a more expended cooperation for mutual benefit.

But there is a reverse connection, too. Negotiations become a lot more difficult to hold, and agreements harder to arrive at, if there are prejudiced political attitudes, blind enmity, and unwillingness to search out ways to establish good, neighborly relations. The final period of the Carter administration and the early days of the Reagan administration saw the rise and, finally, the domination of such attitudes. In a nuclear era this begets additional dangers.

I think chauvinistic vindictiveness toward the world beyond the American borders can explain something in the policies and rhetoric of the present administration, including its feverish rearmament in pursuit of chimerical military superiority over the Soviet Union, its attitudes toward American allies, its hard line in the Third World, its pointed rejection of any opportunities to reduce tension, its attempts to create international crises out of situations which do not amount to such crises (one example is Poland), and its demonstrative belligerency in words and in some deeds. I wonder if they have thought of all the consequences of such a line in Washington. I assume that there are those who have not thought about it, that some American leaders assume that the hysteria they are fanning now can be turned on and off, depending on circumstances, like water in a faucet.

But serious policy making has its own laws, which differ from the laws of American electioneering, as well as from the practice of provincial business. One has to think of the consequences your actions may have in other countries, the policies and public moods of which one can't simply turn on or off. Things are not that simple in America either.

John Foster Dulles, who knew well all the ins and outs of American politics, wrote in 1939 in his book *War, Peace and Change:*

> In order to bring a nation to support the burdens incident to maintaining great military establishments, it is necessary to create an emotional state akin to war psychology. There must be the portrayal of an external menace. . . . This involves the development to a high degree of the nation-hero, nation-villain ideology and the arousing of the population to a sense of sacrifice. Once these conditions exist we have gone a long way on the path toward war. . . . The forces they heretofore set in motion in order to create armament, may compel its use.

Might not Washington's current military hysteria lead in the same direction?

I am raising this point because to reach the goals defined in this book, which are mankind's most important goals (prevention of nuclear holocaust, ending the arms race, strengthening détente), it is necessary to break with quite a few political attitudes to introduce many radical changes in foreign policy.

A Soviet Commentary

To the questions put forward by Arthur Cox, one cannot find easy answers. He himself is aware of it, stressing that the program he advances would require a lot of hard effort.

Yet, for the reasons I have given earlier, I believe that the program should be broadened, even if that would make it more difficult to carry out. There really are no easy answers to the questions confronting us. Nevertheless, the answers will have to be given—given by all of us together. We all have to search for those answers, particularly the United States and the USSR, which bear a special responsibility.

There is perhaps no city in our two countries, and in many other countries as well, that has not become a target for nuclear weapons. But even this does not seem enough, and the arms race is surging ahead. Can we continue to rely on sheer luck when the bets are on the physical existence of whole nations, the fate of whole continents?

Let us think of it, while there is still time.

MR. COX REPLIES TO MR. ARBATOV

The reader should be aware that there are several difficulties involved in conducting a dialogue between a high-ranking figure in the Communist Party of the Soviet Union and a private citizen of the United States. It is apparent that Mr. Arbatov does not present any criticism of his government or his party, while I engage in vigorous criticism of my government and leaders in both political parties. If I were still serving in the United States government, I would not have said many of the things contained in this book.

But as a citizen of a free society I am privileged to speak out as I do here. One of the great tragedies resulting from the demise of U.S.-Soviet détente has been the snuffing out of voices of dissent in the Soviet Union. Most of the dissidents, with the exception of Roy Medvedev and a few others, have been sent to prison, or psychiatric hospitals, or work camps, or have been deported from the country. Andrei Sakharov, the greatest voice of Soviet dissent, is held under house arrest. One of my hopes in seeking the achievement of genuine détente is that the ensuing relaxation of tensions will not only restore but expand the opportunity for dissent in the Soviet Union.

Having said that, I believe that Georgy Arbatov has written much more than a skillful polemic in defense of his government's policies and operations. He clearly has just as passionate a conviction as do I that U.S.-Soviet action is required soon if we are to avert nuclear war. And while Mr. Arbatov and I have some very basic differences of opinion, still, running through all of his remarks is evidence that these differences are negotiable. At no time does he create impasse by setting his positions in concrete.

Most encouraging to me is his assertion that if my proposals for negotiation "were to be embodied in a U.S. foreign policy, they would find an active favorable response in the Soviet Union, and, I am sure, would open the way to far-reaching agreements." He bases this view not only on his own opinion, but on his interpretation of the positions of Leonid Brezhnev and the Soviet Communist Party. I believe Georgy Arbatov is correct—these proposals do provide a basis for negotiating genuine détente and avoiding nuclear war.

Not surprisingly, Arbatov finds most distasteful my analysis of Soviet direct and indirect intervention in the Third World with combat forces. We could continue to argue about the political issues surrounding the events in Angola, Ethiopia, Yemen, Cambodia, and Afghanistan. In fact, I would accept some of the arguments put forward by Arbatov, but that misses the point. The point, which he never squarely faces, is that there is a vast difference between all other forms of assistance and intervention with combat forces. That word "combat" means just what it says. Those are military forces engaged in warfare. As indicated many times, the difference between assistance and warfare is substantial.

Whatever the political justification might have been is not the issue; the issue is that the Soviet Union intervened directly or indirectly with combat forces. Such intervention, no matter how rationalized, will never be accepted by the American people, of either political party, as permissible under the terms of détente or peaceful coexistence. I have already acknowledged Mr. Arbatov's claim that the United States has intervened with combat forces in Lebanon, the Dominican Republic, and Vietnam, and through several paramilitary covert operations. But U.S. misbehavior doesn't justify Soviet misbehavior and vice versa. My point is that both sides should negotiate a halt to such intervention.

Mr. Arbatov accuses me of indulging in "Kremlinological antics," and "scholasticism" in my interpretation of Soviet dogma. He says: "The heart of the matter is that Marxist-Leninist theory rejects the idea of 'exporting revolutions,' i.e., promoting them through military intervention." He goes on to say: "By the same token, we oppose the export of counter-revolution, i.e., attempts to do away with social and national liberation movements with the help of military intervention from abroad." Arbatov justifies Soviet action in the Third World by claiming that such counterrevolutionary activity made Soviet intervention necessary.

In other words, Arbatov is establishing a role for the Soviet Union as the world's policeman. My view is that no matter what ideological differences exist, neither the United States nor the Soviet Union can be granted the role of world police-man. The Third World nations do not want the superpowers to police their affairs. They want them to stay out. But I was pleased to note that there is flexibility in Georgy Arbatov's position. He says: "I am strongly convinced that if détente had been given a real chance, if it had been pursued more vigorously, if we had been more persistent in overcoming the remnants of the cold war, we might have succeeded in avoid-ing its resurgence. Many events of the last five to six years might have taken a different shape; some crises would not have taken place at all, others could have been managed by political means. This refers to Angola, Ethiopia, Afghanistan, and Cambodia." That is an important statement which indi-cates a genuine basis for negotiation.

While Mr. Arbatov does not oppose negotiations to ban U.S.- and Soviet-controlled interventions with combat forces in the Third World, he would prefer to see the scope of negotiations broadened, "even if that would make it more difficult." He would like to include issues of "military meddling in the affairs of other countries by China, Israel, South Africa, France, and others." And he says the Soviet Union would "support an agreement to liquidate military bases of all countries on foreign territories." These proposals are, in my opinion, too sweeping to provide a basis for serious political settlement, at least at the outset. It was because I wanted to avoid making the initial talks "even more difficult" that I proposed the power vacuum area of the Third World as the territory about which to conduct the first round of negotiations.

If a military nonintervention pact for the designated Third World area can be successfully negotiated, it would probably be desirable to move ahead to broaden the terms of reference and to include other states besides the United States and the Soviet Union. In fact, in the concluding chapter I go further than Georgy Arbatov, proposing that we begin to reexamine the security arrangements made in Europe after World War II in order to start the process of resolving the outstanding political and military issues.

Mr. Arbatov agrees thoroughly with the need to negotiate further controls and deep cuts in the nuclear weapons arsenals of the two sides. I think he makes some interesting and important points about the differences in the strategic models of the two sides. He describes a Soviet interpretation of the threat posed by strategic bombers and submarines that is at variance with U.S. theory. He states that in case Soviet ICBM's become vulnerable "there is always a countermeasure—launch on warning and under attack. It can never be ruled out by the side planning a counterforce attack, which apparently serves to reinforce the deterrent." It may, but as discussed in earlier chapters, it greatly increases the risk of accidental launch.

Arbatov urges that we should preserve all the positive elements of SALT I and SALT II in the course of negotiating SALT III. He also favors an agreement which would ban the arms race in outer space. This last raises questions about the space shuttle, but certainly the security issues involved in the new space technology should be high on the negotiating agenda. So should those aspects of SALT I and SALT II which remain relevant, especially the principles of equality and equal security and the requirement for adequate verification of compliance with the terms of the treaties.

On balance, I think Georgy Arbatov and I, while differing fundamentally on many political and ideological issues, are in full agreement on the overriding need to negotiate agreements dealing with the issues of military intervention and arms control, which will provide for genuine détente and reduce, if not eliminate, the growing danger of nuclear war.

Chapter VIII

Conclusions

The United States and the Soviet Union are playing Russian Roulette with nuclear weapons. Soon there could easily be an accident or an unintentional launch of nuclear weapons which would result in the death of both nations. With a great deal of luck we have lived with the bomb for thirty-seven years, but we are rapidly approaching a new era for mankind when the odds will be much shorter. Instead of one missile in the six-chambered Russian Roulette revolver, there will be three or four. For if we move ahead with the next round of nuclear weapons systems, the command of nuclear weapons will spin out of the control of man. There are still a few years left to reverse this insane course through political action and diplomacy.

Partly as a result of a series of direct and indirect Soviet interventions with combat forces in the Third World, and partly as a result of exaggerated estimates of Soviet military power, the Reagan administration is pursuing impossible goals, which were articulated by the Republican National Convention. The GOP platform says: "We will build toward a sustained defense expenditure sufficient to close the gap with the Soviets and ultimately to reach the position of military superiority that the American people demand."

Actually most Americans demand no such thing. In an ABC News/*Washington Post* poll taken three months after Reagan entered the White House, a nationwide sample was

Conclusions

asked whether it supported the President's goal of strengthening U.S. military power so that it has a "margin of safety" over the Soviet Union. In response 31 percent said yes, but 65 percent favored an "agreement that would leave both countries as equal as possible in military strength."[1] Commenting on the Reagan goal of military superiority, Malcolm Toon, who was U.S. ambassador to the USSR from 1976 to 1979, said: "It is totally unrealistic. . . . [The] two nations must continue to negotiate because of the threat of nuclear war. It is vital that we realize that we cannot negotiate a position of superiority over the Soviet Union. We can only negotiate a position of equality."[2]

Thomas J. Watson, Jr., who succeeded Toon as U.S. ambassador to Moscow, had this to say about superiority:

We long for days gone by when the United States had nuclear superiority over the Soviet Union and knew that if push came to shove, we were in a dominant position. There are snake-oil salesmen and medicine men in America today purveying their various and sundry balms with all sorts of promises of quick fixes that would restore us to this position. A basic element in most of these elixirs is a call for a rapid build up of our nuclear forces, accompanied by assurances that the Soviet Union will be unable to match us.

Even if one could achieve meaningful nuclear superiority—and one cannot—I submit that this is a fundamental and dangerous misunderstanding of the Soviet Union. . . . What does all this mean? Simply that we can and should be equal but that neither of us can dominate. . . . Now, for our lives and the lives of everyone in the world we must learn to reason with our opponents and they with us. There is no other alternative.[3]

Another former ambassador to Moscow, one of America's greatest authorities on the Soviet Union, George Kennan, on the occasion of receiving the Albert Einstein Peace Prize, said:

Look at the record. Over all these years the competition in the development of nuclear weapons has proceeded steadily, relentlessly without the faintest regard for all the warning voices. We have gone on piling weapon upon weapon, missile upon missile, new levels of destructiveness upon old ones. We have done this helplessly, almost involuntarily like victims of some sort of hypnotism, like men in a dream, like lemmings heading for the sea, like the children of Hamlin [sic] marching blindly along behind their Pied Piper. And the result is that today we have achieved, we and the Russians together, in the creation of these devices and their means of delivery, levels of redundancy of such grotesque dimensions as to defy rational understanding.[4]

Here are three Americans, with conservative backgrounds and expert knowledge of the Soviet Union, all testifying to the fact that the quest for nuclear superiority is irrational. Yet it continues to be pursued. Kennan is right. Americans are behaving "like the victims of some sort of hypnotism," and in a way, they have been hypnotized. They have been told that the Soviets are acquiring nuclear superiority over the United States. They have been told that there is no point in serious negotiations with the Soviet Union until we have restored our "margin of safety" (a euphemism for superiority) so that we can bargain from strength. They have been told that the Soviet Union is opposed to deep, verifiable cuts in the two nuclear arsenals. All these assertions are false, but because the Soviet Union has indulged in a series of military interventions in the Third World, it has not been difficult for American advocates of military supremacy to manipulate public opinion.

What we are witnessing today is a desperate attempt to make the use of nuclear weapons a rational defense strategy. It won't work. Moreover, it is a gigantic risk which threatens the very survival of our nation. The risk of accidental nuclear war will grow each year. As our security shrinks, the costs of the new weapons will reach astronomical proportions. The effects on the domestic economy and on domestic tranquillity will be devastating, reducing our security even more.

The thinking behind the new strategy goes like this. The Soviet Union has always maintained larger conventional

Conclusions

forces than we have. Our main deterrent has been nuclear weapons. So long as we maintained superiority over the Soviet Union in nuclear weapons, it was unlikely to risk military action. Our NATO policy was based on stopping any Soviet aggression, if necessary, with nuclear weapons. It would have been difficult, and very expensive, to build our conventional forces in Europe to a level which could stop any Soviet attack.

Therefore, we adopted the policy of flexible response, which meant that if necessary, we could respond with nuclear weapons at various levels of escalation, depending on the circumstances. This was the beginning of the concept of limited nuclear war. This theoretically made sense so long as we had nuclear superiority, but once the Soviets achieved strategic nuclear parity, the balance of deterrence was lost. This argument was strengthened by Soviet-supported aggression in the Third World, especially by the invasion of Afghanistan. The Soviets were moving because they were no longer checked by our military power, it was claimed.

All this gave impetus to a revised U.S. doctrine stressing a capacity to fight and win limited nuclear wars. The weapons required would have a counterforce capability, and if we spent the necessary money and took advantage of our lead in technology, we could, in about a decade, restore nuclear superiority. This was the program devised by groups like the Committee on the Present Danger and backed by Democratic neoconservatives such as Paul Nitze, Senator Henry Jackson, and Zbigniew Brzezinski in coalition with the right-wing ideologues who have moved into power with the Reagan administration.

The search for a rational use of nuclear weapons has spawned a new group of so-called strategic thinkers, most of them under forty, who have moved into key policy positions dealing with nuclear weapons in the State and Defense departments or who serve as policy consultants to those departments. Among the most influential are Richard Perle, Colin Gray, Richard Burt, and Edward Luttwak. They are leading philosophers of nuclear war fighting. Tragically, as of today, their views are still being treated seriously and are used to

203

justify the expenditure of what will amount to hundreds of billions of American taxpayers' dollars.

The following are some instructive quotes from Colin Gray:

So long as the world is locked into a threat system that includes nuclear weapons, there is no practical alternative to preparing to wage nuclear war as effectively as possible.

The United States may have no practical alternative to waging a nuclear war.

The United States requires the capability to strike first with strategic forces and dominate any subsequent process of escalation.

Survivable command, control, communications and intelligence assets should permit genuine political direction of the war on an hour-by-hour and day-by-day basis. In practice the fog of battle may not permit this, but the goal is a sound one.

A damage-limitation capability comprising counterforce strikes, multilayer ballistic missile defense, air defense, and civil defense—though not perfect or "leak proof"—should make the difference between a United States which could and a United States which could not survive a nuclear war. By extension such damage-limitation provisions would restore meaning to the concept of strategy so far as U.S. nuclear forces are concerned. [This is credited to Edward Luttwak.] Military power and political purpose would be reunified and the American president would have regained a useful measure of freedom of foreign policy action. The prospect of nuclear war would still be daunting: given what we think we know about probable Soviet strategic targeting "style," American casualties could still easily reach into low tens of millions.[5]

Young Mr. Gray is a brave man. Not only does he consider the prospect of a nuclear war "daunting," but he is also prepared to fight it. General Maxwell Taylor, Army chief of staff under Eisenhower and chairman of the Joint Chiefs of Staff in the Kennedy and Johnson administrations, has a different view. He says:

> After the Soviets had acquired intercontinental missiles it was generally accepted that strategic war would be mutually suicidal and that no defensive means, passive or active, existed that could make it less so.
>
> Not only were defensive measures viewed as futile, but damage control was equally unpromising. One could never hope to foresee where and how to stockpile reserves of food, water, medicines, hospital beds, firefighting equipment and the like needed to deal with hundreds of regional disasters. Even if there were warning of attack, how to relocate senior government officials without closing down government itself, how to evacuate urban populations without creating nationwide panic, and how to disperse industry at a time when all communications might be blotted out by nuclear explosions? And after the attack, how to put out fires, restore order and keep survivors alive while disposing of millions of dead?
>
> Unable to answer such questions, most of my contemporaries concluded, as I did and do, that there is no conceivable way of hedging adequately against a failure of deterrence. We are not dealing with war in any rational, Clausewitzian sense—the use of military force as another means for a government to achieve political ends beneficial to the nation. In any major strategic exchange, the reciprocal damage would create conditions that would make victory and defeat virtually indistinguishable, save perhaps that the victors might survive a bit longer than the vanquished.[6]

The fact is that nuclear war between the superpowers would be mutual suicide.

No matter how much strategists such as Gray may wish it to be otherwise, there can never again be a realistic possibility of using nuclear weapons to coerce the Soviet Union. Hans Morgenthau, one of our greatest authorities on balance of power, pointed out shortly before his death:

Both the United States and the Soviet Union are today able to destroy each other. Neither side gains anything militarily or politically by increasing its ability of destruction beyond the optimum of assured destruction. . . . As long as both sides are in possession of the optimum force assuring mutual destruction, the quality and quantity of the mutual means are irrelevant. To use a conventional metaphor: As long as my enemy has one gun with which to kill me, it is irrelevant that he has also the finest collection of guns in town. . . . What is disquieting and ominous is the reluctance of most of those who do our thinking in these matters to refrain from applying obsolete modes of thought and action to our existence. As Einstein said, "The unleashed power of the atom has changed everything except our way of thinking."[7]

Of course, Einstein and Morgenthau were correct—nuclear weapons have changed everything—but both the Americans and the Russians are still unwilling or incapable of dealing with that reality. We both are still talking about the lessons of World War II. The Soviets still maintain huge conventional forces backed by tanks, artillery, and fighter-bombers much as they were organized and equipped in World War II. The politicians and bureaucrats in the United States constantly warn of the lessons of Munich and Pearl Harbor. As we have also observed, the perception theory has been devised as a means of maintaining the momentum of the arms race. Even though we clearly have the capacity to destroy the Soviet Union, it is maintained that if there is a perception of superior Soviet power, the Soviets will be able to use that perception to blackmail and coerce our allies or us. Just how this is to be accomplished is never explained.

Mr. Gray and like-minded strategic thinkers have been striving to return us to a cold war past when our nuclear weapons had political meaning. But what they don't want to face up to is that since the Soviets have achieved the capability to destroy us, concepts of political and strategic power have changed forever. Such hawks are opposed to genuine arms control based on deep cuts in existing nuclear arsenals and to banning further production of nuclear weapons because they want the United States to be in a position to fight and win nuclear wars.

They believe that if we expend the vast sums of money and resources required and exploit our technological advantages, we can, in about ten years, make nuclear war fighting a credible, rational option. Mr. Gray asserts that "military power and political purpose would be reunified and the American president would have regained a useful measure of freedom of foreign policy action." This is a siren song of disaster. As pointed out, the Soviets will be forced to adopt a policy of launch on warning if we ever appear to have the capability to destroy their nuclear weapons systems or command and control.

THE CHANGE IN EUROPE

Western Europe today is at least three years ahead of the United States in terms of popular awareness and political action with respect to nuclear weapons. Europeans are much more preoccupied with the issues of survival than Americans are, partly because they have had more historical experience, but also because they are located where a nuclear war might begin, between the superpowers. As pointed out in Chapter V, the U.S. concept of limited nuclear war fighting terrifies most Europeans. As a result, the subject of nuclear weapons is no longer left to government leaders, strategic experts, and military officers. In less than three years thousands of Europeans have become expert, or at least well informed, about the complex maze of nuclear information. They have spent so much time educating themselves because they are preparing for political action.

Very few people in Europe, to the extent that they know about them, support the concepts of nuclear war fighting that strategists in the Reagan administration have been developing. As indicated, most European military leaders reject the various scenarios for limited nuclear war fought in Europe. Essentially three positions have emerged: (1) the NATO position; (2) the position calling for strengthening conventional forces, and (3) the position advocating a nuclear-free Europe.

RUSSIAN ROULETTE

The first position is advanced by that group that supports the NATO decision of December 1979 calling for the deployment of 572 nuclear weapons capable of striking targets in the Soviet Union and for U.S.-Soviet negotiations to see whether medium-range nuclear weapons can be substantially reduced. As the months have passed, the support for the deployment decision has eroded considerably.

All the European NATO members have given priority to the negotiating track of the decision, while the United States still emphasizes the weapons deployment track. Interestingly, the Mitterrand government of France, which is not a military member of NATO or a participant in the decision, is the most enthusiastic supporter of the new weapons (none of which will be deployed in France, of course). The other NATO members have unanimously pushed for the zero-option negotiating position, which means that they hope that the talks with the Soviets will go so well that no new nuclear weapons will be placed in Europe. Even if that goal is not achieved, the small governments in NATO will probably oppose deployment.

Mrs. Thatcher's Conservative Party will probably be defeated by the newly merged Social Democrat-Liberal Party, meaning that the British will most likely never accept the cruise missiles. The Social Democrats in Germany are so badly divided that Chancellor Schmidt will probably not survive in office if he accepts the weapons in Germany. As a means of ensuring that the U.S. representatives in Geneva are pursuing a genuine effort for nuclear disarmament, Schmidt agreed with President Brezhnev to have separate, simultaneous German-Soviet meetings. The Italian government still supports the deployment decision; but support has been wavering under growing pressure from political opposition, and it will certainly not be sustained if Chancellor Schmidt backs away. As this is written, the betting must be that the NATO decision will never be consummated.

The second position emerging in Europe is advanced by those who continue to give strong backing for NATO but who want to move away from reliance on nuclear weapons, preferring instead to strengthen conventional forces. Most of the advocates of this position would like to see NATO abandon

208

Conclusions

the concept of first use of nuclear weapons and join with the Soviet Union in an agreement pledging no first use of nuclear weapons. Some supporters of the shift away from nuclear weapons in NATO urge that all tactical nuclear weapons be withdrawn from Europe.

The new approach to NATO defense was well expressed by George Kennan in a prescient lecture delivered at Oxford in 1957. He said:

> The true end of political action is, after all, to affect the deeper convictions of men; this the atomic bomb cannot do. The suicidal nature of this weapon renders it unsuitable both as a sanction of diplomacy and as the basis of an alliance. Such a weapon is simply not one with which one readily springs to the defense of one's friends. . . . A defense posture built around a weapon suicidal in its implications can serve in the long run only to paralyze national policy, to undermine alliances, and to drive everyone deeper and deeper into the hopeless exertions of the weapons race.[8]

In his book *Nuclear Illusion and Reality,* published in 1982, Lord Zuckerman, who was science adviser to Churchill during World War II and has subsequently advised many British prime ministers, carries the argument further. Speaking of possible war in Europe, he says:

> If the Soviet Union were to attack, and our response became nuclear, all would be lost. If the reverse were to happen, the end would be the same. There is no alternative to our deploying enough properly armed conventional forces to fight, if it ever becomes necessary, a real war. Armies are not raised in order to initiate a process that would destroy most of the advanced countries of the world.
>
> It stands to reason that only conventional forces can provide the flexibility that can negate the disastrous rigidity that is implicit in the concept of the automatic first use of nuclear weapons. Only such forces can increase the number of options open to the NATO command. Equally, the concept of "graduated deterrence"—the earlier catchword which is now replaced by the term "flexi-

209

ble response"—is only a confusing abstraction. As I have said, there are no agreed rules for field warfare in which nuclear weapons might be used.[9]

Other top British experts with the same view are Field Marshal Lord Carver, perhaps Britain's most eminent military man today, and strategic expert Michael Howard of Oxford. Field Marshal Carver has condemned

> the concept that an inadequacy in conventional forces can be compensated for by the threat to use, and, if deterrence of that threat failed, actually to use theater nuclear weapons in a first strike to counter a conventional invasion.
>
> That strategy has been incredible and irrational for over 20 years, ever since the Soviet Union gained the capability to answer back in kind. . . . To initiate nuclear war would not redress or restore the situation; it would be an act of unredeemable folly. . . . Unless NATO abandons its unrealistic and suicidal dependence on nuclear response, it will not set about putting its conventional house in order.[10]

Professor Howard also advocates building stronger NATO conventional forces. He says: "The Western strategy of relying on the first use of nuclear weapons to defend ourselves is not only morally dubious, but politically and militarily incredible."[11]

At a conference on Nuclear Weapons in Europe held in Brussels in the fall of 1981 and cochaired by Ambassador Elliot Richardson and former Belgian Foreign Minister Henri Simonet, it was argued that NATO's conventional forces should be strengthened to deter a conventional Soviet attack and lessen the pressure for first use of nuclear weapons by the NATO alliance. The report of the cochairmen said:

> We believe this argument has a great deal of validity. We are aware, of course, that NATO has historically resisted pressure to improve conventional defenses. We believe, however, that the use of new conventional weapons tech-

nologies and tactics emphasizing speed and mobility can improve conventional force capabilities without a major increase in expenditures.[12]

Former Chairman of the U.S. Joint Chiefs of Staff General Maxwell Taylor also gives priority to strengthening conventional forces, as does Senator Sam Nunn of Georgia, the leading expert in the Senate on these matters and a Democrat.

Irving Kristol, one of the most influential of the neoconservatives who have joined the Reagan camp, is also critical of the fact that NATO has not given emphasis to conventional forces. He says:

Neither Western Europe nor the United States took this option seriously. The reason, bluntly, was that it was expensive and politically inconvenient. The Western alliance decided instead to acquire its security "on the cheap," relying on nuclear reprisal while being free to spend money on politically popular social programs, rather than on a large, well-equipped military establishment. It was a tragic error, of a kind that future historians will identify as a clear symptom of political decadence. As things have evolved, NATO's military strategy is no longer cheap, or effective, or credible, or politically popular.

Is it too late to reverse this error? Possibly or even probably. Is there any alternative to attempting to do so? None has even been suggested. Are there any signs that thought is being given to such a basic reconsideration of NATO's structure and posture? No. The State Department and the Pentagon, along with the governments of Western Europe, keep pretending that the present condition of NATO is viable, and that mounting European dissent is but a temporary aberration. They are whistling in the dark.[13]

Kristol is correct; anybody who thinks the dissent which is sweeping through Europe, East and West, is a temporary phenomenon is "whistling in the dark." But is the alternative that he and the other critics propose—the strengthening of NATO's conventional forces—the best one? Is it even realistic? If it could be accomplished, it would certainly be preferable to the present course, which is a political and military nightmare leading in the direction of the dissolution of the Atlantic alliance and of accidental nuclear war.

It is worth examining the merits of the proposition that NATO should shift to reliance on strengthened conventional forces. If this goal could be achieved with sufficient nonnuclear power to deter any potential Soviet conventional invasion, it would mean that NATO could adopt a policy of no first use of nuclear weapons. It would mean that NATO would not rely on nuclear weapons unless attacked by the Soviet Union with nuclear weapons. It would mean that the present NATO plan for deploying additional U.S. nuclear weapons in Europe could be dropped. In fact, it could provide a basis for negotiating an agreement with the Soviet Union to remove most, if not all, nuclear weapons from Eastern and Western Europe. Such an agreement would bring to an end the political pressure of the European nuclear disarmament movement.

In order to build NATO conventional forces to the levels necessary to achieve adequate security without nuclear weapons, all the NATO members would have to increase defense spending considerably. The United States probably would have to contribute an additional $40 billion a year and perhaps another 100,000 troops. In order to fulfill its commitment, the United States would probably have to revert to the draft not only for financial reasons but also to ensure quality manpower.

The present plans of the British for a reduction in conventional ground and naval forces would have to be reversed. The Thatcher government is currently giving emphasis to strategic power with a plan to spend about $15 billion for a British version of the Trident submarine carrying nuclear missiles. The Social Democrats and the Labor Party are opposed to the Trident plans, so that part of British defense policy is likely to be reversed anyhow. Moreover, both the Social Democrats and Labor are pledged to cut defense spending.

Conclusions

In Germany a considerable increase above present levels of defense spending would be required. Given the growing instability in the Social Democratic Party, that is an unlikely prospect. Furthermore, the question of increasing present levels of German military forces raises political problems, not only internally but throughout Europe. There is also the issue of adding more American troops and their dependents to the territory of West Germany. Presently existing problems for both Germans and Americans would increase. How long would the Americans stay in Germany?

Political problems in both Belgium and the Netherlands make it improbable that those governments would significantly increase their NATO financial or manpower commitments. Under the circumstances existing today, it seems most improbable that the alternative of a major buildup in NATO's conventional strength is likely to be adopted, though it would be a step in the right direction, compared to the dangerous and poorly conceived policies being pursued today.

The third position on European policy—other than the current NATO policy and that held by advocates of strengthening conventional forces—is advanced by the antinuclear movement, which has a goal of eliminating nuclear weapons from all Europe, from the Atlantic to the Urals. Since the people of Eastern Europe have relatively little opportunity for independent expression of opinion, most of the political action in this movement comes from Western Europe. It is clear that unless the United States demonstrates a genuine intent to end the nuclear arms race and negotiate meaningful reductions, the nuclear disarmament movement in Europe will continue to grow in both size and power.

The antinuclear movement, though it has established an information clearinghouse and better coordinating machinery, is still not a cohesive political alliance of European organizations. All elements are opposed to any deployment of U.S. missiles in Europe and advocate the dismantling of Soviet SS-20 missiles. They all are opposed to the first use of nuclear weapons as a policy option. Most are opposed to existing

213

nuclear weapons in Europe and would like to see them removed. But beyond the goal of a nuclear-free Europe there is no consensus for an approach to military security.

Many of the organizations support unilateral nuclear disarmament, which means that they are not willing to await the results of U.S.-Soviet negotiations. They want their own nations to be free of nuclear weapons without regard to Soviet action. Some of the organizations support membership in NATO; others oppose it. Some, especially religious organizations, are pacifist. Others advocate neutralism or isolationism. For the most part, though, they see themselves as a European movement.

E. P. Thompson, the leading ideologist for the movement, says: "People have poured onto the streets in response to the saber rattling of the Reagan administration. If the European peace movement has been orchestrated it has been by Reagan, Weinberger and Haig. We must begin to orchestrate ourselves. We must find our own conductor." At a meeting of the movement's leaders in Brussels it was agreed to broaden the appeal to the Communist countries and to the United States. Thompson said: "We must dig tunnels to the East. We must build links with professionals, students, peace groups and dissident movements in Eastern Europe, including the Soviet Union." The leaders agreed to maintain pressure on both the superpowers meeting in Geneva toward the goal of a nuclear-free Europe.[14]

Most of the emphasis has been on banning nuclear weapons, but some elements of the peace movement have pressed for other aspects of détente and nonmilitary measures to strengthen ties between Eastern and Western Europe. They talk of promoting further trade to encourage interdependence of the economies. The special relationship between Austria and Hungary serves as a positive example. Hungary now has the strongest economy in Eastern Europe. There is talk in some neutralist groups about the successful defense strategy of Sweden and Switzerland, based on dissuasion rather than on deterrence with nuclear weapons. Both countries have large citizen armies which are well trained and can be swiftly mobilized to combat and harass any invader. All the talk of Eastern Europe-Western Europe rapprochement looks to a multipolar world with Europe, as an entity, taking its place between the United States and the USSR, but no longer dominated by or dependent on either.

In Germany, especially, the warlike posture of the Reagan administration has inspired growing anti-American feelings. A study prepared in 1981 for the Aspen Institute of Berlin which reviewed seven weeks of German television "didn't observe a single program that was either friendly or clearly positive about the United States." There has been widespread discussion in the press about the Reagan administration's viewing Germany as a battleground. One story filed by a German correspondent in Washington quoted an unnamed member of the National Security Council as saying that the Germans must learn that "if you don't toe the line you get whacked."[15]

The End of the Ideological Age, a book written by Peter Bender, a close friend of Social Democratic leaders Willy Brandt and Egon Bahr, says:

As long as the Atlantic Alliance is the measure of all things for Western Europe, Moscow will hold on to what it has with all its strength. Eastern Europe can't emancipate itself from the Soviet Union without Western Europe emancipating itself from the United States. . . . The perspective exists that the Kremlin will let democracy come to the borders of the Soviet Union when Western Europe no longer serves or seems to serve or could serve America as a base against the Soviet Union —when neither missiles nor radio stations (RFE and Radio Liberty are located in Munich) are allowed that can reach the Soviet Union.[16]

Assistant Secretary of Defense Richard Perle, who is chairman of the NATO High Level Group which develops defense policy, gave a public assessment of the European antinuclear movement, drawing a distinction between Protestant Northern Europe and Catholic Southern Europe. He said:

Protestants are suffering from Angst—a gloomy, often neurotic feeling of anxiety or depression. It's a sense of fear—troubled people, troubled governments, troubled coalitions. . . . When you look at Portugal, Spain and Italy, when you look at Greece and Turkey—which are not Catholic but they're not Protestant either—you find a very different attitude, a much greater awareness of the danger of military imbalance, a greater willingness to make sacrifices for defense.[17]

Two days later Greek Prime Minister Andreas Papandreou announced his intention to withdraw NATO nuclear weapons from Greece. Two weeks later Pope John Paul II announced that he was sending Catholic experts, mostly scientists, to Washington, Moscow, Paris, London, and the United Nations to outline the "terrifying prospects" of the use of nuclear weapons. The Pope said his work for disarmament and against the use of nuclear weapons would be one of the main campaigns of his papacy. He added: "Humanity must make a moral about-face. From now on it is only through a conscious choice and through a deliberate policy that man can survive."[18] Obviously the analytic capabilities of Richard Perle, who is one of the four or five most influential people dealing with U.S. national security, leaves something to be desired. But what is much more troubling is Perle's apparent insensitivity to and lack of awareness of the causes of fear and disenchantment in Europe. Such thinking contributes to the growing gulf between the United States and Europe.

U.S. Ambassador to West Germany Arthur Burns called the current European debate about nuclear weapons "a battle for the soul of Europe with clear alternatives," indicating the choice would determine to what extent the United States continued to help defend Europe:

There may well be a growing sentiment in America to turn back upon itself and let Europe depend for its security and freedom upon its own resources or upon Soviet good will. . . . [Many] Americans are now wondering whether Europeans are sufficiently mindful of the fact that the Atlantic Alliance has made a free, prosperous and peaceful Western Europe possible during the past 30 years.[19]

Democratic Representative Les Aspin of Wisconsin, an expert on U.S. defense matters for years, says that:

> if the Europeans want to reverse field and stop relying on nuclear weapons they should realize that means heavier outlays for conventional forces or no defense at all. ... If we emerge from this exercise with neither nuclear modernization nor higher defense budgets in Europe a proposal to withdraw our troops would go through Congress like a prairie fire.[20]

James Reston of *The New York Times* asked Senate Majority Leader Howard Baker what would happen if another Mansfield resolution were proposed in the Senate calling for the withdrawal of U.S. troops from Europe. Baker said he hoped it would be defeated, but he wasn't sure.[21] *The Wall Street Journal* printed a long editorial proposing that the United States reconsider its commitment to Europe and turn its attention to the Pacific. The Pentagon floated a story that plans were being developed for greater reliance on the Navy while shifting away from land-based military arrangements.

The trouble with all these reflexes is that they are so short-sighted and knee-jerk. It is as though there were no leadership on either side of the Atlantic willing to do the hard thinking and hard work required to repair the alliance. Both sides seem to be behaving like spoiled brats—"either you play the game my way, or we don't play." Half-baked military ideas such as the NATO decision of December 1979 and the British Trident decision have eroded the alliance. The alternatives need to be developed and pursued.

THE MOVEMENT IN THE UNITED STATES

Europeans often ask why Americans are lagging so far behind in doing anything about the looming peril of nuclear holocaust. As one American writer put it:

217

For those of us who stand so little chance of becoming anything other than a statistic should the unthinkable prove a reality, the wonder is that the debate over the use of nuclear weapons has been so muted. . . . At least in this country the political means exist—however difficult they might be—to act upon that which can be understood.[22]

There are several reasons why awareness in the United States has been behind that of Europe. Europe is in the middle, between the superpowers. Not only do Europeans see themselves as the first nuclear battlefield, but they feel also a sense of frustration because they have so little direct influence over the nuclear arsenals of the great powers. The Europeans also have a well-developed sense of survival because they have been through so many wars. Most European nations, since World War II, have seen their empires disintegrate. They have no illusions of world power, no "Vietnam syndrome," no Committee on the Present Danger.

However, in spite of the important differences from the European experience, an antinuclear movement of consequence is developing in the United States. Unless the Reagan administration demonstrates that it is putting the brakes on the nuclear arms race, the American movement will begin to have political impact by the November election in 1982. The best organized and most influential antinuclear force in the United States consists of doctors. They are generally respected, usually conservative, with a profession which, more than any other, deals with human life and survival.

The Physicians for Social Responsibility started in 1980 with a few hundred members. Now there are more than 9,000. They have sponsored in most of the major cities in the United States well-attended conferences dealing with the medical consequences of nuclear war. Dr. Helen Caldicott, one of the founders of the organization, gave up her medical work so that she could devote full time to the movement. She said: "I'd go into work and think what am I doing this for, when everyone is going to be killed within 10 years." Doctors now look at nuclear war as the ultimate medical issue, the final epidemic.

Conclusions

Another medical group organized in the United States is called International Physicians for the Prevention of Nuclear War and includes prominent doctors from Britain, France, Japan, and the Soviet Union. They hold international conferences discussing in graphic detail the horrors of the medical consequences of nuclear war. One of the Soviet doctors is President Brezhnev's personal physician. The results of these meetings are published extensively in the Soviet Union and discussed on nationwide television. Dr. Bernard Lown, one of the cochairmen, writing in the *Journal of the American Medical Association* (AMA), said: "Only an aroused public opinion can compel political leaders to stop the spiraling nuclear arms race."[23]

And in regard to the AMA, which is one of the more conservative organizations in the United States, at its 1981 national convention it passed a resolution calling on doctors to inform President Reagan and members of Congress about the medical consequences of nuclear war. Dr. James Muller, a cardiologist at Harvard, says the doctors are in the mainstream of the nuclear arms movement, which he thinks is about to take off "like the civil rights movement in the 1960's." Another leader of the movement, Dr. Howard Hiatt, dean of the Harvard School of Public Health, was in the delegation sent by the Pope to speak to President Reagan about the growing danger of nuclear war.

In addition to the doctors, church leaders have become much more active. Billy Graham, the most widely heard religious leader in America, has been speaking about the need to end the nuclear arms race and drastically reduce nuclear stockpiles. The Pope has taken a similar position, which has been pressed by the Catholic Bishops of the United States. In Amarillo, Texas, Bishop Leroy Mathiesen told Catholics working at a nuclear weapons assembly plant to consider switching to more peaceful jobs. Archbishop Raymond Hunthausen of Seattle denounced the nuclear arms race and said he had a vision of thousands of U.S. citizens refusing to pay part of their federal taxes to protest the nuclear buildup if it isn't curbed soon.

Partly as a result of the aborted attempt to deploy MX

missiles in Utah, the Mormon Church has taken a strong stand against the nuclear buildup. The Episcopal Church has been active in sponsoring antinuclear meetings. A coalition of church and peace groups organized the huge weekend demonstration in New York during the United Nations special session on disarmament.

Scientists, including most American Nobel prizewinners, have taken a more active role through the activities of such organizations as the Union of Concerned Scientists and the Federation of American Scientists. The Union of Concerned Scientists sponsored a teach-in at hundreds of colleges and universities on Armistice Day 1981 to discuss the implications of the continuing nuclear arms race. For the first time since the Vietnam War political activism is stirring on American campuses.

A new movement spawned in Cambridge, Massachusetts, calling for a freeze on the production, testing, and deployment of nuclear weapons, is spreading across the country. Hundreds of thousands of citizen signatures have endorsed the freeze, as have town meetings in New England and city councils in several parts of the country. In California a group led by Los Angeles businessman Harold Willens and actor Paul Newman has gathered 350,000 signatures to place a resolution on the California ballot for the November election. The resolution calls for the USSR and the United States to freeze the deployment of all nuclear weapons. Willens and Newman hope that this bilateral weapons freeze initiative will be adopted by other states across the country.

In April 1981 meetings were held all over the United States to discuss the alternatives for action to avoid nuclear war. Attended by thousands of people, these sessions—called Ground Zero—were organized by Roger Molander, an expert on nuclear weapons, formerly on the staff of the National Security Council. Molander had become so concerned about the lack of real progress toward curbing nuclear weapons that he decided to take the issues to the grass roots of America.

Other organizations which support a nuclear freeze and deep cuts in the nuclear arsenals, some of which have existed for several years, have experienced a surge in membership and growing financial support. The American Committee on East-West Accord is probably the closest thing to a major organization with opposite views to those of the Committee on the Present Danger. It is a bipartisan organization of invited members, most of whom have had direct experience with the Soviet Union. Its cochairmen are Donald Kendall, president of the U.S. Chamber of Commerce; George Kennan, former ambassador to Moscow; and John Kenneth Galbraith, Harvard economist and author. Other members include Averell Harriman, Robert McNamara, George Ball, former Senator Jacob Javits, and former chairmen of the Senate Foreign Relations Committee J. William Fulbright and Frank Church. A nationwide Gallup poll taken in December 1981 showed that 76 percent of those polled favor George Kennan's proposal for a 50 percent cut across the board of all types of nuclear weapons and their launchers.

Other important organizations in the movement are: the Arms Control Association, the president of which, Herbert Scoville, wrote an excellent book demonstrating why the plans for the MX missile won't work; the Center for Defense Information, directed by Admiral Gene La Rocque; the Committee for National Security; the American Friends Service Committee; the Council for a Livable World; and SANE. Parts of the American labor movement, including the United Auto Workers under Douglas Fraser and the machinists led by William Winpisinger, have become active in the antinuclear movement. These and other organizations have established a network of communication across the country, developing political action. It is not as yet as powerful as the European movement, but its impact will soon be felt in American politics.

WHERE DO WE GO FROM HERE?

There is a growing awareness that the superpowers have failed to control the nuclear arms race and that unless drastic action is taken, we may not survive this decade. But there is not much evidence of leadership in Moscow, Washington, or the capitals of Europe stepping forward with the required drastic action. There is very little evidence of the hard political thinking and diplomacy which are needed. The prognosis is grim.

Certain things must be very clearly understood. If we are to survive, the United States and the Soviet Union must never have a war. This means that the highest priority of both governments should be the search for political arrangements to prevent and avoid war. The Soviets know this better than the Americans, but their totalitarian system, their secrecy, and elements of their archaic ideology have so far blocked the necessary action. It is clear that the action will come only from a two-way process—resulting from continuous U.S.-Soviet negotiation.

It is clear, also, that the present U.S. course is disastrous and must be reversed. There is no such thing as nuclear superiority. Building more nuclear weapons reduces our security and increases the risk of nuclear war and especially the risk of nuclear accident. It is important that the American people know this—know that those who are advocating continuation of the nuclear arms race for reasons of power or profit are endangering our nation's security. They are taking the ultimate risk—our very survival.

It is essential that we reject the doctrine of limited nuclear wars. There can be no such thing. All the elaborate concepts and scenarios of nuclear war fighting are dangerous nonsense. It is almost unbelievable that so many intelligent people could indulge in so many learned words and participate in so many so-called war games, trying to make nuclear war fighting a rational option. It is impossible. Nuclear weapons are rational only for deterrence. That is why the policy of mutual assured destruction makes sense. Any attempt to develop offensive or defensive weapons to change the balance of deterrence is destabilizing and thus insane.

Bernard Brodie, one of our first and best thinkers about nuclear weapons, said it well:

Thucydides was right . . . peace is better than war, not only in being more agreeable but also in being very much more predictable. A plan and policy which offers a good promise of deterring war is therefore by orders of magnitude better in every way than one which depreciates the objective of deterrence in order to improve somewhat the chances of winning.[24]

Today we are doing the opposite, eroding deterrence in pursuit of the chimera of winning.

We have not kept our eye on the most realistic and highest-priority goal—devising plans and policies which offer good promise of deterring war, especially plans for political negotiation. Instead, we have been absorbed with worst-case scenarios. As former Secretary of Defense Harold Brown says, "A Soviet nuclear attack on the United States is the least likely military contingency we face." Another remote contingency is a Soviet invasion of West Germany. Nevertheless, we continue to spend billions of dollars building weapons to respond to these two contingencies.

Our goal should be to freeze the nuclear arms race and to cut existing levels of all forms of nuclear weapons to the lowest level possible, while still maintaining deterrence. The nuclear genie cannot be put back in the bottle, but we certainly can eliminate the threat of counterforce and substantially reduce the risk of accidental or unintentional war. We should avoid any weapons which would make it difficult to verify treaty compliance with existing means of intelligence.

Also, as described in Chapter VI, we should negotiate, on a separate track, a military nonintervention pact which would ban the use of combat forces in the Third World by either superpower. The present course of both sides is militarization. That will have only one outcome. In time there will be confrontation, conflict, and probably nuclear war. Political ground rules are essential to provide for mutual restraint and genuine détente.

We should also start in motion talks first with our European allies and then together with the Soviet Union to begin exploration of new political and security arrangements for Europe. History has overtaken the agreements reached after World War II and the security concepts of NATO and the Warsaw Pact. Even the Helsinki accords are already out of date and essentially unworkable. The events in Poland and the mass marches in Western Europe demonstrate the extent of unrest. Military measures can no longer be relied upon to provide stability. This is particularly true in Eastern Europe, where aspirations for political freedom have remained in check too long. Solidarity in Poland has demonstrated decisively the longing of the workingman for freedom.

The only solution that will give Eastern Europeans their freedom and Western Europeans their security is the demilitarization of Europe. This means that the Red Army will gradually have to move out of East Germany, Poland, Hungary, and Czechoslovakia, and the United States forces will gradually have to move out of Europe. NATO and the Warsaw Pact will be abolished. As always, the crucial question is Germany. Should it be reunified? How far should it disarm? The Soviets obviously will not leave Eastern Europe until they feel secure about the future of Germany.

The Germans themselves can be very helpful in the resolution of these vital political and security issues. Just as the leadership of Willy Brandt gave impetus to the first stages of détente in Europe, so German leadership again can provide the imagination and spirit needed to move to the final stage of détente. All these are matters that can be negotiated to fruition, provided the parties have sufficient will and vision. The same is true of the control of nuclear weapons.

The mutual and balanced force reduction (MBFR) talks in Vienna have gotten nowhere because the will has not been there. The parties have preferred to dance lightly around the central issues. Diplomats have been saying that it is better not to rock the boat so long as there is relative equilibrium. Well, the boat is rocking and soon will sink. The events in Poland have demonstrated conclusively that a major new effort must be made to resolve the political and military issues that have been skirted since World War II. There are obvious risks in opening these subjects to negotiation, but the risks of not doing so are greater.

General Omar Bradley, who died in 1981, the last of our great World War II five-star generals and the man chosen by

Conclusions

President Reagan to represent the military at his inauguration, put it well in one of his speeches:

It may be that the problems of accommodation in a world split by rival ideologies are more difficult than those with which we have struggled in the construction of ballistic missiles. But I believe, too, that if we apply to these human problems the energy, creativity and the perseverance we have devoted to science, even problems of accommodation will yield to reason. Admittedly the problem of peaceful accommodation in the world is infinitely more difficult than the conquest of space, infinitely more complex than a trip to the moon. But if we will only come to the realization that it must be worked out—whatever it may mean even to such sacred traditions as absolute national sovereignty—I believe that we can somehow, somewhere, and perhaps through some as yet undiscovered world thinker and leader find a workable solution.[25]

Notes and Sources

CHAPTER I

1. Richard Thaxton, "Nuclear War by Computer Chip," *The Progressive* (August 1980).
2. Stephen Talbot and Jonathan Dann, "Broken Arrows, Broken Sleep," *Los Angeles Times*, March 18, 1981. Talbot and Dann received the 1981 George Polk Award for local television reporting for their documentary *Broken Arrow: Can a Nuclear Weapon Accident Happen Here?*
3. "Problems Associated with the World Wide Military Command and Control System," Richard W. Gutmann, director, Logistics and Communications Division, General Accounting Office, Before the Subcommittee on Research and Development, Committee on Armed Services, U.S. House of Representatives, April 23, 1979.
4. "The Navy's Strategic Communications Systems—Need for Management Attention and Decisionmaking" (Washington: General Accounting Office Report, May 2, 1979).
5. Richard Halloran, "Weinberger Said to Offer Reagan Plan to Regain Atomic Superiority," *The New York Times*, August 14, 1981.
6. Richard Halloran, "Reagan Arms Policy Said to Rely Heavily on Communications," *The New York Times*, October 12, 1981.
7. Ernest Conine, "Alarm Bells on America's Defense," *Los Angeles Times*, November 2, 1981.
8. Jim Bencirenga, "C Cubed: New U.S. Entrant in Military Technology Race," *The Christian Science Monitor*, October 16, 1981.
9. Desmond Ball, "Can Nuclear War Be Controlled?" *Adelphi Paper* 169 (London: International Institute of Strategic Studies, October 1981).
10. Vice Admiral Gerald E. Miller, statement before Subcommittee on International Security and Scientific Affairs, Committee on International Relations, House of Representatives, in report entitled "First

Use of Nuclear Weapons: Preserving Responsible Control," March 18, 1976.

11. Conine, *op. cit.*
12. *CBS Reports, The Defense of the United States,* Part I: "Ground Zero," June 14, 1981.
13. Phil Stanford, "Who Pushes the Button?," *Parade* magazine (March 28, 1976).
14. *Ibid.*
15. *CBS Reports, op. cit.*
16. James Schlesinger, testimony before the Senate Foreign Relations Committee, April 4, 1974.
17. Arthur Macy Cox, "The Way the West and East Can Be Lost," *Newsday*, September 28, 1980.
18. "Rethinking U.S. Security Policy for the 1980's," *Proceedings of the Seventh Annual National Security Affairs Conference,* July 21–23, 1980 (Washington, D.C.: National Defense University) p. 162.
19. Hearings, International Relations Committee, House of Representatives, March 18, 1976, *op. cit.*
20. Fred Charles Ikle, "The Growing Risk of War by Accident," *The Washington Post,* June 24, 1980.
21. Kenneth Bacon and Thomas Bray, "An Interview with Harold Brown," *The Wall Street Journal,* July 1, 1980.
22. Michael Getler, an interview with Richard De Lauer, *The Washington Post,* November 12, 1981.
23. *CBS Reports, op. cit.*
24. George Kistiakowsky, "Frightening Quotation," *Parade* magazine (March 9, 1980).

CHAPTER II

1. Henry Trofimenko, "The Third World and the U.S.-Soviet Competition: A Soviet View," *Foreign Affairs* (Summer 1981). Trofimenko heads the department for the study of U.S. foreign policy in the Institute of U.S. and Canadian Studies of the Academy of Sciences of the USSR.
2. Arthur Macy Cox, *The Dynamics of Détente* (New York: Norton, 1976), pp. 31–32.
3. Boris Rabbot, "Détente: The Struggle Within the Kremlin," *The Washington Post,* July 10, 1977.
4. John A. Marcum, "Lessons of Angola," *Foreign Affairs* (April 1976).
5. Walter Stoessel, who was U.S. ambassador to Moscow at the time. Stoessel is currently deputy secretary of state.
6. Henry Kissinger, testimony before the Subcommittee on Africa, Senate Foreign Relations Committee, January 29, 1976.
7. Henry Kissinger, "The Permanent Challenge of Peace: United States Policy Toward the Soviet Union," speech before the Commonwealth Club and the World Affairs Council, San Francisco, February 3, 1976.
8. Leonid Brezhnev, keynote speech at Soviet Communist Party's Twenty-fifth Congress, Moscow, February 25, 1976.

Notes and Sources

9. Leonid Brezhnev, reported in *The Washington Post*, January 16, 1976.
10. "Soviet Policy and United States Response in the Third World," report prepared for the Committee on International Affairs, U.S. House of Representatives, by the Congressional Research Service, Library of Congress, March 1981.
11. Murrey Marder, "U.S. Links SALT Fate, Horn of Africa," *The Washington Post*, March 2, 1978.
12. "SALT on Its Own Merits," *The Economist*, March 18, 1978.
13. Murrey Marder, "GOP Hits Carter Soviet-Cuban Policy," *The Washington Post*, March 23, 1978.
14. Georgy Arbatov, "Soviet-American Relations: Time of Crucial Decisions," *Pravda*, March 28, 1978.
15. Murrey Marder, "Brzezinski Delivers Attack on Soviets," *The Washington Post*, May 29, 1978.
16. Jimmy Carter, address to the graduating class of the U.S. Naval Academy, Annapolis, Maryland, June 7, 1978.
17. "Soviet Policy and United States Response in the Third World," p. 53.
18. Christopher Ogden, an interview with Henry Kissinger, *Time* magazine (January 15, 1979).
19. The editors of *Time* magazine, an interview with Leonid Brezhnev, *Time* magazine (January 15, 1979).
20. Jimmy Carter and Leonid Brezhnev, remarks reported in Robert Kaiser, "Prospects Now Poor for Improved U.S.-Soviet Relations," *The Washington Post*, May 18, 1980.
21. Jimmy Carter, address to the nation, October 1, 1979.
22. Cord Meyer, "The Ghost of Détente," *Washington Star*, January 18, 1980.
23. Vernon Aspaturian, "Soviet Global Power and the Correlation of Forces," *Problems of Communism* (May–June 1980).
24. Trofimenko, *op. cit.*
25. Don Oberdorfer and Michael Getler, "Soviet Restraint a Condition for Pacts," *The Washington Post*, February 13, 1981.

CHAPTER III

1. Arthur Macy Cox, *The Dynamics of Détente* (New York: Norton, 1976), p. 142.
2. Dean Acheson, *Present at the Creation* (New York: Norton, 1969), p. 374.
3. Leslie H. Gelb, "Schlesinger for Defense," *The New York Times Magazine* (August 4, 1973).
4. Robert G. Kaiser, "Behind-Scenes Power Struggle over Arms Policy," *The Washington Post*, June 26, 1977.
5. Cox, *op. cit.*, p. 47.
6. James Schlesinger, quoted in Richard J. Whalen, "The Ford Shakeup: Politics vs. Policy," *The Washington Post*, November 9, 1975.
7. Murrey Marder, "Carter to Inherit Intense Dispute on Soviet Intentions," *The Washington Post*, January 2, 1977.
8. Henry S. Bradsher, "How New Study of Soviet Arms Affects Carter," *Washington Star*, December 27, 1976.

9. Marder, *op. cit.*
10. Richard Barnet, "The Search for National Security," *The New Yorker* (April 27, 1981).
11. Lynn Rosellini, "Richard Perle and the Inside Battle Against SALT," *Washington Star*, May 21, 1979.
12. Strobe Talbott, *Endgame: The Inside Story of SALT II* (New York: Harper & Row, 1980), p. 53.
13. *Ibid.*, p. 66.
14. Jimmy Carter, address delivered at Notre Dame University, Notre Dame, Indiana, May 22, 1977.
15. Juan de Onis, "Lobbying Body to Push Congress for a Nuclear Edge over Soviets," *The New York Times*, January 6, 1981.
16. Henry Jackson, quoted in Talbott, *op. cit.*, p. 5.
17. Richard Burt, "In the Washington Shake-Up, No Tremors for Brzezinski," *The New York Times*, July 20, 1979.
18. Anthony Lewis, "The Brzezinski Puzzle," *The New York Times*, August 18, 1980.
19. Bernard Gwertzman, an interview with Cyrus Vance, *The New York Times*, December 3, 1981.
20. Carnes Lord, a letter to the Coalition for a New Foreign and Military Policy, April 14, 1981.
21. Richard Pipes, "The Soviet Strategy for Nuclear Victory," *The Washington Post*, July 3, 1977.
22. Jonathan Alter, "Reagan's Dr. Strangelove," *The Washington Monthly* (June 1981).
23. Hedrick Smith, "Discordant Voices," *The New York Times*, March 20, 1981.
24. Colin S. Gray and Keith Payne, "Victory Is Possible," *Foreign Policy* (Summer 1980).

CHAPTER IV

1. Arthur Macy Cox, *The Dynamics of Détente* (New York: Norton, 1976), pp. 29–30.
2. Edward Luttwak, "SALT and the Meaning of Strategy," *The Washington Review* (April 1978).
3. James Schlesinger, Annual Defense Department Report to Congress, for the year 1976, quoted in Cox, *op. cit.*, p. 43.
4. Ray S. Cline, *World Power Assessment* (Washington, D.C.: Center for Strategic and International Studies, Georgetown University, 1976).
5. Strobe Talbott, "The Vulnerability Factor," *Time* magazine (August 31, 1981).
6. Harold Brown, speech at the Commonwealth Club, San Francisco, June 23, 1978.
7. Murrey Marder, "Carter to Inherit Intense Dispute on Soviet Intentions," *The Washington Post*, January 2, 1977.
8. Harold Brown, interview on *Issues and Answers*, ABC-TV, August 17, 1980.

Notes and Sources

9. Stansfield Turner, testimony before the Joint Economic Committee, U.S. Congress, February 17, 1978.
10. Donald L. Clark, "Who Are Those Guys?," *Air University Review* (May–June 1979).
11. Lee Lescaze, "In Event of Nuclear War, Health Prognosis Is Hopeless, Doctors Say," *The Washington Post*, November 21, 1980.
12. Arthur Macy Cox, "The CIA's Tragic Error," *The New York Review of Books* (November 6, 1980).
13. Daniel Yergin, "The Arms Zealots," *Harper's* (June 1977).
14. W. Graham Claytor, speech at the National Press Club, Washington, D.C., February, 1979.
15. Charles W. Duncan, Jr., "U.S. Defense: Our State of Readiness," speech before the Association of the U.S. Army, Washington, D.C., October 18, 1978.
16. Harold Brown, speech at the Naval War College, Newport, Rhode Island, August 20, 1980.
17. Daniel O. Graham, testimony before the Senate Subcommittee on Arms Control, Oceans, and International Environments, Senate Foreign Relations Committee, March 16, 1977.
18. Paul Marantz, "Prelude to Détente," *International Studies Quarterly* (December 1975). An analysis of Khrushchev's doctrinal revision.
19. Richard Pipes, "The Soviet Strategy for Nuclear Victory," *The Washington Post*, July 3, 1977, reprinted from *Commentary* (July 1977), by permission of the American Jewish Committee.
20. Leonid Brezhnev, speech at Tula, reported in *Pravda*, January 19, 1977.
21. Raymond L. Garthoff, "Mutual Deterrence and Strategic Arms Limitation in Soviet Policy," *International Security* (Summer 1978). I am indebted to Raymond Garthoff for much of the material on Soviet military doctrine, especially the quotes from Soviet military commanders. Garthoff is a specialist in Soviet military affairs, was on the U.S. delegation which negotiated SALT I, was U.S. Ambassador to Bulgaria, and is presently a senior fellow at the Brookings Institution.

CHAPTER V

1. Subcommittee on European Affairs, Committee on Foreign Relations, U.S. Senate, *SALT and the NATO Allies*, (Washington, D.C.: GPO, October 1979), p. 6.
2. Bradley Graham, "10 Years Later, West German Ostpolitik Flourishes in Rocky Soil," *The Washington Post*, April 7, 1980.
3. *SALT and the NATO Allies*, p. 53.
4. Henry Kissinger, speech at a seminar in Brussels organized by the Center for Strategic Studies, Georgetown University, the Atlantic Institute, and the Atlantic Treaty Association, September 1, 1979.
5. Richard Burt, "Among Allies: Doubt on U.S.," *The New York Times*, September 7, 1979.
6. McGeorge Bundy, "Strategic Deterrence After Thirty Years; What Has Changed?" speech at the annual conference of the International

Institute of Strategic Studies, Villars, Switzerland, September 7, 1979.

7. Communiqué of the special meeting of NATO foreign and defense ministers, December 12, 1979.
8. Communiqué of NATO ministerial meeting in Rome, May 5, 1981.
9. Jan-Miendt Faber, head of Dutch Interchurch Peace Council, "Dutch in the Vanguard of Europe's Missile Skeptics," *The New York Times,* September 18, 1981.
10. John Vinocur, "The German Malaise," *The New York Times Magazine,* (November 15, 1981).
11. E. P. Thompson, "A Letter to America," *The Nation* (January 24, 1981).
12. Edward Heath, "Pursing Détente and Deterrence," *The New York Times,* November 5, 1981.
13. Elizabeth Pond, "Kremlin—like U.S.—Feels Sting of European Protests," *The Christian Science Monitor,* November 12, 1981.
14. Bradley Graham, "East, West Germans Join in Appeal to Brezhnev for Neutralization," *The Washington Post,* October 8, 1981.
15. Pond, *op. cit.*
16. *CBS Reports, The Defense of the United States,* Part II: "NATO," June 15, 1981.
17. Ronald Reagan, excerpts from press conference of November 10, *The New York Times,* November 11, 1981.
18. Lord Louis Mountbatten, "A Military Commander Surveys the Nuclear Arms Race," *International Security* (Winter 1979–1980).
19. Lord Hill-Norton, letter to the *Times* (London), May 13, 1980.
20. Lord Carver, *Hansard,* House of Lords, April 23, 1980, Col. 843.
21. Desmond Ball, "Can Nuclear War Be Controlled?," *Adelphi Paper* 169, (London: International Institute of Strategic Studies, November 1981).
22. Leonid Brezhnev, an interview in *Der Spiegel,* (November 1, 1981).
23. *Ibid.*
24. Ronald Reagan, address on arms reduction, reprinted in *The New York Times,* November 18, 1981.
25. Michael Howard, "Case for Keeping a Strong Conventional Arms Capability," letter to the *Times* (London), November 3, 1981.

CHAPTER VI

1. Andrei A. Gromyko, "Leninist Foreign Policy in the Modern World," speech in Moscow, January 5, 1981.
2. Viktor Kortunov, "The Leninist Policy of Peaceful Co-existence and Class Struggle," *International Affairs* (May 1979).
3. Henry Trofimenko, "The Third World and the U.S.-Soviet Competition—A Soviet View," *Foreign Affairs* (Summer 1981).
4. James Reston, an interview with Alexander Haig, *The New York Times,* February 4, 1981.
5. David Aaron, quoted in Leon V. Sigal, "Kennan's Cuts," *Foreign Policy* (Fall 1981).

6. Andrei Gromyko, memorandum to the Secretary-General of the United Nations on ending the arms race and disarmament, September 28, 1976.
7. Nikolai Tikhonov, speech at the Sixty-third Anniversary of the Bolshevik Revolution, Moscow, November 6, 1980.
8. Barry M. Bleckman, "The Comprehensive Test Ban Negotiations—Can They Be Revitalized?" *Arms Control Today* (June 1981).
9. George F. Kennan, address on the occasion of his receiving the Albert Einstein Peace Prize, Washington, D.C., May 19, 1981.

CHAPTER VIII

1. ABC News/*Washington Post* polls, April 20–22, published in *The Washington Post*, April 25, 1981.
2. Malcolm Toon, from a speech carried on the Associated Press wire, March 16, 1981.
3. Thomas J. Watson, Jr., "Dealing With Moscow," *The New York Times*, January 19, 1981.
4. George F. Kennan, address on the occasion of his receiving the Albert Einstein Peace Prize, Washington, D.C., May 19, 1981.
5. Colin Gray, "Presidential Directive 59: A Critical Assessment," *Parameters: The Journal of the U.S. Army War College* (March 1981).
6. Maxwell D. Taylor, "Can We Depend on Deterrence?" *The Washington Post*, June 30, 1981.
7. Hans J. Morgenthau, "The Mutual Ability of Utter Destruction," *Baltimore Sun*, August 9, 1979, reprinted from the newsletter of the National Committee on American Foreign Policy, of which Morgenthau was chairman.
8. George F. Kennan, the 1957 Reith Lectures, reprinted in Kennan's *Memoirs: 1950–1963*, (Boston: Little Brown, 1972) pp. 244–45.
9. Solly Zuckerman, *Nuclear Illusion and Reality* (London: Collins, 1982), p. 77.
10. Field Marshal Lord Carver, quoted in Anthony Lewis, "Absurd and Suicidal," *The New York Times*, November 18, 1981.
11. Michael Howard, "Case for Keeping a Strong Conventional Arms Capability," letter to the *Times* (London), November 3, 1981.
12. Elliot Richardson and Henri Simonet, "Nuclear Weapons in Europe," *Arms Control Today* (November 1981).
13. Irving Kristol, "NATO at a Dead End," *The Wall Street Journal*, July 15, 1981.
14. Gary Yerkey, "Europe's Peace Movement Targets U.S. and USSR for 82," *The Christian Science Monitor*, December 8, 1981.
15. John Vinocur, "The German Malaise," *The New York Times Magazine* (November 15, 1981).
16. *Ibid.*
17. Robert Scheer, "Arms Aide Links Protestant Fears, Europe Protests," *Los Angeles Times*, November 26, 1981.
18. "Pope to Send Out Aides in Bid to End Atomic Arms Race," *The New York Times*, December 13, 1981.

Notes and Sources

19. "Ambassador Warns of U.S. Backlash," *The Washington Post,* December 2, 1981.
20. Les Aspin, in Philip Geyelin, "Bringing the Troops Home," *The Washington Post,* December 11, 1981.
21. James Reston, "The New Isolationists," *The New York Times,* December 15, 1981.
22. Tad Szulc, "The Unthinkable," *The Washingtonian* (June 1981).
23. Bernard Lown, M. D., quoted in Tom Wicker, "A New Political Reality," *The New York Times,* December 9, 1981.
24. Bernard Brodie, *Strategy in the Missile Age* (Princeton, N.J.: Princeton University Press, 1959).
25. General Omar N. Bradley, address at St. Albans School, Washington, D.C., November 5, 1957.

Index

Aaron, David, 164
Acheson, Dean, 64, 77
Adenauer, Konrad, 121
Afghanistan:
  history of Soviet relations with,
    54–55
  tribal rebellions in, 55, 57
Afghanistan, Soviet invasion of, 54,
    55–59, 84, 131, 161
  Arbatov's commentary on, 177
  reasons for, 56–57
  Soviet ideology and, 57–59
  Third World reaction to, 55–56,
    60
  U.S. reaction to, 56, 62, 88, 132,
    156, 176
Agt, Andreas van, 133–134
airborne command centers (E-4's),
    4, 9, 11
Allen, Richard, 77, 90
American Committee on East-
    West Accord, 221
American Friends Service Com-
    mittee, 221
American Medical Association
    (AMA), 219
American Security Council, 84–85
Amin, Hafizullah, 55, 57
Amin, Idi, 177*n*

Angola:
  political organizations in, 35
  South African troops in, 35, 36
  U.S. business interests in, 60
  U.S. involvement in, 35, 36,
    37–38
Angola, Soviet intervention in, 34–
    40, 41, 48, 49, 57
  Arbatov's commentary on, 176
  Cuban troops in, 34, 35, 36–37,
    38, 39, 60
  détente disrupted by, 39–40, 72
  events leading to, 34, 35–36
  Soviet foreign policy goals and,
    38–40, 41
  as test of U.S. will, 37–38
antiballistic missile (ABM) treaty
    (1972), 18–19, 31, 67
antinuclear movement, 207, 213–
    221
  church leaders in, 216, 219–220
  conventional forces advocated
    by, 207, 208–211
  doctors in, 218–219
  in Eastern Europe, 137–138
  Eastern Europe-Western Europe
    rapprochement as goal of, 214–
    215
  grass roots organizing in, 220

235

Index

antinuclear movement (cont'd)
nuclear-free zones formed by,
137
scientists in, 220
in Soviet Union, 138–139
unified approach lacked by, 213–
214
in U.S., 217–221
U.S. public opinion on, 221
as viewed by U.S. officials, 215–
217
in Western Europe, 133–137,
139–140, 143, 148, 213–217
antitank weapons, 108–109, 123
Arbatov, Georgy, 43–44, 156, 173–
195
on alleged Soviet military "superiority," 179–180
Cox's reply to, 195–199
on political negotiations, 188–
191, 197–198
on prevention of nuclear war,
181–182, 185–187, 191–193, 198
on regression to cold war tensions, 175–181, 182–185, 193–
194
on Soviet adventures in Third
World, 176–178, 190, 196, 197
Arms Control Association, 221
Aspin, Les, 217
Austria, 137, 214

Backfire bombers, 80, 81, 131, 170
dispute over classification of, 71–
72, 79, 99
Baker, Howard, 43, 217
Ball, George, 221
Barry, John, 141
"Basic Principles of Relations be-
tween the USSR and the
USA," 31, 51, 153, 155, 157
Belgium, 213
antinuclear movement in, 134
nuclear weapons deployed in,
125, 126, 130–131
Bender, Peter, 215

Boeing, 64
bomber gap (1950s), 65, 94
Boston Globe, 74
Bradley, John H., 7
Bradley, Omar, 224–225
Brandt, Willy, 31–32, 108, 122, 134–
135, 224
Brezhnev, Leonid, 55, 138, 186, 196,
208, 219
Angolan intervention and, 34,
36, 37, 39, 40
arms reduction proposed by, 53–
54, 88, 129–130
on inevitability of superpower
rivalry, 40
limited nuclear war concept rejected by, 115, 143
peaceful coexistence (détente)
policy of, 29, 31, 34, 38–39, 50
SALT and, 31, 33, 50–51, 53–54,
72, 81–82, 86, 126, 155, 165
on solidarity with liberation
struggles, 39, 50, 51, 155–156
zero-based option rejected by,
144
Brezhnev doctrine, 57
Brodie, Bernard, 222–223
"broken arrows," 4–5
Brown, Harold, 5, 77, 89, 110, 223
on launch on warning, 25, 26–27
limited nuclear war concept accepted by, 20–22
on Soviet strategic doctrine, 111–
112
Team B and, 101, 102
Brussels conference on Nuclear
Weapons in Europe (1981),
210–211
Brzezinski, Zbigniew, 59, 82, 90,
100–101, 112, 126, 203
linkage adopted by, 42–43, 45–46,
85
power shift toward, 87–88
SALT and, 80, 84, 85
stories leaked to press by, 86
strategic doctrine paper prepared by, 89

Index

Index

Index

Ikle, Fred, 25–26, 43, 71, 90, 124
Interchurch Peace Council, 134
intercontinental ballistic missiles
(ICBMs), 18, 19, 25, 64, 70, 95,
191, 192
  formula proposed for, 168–169
  in launch on warning policy, 17,
168
  launch procedures for, 3–4
  missile gap and (1959), 65–66
  in SALT, 31, 67, 79, 81, 82, 95
International Institute of Strategic
Studies, 10–11, 108, 142–143,
179–180
International Physicians for the
Prevention of Nuclear War,
219
Ismail, Abdel Fattah, 48
Israel, 32
  U.S. military aid to, 158–159
Italy, 137, 208
  antinuclear movement in, 134
  nuclear weapons deployed in,
125, 126, 130, 134
Ivanov, Semyon P., 116
Izvestia, 117

Jackson, Henry M., 90, 203
  as cold warrior, 63–64, 65
  emigration of Soviet Jews and,
33–34, 68–69
  Kissinger's struggle with, 68, 70,
71, 72, 79
  power in Senate of, 63–64, 67
  SALT and, 43, 67, 70, 79–80, 81,
82, 86–87, 95, 97, 99
  staff of, 67–69
  Warnke nomination and, 78, 79
  Yom Kippur War and, 32, 68
Jackson-Vanik amendment, 33–34,
68–69, 162
Jaicks, Frederick, 28
Japan, as potential Soviet adversary, 179, 180
Javits, Jacob, 221
John Paul II, Pope, 216, 219

Johnson, Lyndon B., 66, 67
Joint Chiefs of Staff, SALT II sup-
ported by, 20, 51–52
"Joint Statement of Principles for
Subsequent Negotiations,"
126, 165–166

Karmal, Babrak, 55
Kendall, Donald, 221
Kennan, George, 171–172, 201–202,
209, 221
Kennedy, Edward, 64
Kennedy, John F., 52, 66, 95
Kent, Bruce, 135
Khrushchev, Nikita, 52, 66
  nuclear war doctrine of, 112–113
Kirkland, Lane, 76
Kissinger, Henry, 24, 42, 74, 150
  Angolan War and, 36, 37–38, 41,
59
  détente policy of, 62, 63, 67, 150,
153
  on halting of Soviet expansion-
ism, 49
  Jackson's struggle with, 68, 70,
71, 72, 79
  linkage concept of, 37, 42
  MIRV technology and, 18
  on NATO vulnerability, 127–
128, 129, 139
  popularity of, 62–63
  repudiated at Republican Na-
tional Convention, 73
  SALT and, 33, 37, 49, 59, 67, 69,
70, 72, 79, 80, 81–82, 83, 95
  in trade negotiations, 33–34
Kistiakowsky, George, 28
Kohler, Foy D., 73–74
Kommunist, 58, 138
Korean War, 36
Kortunov, Viktor, 152
Kristol, Irving, 69, 211
Krylov, Nikolai I., 116
Kulikov, Viktor, 117

Index

Laird, Melvin, 68
La Rocque, Gene, 221
Latin America, uprisings in, 160–161
launch authority, 11–15
  of NORAD Commander, 12–13
  of President, 11–12, 15
  of strategic submarines, 13–14
  succession to presidency and, 12, 14
launch on warning (launch under attack), 6, 25–28, 114, 126, 192
  accidental nuclear war as risk of, 25–27, 168
  defined, 9, 17
  warning system proposed for, 9
Leahy, Patrick, 109
Lebanon, Israeli incursions into, 159
Lehman, John, 71, 79, 90
Lenin, V. I., 112, 113, 117, 149, 186n
"Letter from Exile" (Sakharov), 172
limited nuclear war concept, 20–25, 139, 174, 222
  casual treatment of, 15–16
  criticized in Europe, 142–143, 207
  deterrence capability reduced by, 20–21, 22, 25
  implausibility of, 21–22
  misperceptions of Soviet strategic doctrine and, 91–92, 111–117
  origins of, 19–20, 203
  Reagan's acceptance of, 140, 141–142
  Soviet views on, 10, 11, 24–25, 128, 143
  as suicidal fantasy, 24
linkage concept, 155
  debated in Carter administration, 42, 46
  Kissinger as proponent of, 37, 42
  Reagan's acceptance of, 59

  in SALT II, 37, 42–46, 47–48, 85, 88
  Soviet rejection of, 37, 39, 44
Lown, Bernard, 219
Luttwak, Edward, 24–25, 96, 97, 203, 204

McGovern, George, 78
McNamara, Robert, 221
Mansfield, Mike, 122–123
Mansfield Resolution, 123, 217
Mark 12A warheads, 71, 168, 169
Marshall Plan, 121
Marxism-Leninism, 189, 197
  as rationalization for Third World interventions, 57–59
Mathiesen, Bishop Leroy, 219
MBFR talks. See Geneva
Medvedev, Roy, 195
Meet the Press, 46
Mengistu Haile Mariam, 41
Middendorf, William, 85
Military Balance 1981–82, The, 179–180
Military Thought, 115
Miller, Gerald E., 12–13
Milshtein, Mikhail A., 115
Minuteman III missiles, 19, 64, 71, 168, 169
MIRVs. *See* multiple independently targeted reentry vehicle warheads
missile gap (1959–1960), 65–66, 95
Molander, Roger, 220
Mondale, Walter, 53
Monnet, Jean, 121
Morgenthau, Hans, 205–206
Mormon Church, antinuclear stance of, 220
Mountbatten, Lord, 142
Moynihan, Daniel Patrick, 69
Muller, James, 219
multiple independently targeted reentry vehicle (MIRV) warheads, 70

242

Index

proletarian internationalism, 152–153, 189

Putzel, Michael, 7

"Quest for Détente, The" (Rostow), 69

Rabbot, Boris, 34

Rather, Dan, 28

Reagan, Ronald, 105, 109, 187, 188, 225
  antinuclear movement and, 214, 215, 218, 219
  attempted assassination of, 12
  C³ system improvements, 8–9
  in election of 1976, 72–73
  hawkish administration of, 89–93, 94, 132, 139–140, 193–194
  limited nuclear war concept accepted by, 140, 141–142
  military superiority as goal of, 91, 200, 201
  negotiating position of, 144–147, 164, 167
  SALT II treaty rejected by, 22–23, 59
  on Soviet strategic doctrine, 112

Real War, The (Nixon), 63, 103–104

Republican National Committee, 43

Republican National Convention of 1976, 73

Republican National Convention of 1980, 200

Reston, James, 153–154, 217

"Rethinking U.S. Security Policy for the 1980's," 23

Richardson, Elliot, 210

Robaye, Salem Ali, 48

Roberto, Holden, 35

Rostow, Eugene, 69, 71, 73, 76, 90, 146, 178

Rowny, Edward L., 23, 90

Rumania, antinuclear movement in, 137–138

Rumsfeld, Donald, 72, 99

Rybkin, Ye, 117

Sadat, Anwar, 32

Sakharov, Andrei, 56, 172, 195

SALT (strategic arms limitation talks), 150
  counterforce weapons incompatible with, 23
  Munich agreement equated with, 70
  Soviet position in, 116, 117
  U.S. opponents of, 43, 44, 47, 48, 49, 52, 62, 63, 69, 79, 84

SALT I, 70, 146, 167, 193, 198–199
  achievements of, 18–19, 31
  Jackson's qualification to, 67, 68
  public misperception of, 95–97
  U.S. strategic advantages in, 95–96

SALT II, 20, 31, 42–54, 57, 77–88, 90, 124, 146, 167, 193, 198–199
  breakthrough in, 50–51
  European-based nuclear weapons and, 53–54, 81–82
  furor over Soviet combat troops in Cuba and, 52–53, 88
  harmed by Soviet adventures in Third World, 37, 43, 44–46, 47, 48–49, 56, 59, 84, 88
  impasses in, 71–72, 99
  Jackson's policy paper on, 79–80
  linkage concept in, 37, 42–46, 47–48, 85, 88
  protocol to, 126, 165–166
  Reagan's rejection of, 22–23, 59, 132, 140
  Senate and, 24, 43, 51–53, 86–87, 88
  signed at Vienna summit, 86, 87, 88, 155–156, 165–166
  Soviet rejection of, 42, 81–82
  U.S. public opinion on, 52
  Vladivostok numbers and, 33, 70, 72, 79, 80, 81–82, 83

SANE, 221

245

Index

Savimbi, Jonas, 35, 60
Schieffer, Bob, 13–14, 15–16, 27–28
Schlesinger, James, 24, 73, 76
  appointed secretary of defense, 68
  counterforce doctrine and, 19–20, 22, 70–71
  firing of, 72
  perception theory and, 97, 98
  SALT and, 70
Schmidt, Helmut, 124, 125, 134, 208
Schuman, Robert, 121
scientists, in antinuclear movement, 220
Scoville, Herbert, Jr., 75, 221
Scowcroft, Brent, 72
Senate, U.S.:
  SALT I and, 67, 68
  SALT II and, 24, 43, 51–53, 86–87, 88
Senate Armed Services Committee, 4, 27, 69
Senate Foreign Relations Committee, 20, 52, 88, 112
Shelepin, Alexander, 34
Shulman, Marshall, 42, 77, 87
Siad Barre, Muhammad, 40
Simonet, Henri, 210
SLBMs (submarine-launched ballistic missiles), 31, 191, 192
Smith, Gerard, 116
Solzhenitsyn, Alexander, 114
Somalia:
  Ogaden claimed by, 176–177
  Soviet ties with, 40–41
South Africa, 158, 160
  troops from, in Angola, 35, 36
Soviet Union:
  allocation of military forces in, 106–107
  antinuclear movement in, 138–139
  China as potential adversary of, 106–107, 131, 159–160, 170–171, 179, 180
  China-U.S. relations and, 45, 53, 57, 160, 182

civil defense program in, 76, 101–102
C³ system of, 10, 26
defense spending in, 45, 76, 101, 104–106, 109, 179–180
dissidents in, 56, 195–196
emigration of Jews from, 33–34
estimates of military strength of, 65–66, 73–76, 94–95, 100–111, 179–180
failed foreign policy of, 59–61
first-strike capability of, 19
hawks vs. doves in, 34
inefficient defense production in, 104
naval superiority ascribed to, 109–110
policy toward liberation movements of, 39–40, 41–42, 50, 51, 57–59, 152–156, 161, 189–190
strategic doctrine of, 75–76, 91–92, 111–119
Third World adventures of, 29–30, 32, 34–61, 62, 63, 84, 85, 88, 131, 132, 152–156, 176–178, 190, 196, 197
U.S. trade with, 33–34, 162, 182
Spiegel, Der, 143, 144
Sputnik, 95
SS-18 missiles, 19, 79, 81, 169
SS-19 missiles, 19, 79
SS-20 missiles, 124, 130, 138, 139, 147, 193
  aimed at China, 131, 170–171
strategic arms limitation talks. *See* SALT
strategic arms reduction talks (START), 145, 167
strategic bombers, 18, 19, 84, 96, 168, 169, 191, 192
  alleged gap in (1950s), 65, 94
"Strategic Stability Reconsidered" (Gray), 23–24
strategic submarines, 18, 19, 67, 110, 168, 169, 192
  communications with, 8, 13
  launch authority of, 13–14

246

Index

strategic thinkers, 203–204, 206–207

submarine-launched ballistic missiles (SLBMs), 31, 191, 192

Sweden, defense strategy of, 214

Switzerland, defense strategy of, 214

Syria, in Yom Kippur War, 32, 36

TACAMO aircraft, 8

Taraki, Nur Mohammad, 54–55

Taylor, Maxwell, 204–205, 211

Team B, 73–76, 100–102, 104, 109, 117

   accepted by Carter administration, 76, 100–101, 102

   CIA damaged by, 75, 100

   CIA findings reviewed by, 73, 74–75, 76, 100, 101, 102

   conclusions of, 75–76, 91, 101–104, 111, 112, 114

   members of, 73–74

   press leaks and, 74–75, 100

   in Reagan administration, 90

Teng Hsiao-ping, 85

Thatcher, Margaret, 136, 208, 212

Third World:

   Arbatov's commentary on, 176–178, 190–191, 196, 197

   arms race opposed by, 163

   Marxist-Leninist ideology and, 57–59

   military nonintervention pact proposed for, 156–164, 196–198, 223

   postwar power vacuum in, 157

   Soviet adventures in, 29–30, 32, 34–61, 62, 63, 84, 85, 88, 131, 132, 152–156, 176–178, 190, 196, 197

   Soviet setbacks in, 55–56, 60–61

   superpowers as world policemen in, 197

   as tinder box for World War III, 162

Thompson, E. P., 135, 214

Tikhonov, Nikolai, 166

Time, 49–50, 98

Titan II missiles, 19, 170

Tito, Marshall (Josip Broz), 56

Toon, Malcolm, 201

Trident submarines, 64, 68, 212

Trident II missiles, 9, 20, 23, 71, 84, 168, 169

Trofimenko, Henry, 32, 58–59, 152

Turkey, deployment of nuclear weapons in, 125

Turner, Stansfield, 102

Union of Concerned Scientists, 220

United Auto Workers, 221

United Nations, 55, 163, 165

United Nations Charter, 156

United Nations Special Session on Disarmament, 45, 220

Ustinov, Dimitri, 10

Vance, Cyrus, 52, 77

   Brzezinski as rival of, 42, 44, 46, 85, 86, 88, 89

   resignation of, 88

   SALT and, 42, 46, 81–82, 99, 164

Van Cleave, William R., 73

verification issues, 23, 126, 145–146, 168, 170, 171

Vietnam, Cambodia invaded by, 49, 60, 84, 159, 176, 177*n*

"Vietnam syndrome," 30–31, 63

Vietnam War, 11, 36, 45, 63, 66, 78, 106, 108, 182

   noninterventionism as result of, 30–31, 150

   repercussions of U.S. defeat in, 29, 57, 62, 178

Vogt, John W., Jr., 74

Vries, Klaus de, 127

Wall Street Journal, The, 217

War, Peace and Change (Dulles), 194

Warnke, Paul, 42, 77, 79–80, 81

Index

Warnke, Paul (cont'd)
  resignation of, 86, 87, 88
  Senate confirmation of, 78–79
War Powers Act (1973), 11
Warsaw Pact, 107–109, 120, 161, 224
  anti-Soviet sentiments in, 107–108
  defense spending in, 108, 179–180
  formation of, 121
  strength of NATO vs., 107, 108–109
Washington *Star*, 75
Watergate, 15, 33, 69
Watson, Thomas J., Jr., 201
Wattenberg, Ben, 69
Weinberger, Caspar, 8, 28, 214
  NATO policies and, 141, 143–144
Weiss, Seymour, 73
Welch, Jasper A., Jr., 74
Willens, Harold, 220
Wimex (World Wide Military Command and Control System), 7–8

window of vulnerability, 168
Winpisinger, William, 221
Wolfe, Thomas, 74
Wolfowitz, Paul D., 73, 90
World War II, 206
  European order established after, 120–122
  superpower rivalry established after, 157
World Wide Military Command and Control System, *See* Wimex

Yemen, People's Democratic Republic of (South Yemen):
  coup in (1978), 48
  Soviet involvement in, 48–49, 57, 84
Yom Kippur War, 32, 33, 36, 68, 69
Yugoslavia, antinuclear movement in, 137

Zraket, Charles A., 9
Zuckerman, Solly, Lord, 209–210